The Home Buyer's Question and Answer Book

Bridget McCrea

AMACOM

American Management Association

New York • Atlanta • Brussels • Chicago • Mexico City • San Francisco
Shanghai • Tokyo • Toronto • Washington, D.C.

Special discounts on bulk quantities of AMACOM books are available to corporations, professional associations, and other organizations. For details, contact Special Sales Department, AMACOM, a division of American Management Association, 1601 Broadway, New York, NY 10019.
Tel.: 212-903-8316. Fax: 212-903-8083.
Web site: www.amacombooks.org

This publication is designed to provide accurate and authoritative information in regard to the subject matter covered. It is sold with the understanding that the publisher is not engaged in rendering legal, accounting, or other professional service. If legal advice or other expert assistance is required, the services of a competent professional person should be sought.

Various names used by companies to distinguish their software and other products can be claimed as trademarks. AMACOM uses such names throughout this book for editorial purposes only, with no intention of trademark violation. All such software or product names are in initial capital letters or ALL CAPITAL letters. Individual companies should be contacted for complete information regarding trademarks and registration.

REALTOR® is a Registered collective membership mark that identifies a real estate professional who is a member of the National Association of REALTORS® and subscribes to its strict Code of Ethics. AMACOM uses these names throughout this book in initial capital letters or ALL CAPITAL letters for editorial purposes only, with no intention of trademark violation.

Library of Congress Cataloging-in-Publication Data

McCrea, Bridget.
        The home buyer's question and answer book / Bridget McCrea.
            p.   cm.
        Includes index.
        ISBN 0-8144-7236-2 (pbk.)
        1. Residential real estate—Purchasing—United States.   2. House buying—United States.   3. Condominiums—Purchasing—United States.   4. Mortgage loans—United States.   I. Title.

HD259.M33 2005
643'.12'0973—dc22   2004011986

Printing number

10   9   8   7   6   5   4   3   2   1

Contents

Introduction

Welcome to one of the most exciting and confusing financial transactions you'll ever make in your life. Because you have this book in your hands, I'll assume that you've already set your sights on achieving this integral part of the American Dream. Buying a home is not only about leaving the ranks of renters (or those living with their family or roommates); it's also about making an investment in something that will grow in value as you maintain and improve it, allowing you to "move up" in a few years to a larger home, or if you prefer, hold on to this one for as long as you like.

Soon, instead of putting money in your landlord's pocket every month, you'll be building equity that can either be tapped in the future or allowed to accumulate for your golden years and your heirs. When you walk away from the closing table with the keys to your new home clenched in your fist, you'll join the nearly 74 million households in the United States that already own their own properties, according to the National Association of REALTORS® (NAR).

In its 2003 Profile of Home Buyers and Sellers, NAR pegs the U.S. homeownership rate at 68 percent, up from 64 percent a decade ago. But even in a low mortgage interest rate environment where lenders are offering a wide variety of mortgage programs, NAR says buying a home remains a challenging endeavor. Establishing where to buy, how to search, and just how much home you can afford can all present stumbling blocks, particularly for first-time buyers.

A recent survey from national title insurance firm LandAmerica Financial Group confirmed those challenges when it found that 86 percent of home buyers report difficulty and confusion in the process. More than one-third of respondents reported delays in closing on their home purchase, with the hardest aspect being the management of the sheer number of steps or processes necessary to get to the closing table without delay. The survey of LandAmerica's customers from 700 offices worldwide pinpointed the top four problem areas: establishing an escrow account, negotiating a contract, property appraisals, and purchasing title insurance.

Despite the challenges, a steady stream of buyers is willing to take the risk to get to the ultimate reward, with most first-time purchasers focused on the advantages of home ownership versus renting, according to NAR. The association reports that more than four out of five first-time buyers reported that their primary reason for purchasing a home was the desire to own a home of their own, while 6 percent indicated that they purchased a home for more living space.

Where home buyers have a distinct advantage right now is in the sheer amount of information available at their fingertips. Thanks to the Internet, buyers can search for homes, view virtual tours of those properties, tap into their local multiple listing services, locate competent real estate professionals, and even apply for a mortgage from the comfort of their own computer keyboards. Where consumers were once at the mercy of their real estate providers and lenders, who held information close to the vest, they now have a plethora of information sources at their avail.

With this book in your homebuying arsenal, you'll be even better equipped to deal with the challenges as they arise. I've selected more than 170 different questions that can come up during the homebuying process and divided them into ten different chapters, grouped by subject. I start at the beginning by helping you determine if home ownership is right for you, walk you through the preliminary financial aspect of the transaction, and then help you find a home that meets your specific needs. You'll find in-depth information on the types of properties available, including single-family homes, condominiums, townhouses, and cooperatives.

From there, you'll learn exactly how the financing process works, what government and special financing programs are available right now, and how factors like your credit rating and past payment history come into play. With down-payment funds being one of the main obstacles on the path to home ownership, I've also highlighted a number of programs that can help you over that barrier. You'll also learn about important issues like keeping emotions out of the process, spotting predatory lenders, and the value of obtaining a professional home inspection.

The last section of the book will help you close the deal without falling prey to the unscrupulous practices of some companies in the industry. Read about your legal rights as a home buyer in Chapter 8, take a walk through the entire closing process in Chapter 9, and find out what your and the seller's post-sale responsibilities are in Chapter 10.

With this book in hand, I'm confident that you will soon become one of the millions of people who will switch from renting to buying over the next few years. Depending on what stage of the game you're at, this book can either answer specific questions or help you through the entire process, from the time you visit your first open house until moving day. Through it all, I wish you the best of luck in your homebuying endeavor.

PART I

HOME BUYING
101

COMMON QUESTIONS ABOUT THE HOMEBUYING PROCESS

1. Why should I buy a home?

Home ownership is one of the key components of the American Dream and a universal symbol of financial stability. You may be shelling out more money per month for a great apartment, but it's still not the same as owning a home, which is associated with stability, security, and even wealth. The National Association of Realtors® (NAR) says first-time home buyers generally buy homes because they are (in order of importance):

1. Tired of paying rent to landlords
2. Ready to tap the tax advantages associated with home ownership
3. In need of more living space, be it indoor, outdoor, or both

Of course, home ownership brings with it both positives and negatives that must be considered, particularly if this is your first time out. Despite the challenges it presents, home ownership is undeniably one of the most sought-after dreams that Americans pursue on a daily basis.

Tell me more

If you're not sure whether home ownership is the right choice for you, take out a piece of paper, draw a line vertically down the middle of it, and write the words "pros" and "cons" as headers on each column. Then, take your time comparing the good and the bad aspects of your current living situation against the pros and cons of home ownership. If things are too heavily weighted in either column, it could be time to buy a home.

For starters, right now you're probably putting money in your landlord's pocket—and helping him pay down his own mortgage—without reaping any of the benefits of that money. You're not building equity in a home, and you probably have little or no say in the permanent decor, landscaping, and repairs on your home, even though you live there.

If the home were yours, you'd be making modifications (some of which can add value to the property), enjoying your own wall paint colors, and tapping one of the best tax advantages that Uncle Sam affords Americans: deducting points paid on a home purchase, mortgage interest paid (which can be a pretty hefty sum, particularly during your first few years as an owner), and property taxes. And because properties nearly always appreciate in value, you would also be building a nest egg for yourself that can be tapped when needed (in the form of, say, a home equity line of credit) or saved for future use.

As NAR discovered in its survey, people also buy homes because their lifestyles change and families grow, which means the need for larger yards, more bathrooms, or extra bedrooms. Those who do go in search of homes often find a much better selection than their renting counterparts, since single-family homes, town homes, condominiums, and co-ops come in all shapes and sizes. Other reasons for purchasing a home include the ability to build or improve a credit history, an investment in your future, and more control of your surroundings.

Overall, home ownership can give you a feeling of accomplishment in reaching a goal while also helping you establish deep roots in your community. Unlike renters, who tend to be more transient in nature and less conscientious about their physical surroundings (they don't own them, after all), home owners have plunked down one of the biggest investments of their lives in their communities.

The Department of Housing and Urban Development (HUD) advises first-time home buyers to ask themselves these questions before making their decision. If you can answer "yes" to the following questions, HUD says you're probably ready to buy your own home:

- ❑ Do I have a steady source of income (usually a job)?
- ❑ Have I been employed on a regular basis for the last two to three years?
- ❑ Is my current income reliable?
- ❑ Do I have a good record of paying my bills?
- ❑ Do I have few outstanding long-term debts, like car payments?
- ❑ Do I have money saved for a down payment?
- ❑ Do I have the ability to pay a mortgage every month, plus additional costs?

On the downside, home ownership does bring with it significant responsibilities that renters generally don't have to deal with. Once you've walked away from the closing table with those keys in your hand, you can no longer dial up the landlord when a pipe breaks or when the furnace stops producing heat. You are your own "go to" person on the chain, which means outside chores like cutting grass and cleaning roof gutters are suddenly in your lap. Owning a home also means not being as mobile as you once were, since selling a home and giving thirty days' notice to a landlord are two completely different things.

Here's a rule of thumb for renters wondering if ownership is right for them: In general, the longer you are likely to remain in a residence, the more advantageous it is to own rather than rent. If your career, family status, and other variables are likely to be stable for the next three to five years, then your housing needs should be equally stable. That's not to say that a mobile professional shouldn't buy a home (in fact, many relocating professionals never rent and simply buy and sell as they make their way around the country to different positions), but it does give you something to think about before making your decision.

For some folks, renting is going to be the right choice. For others, the positives of owning their own "home sweet home" will far outweigh the negatives.

2. How difficult are the financial aspects of purchasing a home?

The factors that mortgage lenders look at when doling out money are far different from the criteria landlords use to rent out a property.

Let's compare: When you rent an apartment, a decent credit rating and steady income source usually result in a lease signing and the forking over of first and last month's rent. Within a few days, you're in your new apartment. Home buying is not as simple. The process itself is time-consuming because there's more at stake and because mortgages simply aren't as easy to obtain as leases.

Still, the overall consensus is that the homebuying process is easier than it was, say, ten years ago. The fundamentals are the same: You need some cash reserve for a down payment and/or closing costs; you need the cleanest credit history you can provide (a variable that factors heavily into the interest rate that a lender will offer you); and you need a source of steady income that proves your ability to pay your monthly mortgage payment.

Tell me more

Everyone from mortgage lenders to real estate agents has created programs for first-time buyers like yourself, who need a bit more hand-holding during the purchase process. Still, the biggest challenge that most first-time home buyers face is the same as it was ten years ago: scraping up the money for the down payment. Most lenders offer an array of lending options. Wells Fargo of San Francisco, for example, is the nation's top originator of residential mortgages and offers programs that include closing cost saver, down-payment assistance services, as well as 3 percent and 5 percent down-payment programs. Visit the lender online at www.wellsfargo.com/mort gage, to read more about the homebuying process, mortgage options, and getting preapproved for a mortgage.

That's the financing aspect of the purchase.

3. What's the process for buying a new home?

As for the homebuying process itself, it generally goes something like this:

- ❑ Consult with a lender or real estate professional about how much home you can afford (obtain a "prequalification" estimate).
- ❑ Select a region and/or community where you'd like to live.
- ❑ Decide what type of home you'd like to purchase (single family? town home? condominium? co-op?).
- ❑ Either work on your own (using the newspaper, Internet, and "for sale" yard signs) or enlist the help of a buyer's real estate agent to see what on the market fits your criteria.
- ❑ Find your home and make an offer.
- ❑ Negotiate the price and fine points, such as repairs that need to be made by the current owner.
- ❑ Determine a closing date and set the wheels in motion (start packing!).
- ❑ Finalize your financing while home inspectors, appraisers, and other required inspections or reports are completed.
- ❑ On closing day, take possession of your new home and start moving your stuff in!

Tell me more

Any number of challenges can crop up as you move through these various stages of the homebuying process. The title company might uncover liens on the home that need to be cleared up, you and the owner may not come to terms on which repairs she will rectify prior to closing, or the home inspector may uncover an expensive structural defect like toxic mold. The key is to surround yourself with competent professionals (real estate agents, title companies, appraisal firms, lenders, and even attorneys—

which are required in some states) and books like this to help you navigate the process.

4. What's the market like for first-time home buyers?

The answer to that question depends on a few different factors, like your geographic location, whether your region is experiencing a "seller's" or "buyer's" market right now, and what the average home sales prices are. Working in your favor are low mortgage interest rates, flexible loan programs, and a variety of homes to select from as "move up" buyers (those moving from starter homes to larger dwellings) also take advantage of low interest rates to upgrade their own living situations. Also in your corner is the fact that the supply of housing—including single-family, multifamily, and manufactured housing—is expected to increase by nearly 2 million units (or 1.6 percent) in 2004 alone, according to a Merrill Lynch & Co. housing report. That means more available properties to purchase, and a better selection of housing options for first-time and experienced home buyers.

Working against the first-time buyer are property appreciation rates that range from zero to a staggering 25 percent nationwide, depending on where you're located. In some areas, that kind of appreciation has bumped up the prices of starter homes to $75,000 to $150,000 (in some metro areas that number can be much higher) while stoking a great demand for such properties. In metro areas like Houston and Miami, and throughout much of the State of California, such properties are either hard to come by or hard to purchase, since they sell within a day or two of hitting the market.

Tell me more

A seller's market exists because the quantity demanded by the buyers at a given market price exceeds the quantity supplied by the sellers at that price. In real estate, that means buyers are seeking out more of the goods than sellers are willing to sell, so sellers can pick and choose whom they sell to among prospective buyers. Buyers are lucky to find a desirable home at the right price in such a market.

A buyer's market is just the opposite, and one you should be hoping for as you go out in search of a home. It exists because the quantity supplied by the sellers at a given market price exceeds the quantity demanded by the buyers at that price. In this situation, sellers are seeking to sell more of the goods than buyers are willing to buy, so buyers like you can pick and choose the goods purchased from the sellers, who are typically eager to unload their homes at a fair price.

5. How can I determine my local market conditions?

Timing counts when it comes to buying a home. The last thing you want to do is get stuck in the middle of a hot seller's market, but the good side is that real estate—like all economic forces—is cyclical. A way to find out what your market is like on your own is by flipping through the Sunday real estate section of the newspaper for a few weeks, running your finger down the list of single-family homes and attached housing options (condos, town homes, etc.) available in your targeted area.

You can also log on to a local real estate brokerage's Web site to gain access to certain parts of the MLS (multiple listing service, where all of the properties for sale in an area are compiled) system via a system known as "broker reciprocity." Use the service by first finding a local real estate site, then clicking on a link that will be labeled something like, "view all local MLS listings." After putting in some parameters (house size, number of bathrooms, etc.), you'll get a listing of homes available in the area. Individual real estate offices, agents, and companies like BuyOwner.com (www. buyowner.com) also list homes for sale, searchable by geographic region.

Tell me more

During your newspaper or Internet search, ask yourself the following questions:

❑ Are the homes in my desired range (size, location, amenities) also in my budget?

❑ Are the sources featuring many of the same homes week after week? (This is a sign of a hard-to-sell or overpriced property, or a buyer's market.)

❑ Is there a fresh batch of properties coming on the market each week? (This is a sign of a seller's market.)

❑ Are there certain up-and-coming neighborhoods or communities where homes sell quickly, versus those in which homes are not selling as well?

❑ Does it look as if home prices in the area have gone up, gone down, or stayed the same over the last two years? (This is another good indicator of a seller's or buyer's market, both of which are based on supply and demand.)

If you don't have the time to assess your market, one of your best tools is a good real estate agent who is immersed in the market on a daily basis, and who can usually give a candid picture of whether agents are operating in a buyer's or seller's market. Two easily accessible sources are your local business journal or your local Board of Realtors, both of which publish regular reports on state and local home sales, average sales prices, and year-over-year comparisons.

If you're really interested in buying only when the market is right, keep an eye on fluctuating mortgage interest rates, since low interest rates are one of the key drivers of the real estate market. Other indicators to watch include the rate of U.S. Treasury Bills and the national discount rate, both of which can help you predict the rise and fall of mortgage rates. When the latter drops, for example, the nation's banks pay less to borrow money and, in turn, typically reduce mortgage rates to the borrower.

6. How do I determine my housing needs?

Start by not letting yourself get overwhelmed by the choices and by not getting too emotional about the process. Look at it as an investment, and treat it as if you were making an investment in your family's future. With that in mind, use the information gathered during your market research or from a real estate agent to see what types of homes are available in your market, then whittle down the choices based on your own preferences. For example, do you need a single-family home with a large yard? Would you prefer a lower-maintenance condominium? Do you need an extra bedroom for a home office? Do you have a preference on the number of bathrooms? Having all of these details nailed down before you start house hunting will result in a much more focused, efficient search.

Tell me more

There are many variables that will come up during the homebuying process. Existing homes can be the biggest challenge, since they were built for someone else—someone who might not share your tastes. To avoid getting overwhelmed when you see the home that looks perfect on the outside but that has rooms painted purple with carpeting to match, ask yourself the following questions first:

1. How many bedrooms do I want?
2. How many bathrooms do I want?
3. What size kitchen would I prefer?
4. Do I want a new home or an existing home?
5. What type of home do I want? Single family? Town home? Condominium? Co-op?

6. How important are outdoor amenities like decks, lanais, pools, and patios? And, am I willing to add any of these if they don't come with the existing home?

7. How important are indoor amenities like fireplaces, vaulted ceilings, and crown moldings?

8. Am I willing to do fix-up work (either myself, or by hiring someone) in the home such as painting walls, to make it right for me? (If not, then a home in "move-in condition" is your goal.)

9. How important is the home's proximity to the following: other houses, the street or major intersections (for the noise and safety factor), my place of work, my children's school, and our favorite activities (community pools, movie theaters, workout centers, etc.)?

Answering these nine straightforward questions should help you create a rough sketch of your desired home, and it should give you some indication of your "home hot buttons" (those issues of utmost importance to you, typically those that could ultimately make or break the deal). That's not to say you can't change your mind about wanting a pool if you find the right house with a large backyard with no pool, but it will give you some solid parameters to use when either viewing homes on your own or working with an agent who is trying to nail down a few good candidates.

7. How can emotions affect the homebuying process?

While it's true that you're about to make one of the biggest financial decisions you'll ever make in your life, it's important not to allow emotions to get the better of you during this process. When you walk into that absolutely perfect home, for example, bottle your enthusiasm a bit and instead look at the structure as an investment instead of a place where you'll spend the next ten or twenty years of your life.

Tell me more

When you see the sign go up on that home around the corner that you've always dreamed of living in, try to approach every home with a critical eye and examine every inch, without shame. The seller who knows that a home has you by the heartstrings could use that knowledge to ask more than a fair price and/or avoid making necessary repairs prior to closing.

Once you've given the home a critical review, have a home inspector do the same (should you decide to make an offer and sign a purchase agreement on it). Doing so will save you both money and grief in the long run.

8. What is a REALTOR®?

A real estate agent is a real estate professional who has affiliation to a real estate office or "brokerage" and who is charged with helping home buyers sell homes and with helping home owners sell their homes. REALTOR is a trademarked name used by agents who are members of the National Association of REALTORS®, and who abide by the group's code of ethics and standards. These days, most agents are Realtors.

9. What is the difference between a buyer's agent and a seller's agent?

Traditionally, Realtors only represented sellers in the transaction, but in the last few years a significant number of agents have become what are known as "buyer's agents." These individuals often have the initials "ABR" after their names (Accredited Buyer Representative) and specialize with helping buyers find the homes of their dreams.

Tell me more

Buyer's agents are probably one of the best things to happen for home buyers in a long time. Many will ask you to sign a buyer's agency agreement before they take off with your hot button list in hand to look for suitable properties. The agreement is not exclusive and typically states that the agent will work to find and secure the perfect home for you.

The beauty in all of this is that the agent's commission comes out of the seller's pocket, so you don't have to pay for the valuable services that they offer. If, however, you decide to purchase a "for sale by owner" (FSBO) property and wish to have representation on the sale, most buyer's agents will negotiate a fee with either the seller (most commonly) or buyer.

Because they don't typically list properties for sale, most are eager to work with qualified buyers who are ready to buy now, rather than later. Here are a few advantages of working with a buyer's agent:

- ❏ *Someone in Your Corner:* A buyer's agent works on your behalf, unlike seller's agents, who are accountable by law to the seller. Buyer's agents can not only help you pick out a home, but can also negotiate your best interest and spot potential hurdles before they become real problems.
- ❏ *Benefit of Experience:* An experienced agent will look objectively and carefully at a property, spot potential problems, and point out material defects as well as the positives of a property.

❏ *Negotiating Prowess:* A good buyer's agent will help you draw up an offer based on recent sales in the neighborhood or community, thus allowing you to make better-educated decisions during the negotiating phase.

10. How are Realtors paid?

Today's Realtors operate in a number of different ways, although most "traditional" agents (from companies like Coldwell Banker, Century 21, RE/MAX and ERA) work on a certain percentage (usually 6 percent or 7 percent) of the home's sales price, paid by the seller at closing. Buyer's agents work in the same manner (the buy-side and sell-side agents split the commission 50/50) and operate as fiduciaries or "trusted advisers" in the transaction.

Tell me more

The good news for you, the buyer, is that most Realtors turn to the seller for payment at the closing table. The transaction coordinator (see Question 56) usually does too, unless it's the buyer who enlisted her services and therefore is the person responsible for payment.

11. How do I choose a buyer's agent?

Choose a buyer's agent with the ABR or EBA (Exclusive Buyer Agent) designation after his or her name; "EBA" means the agent doesn't ever represent sellers. The ABR designation is awarded to real estate practitioners by the Real Estate Buyer's Agent Council (REBAC) of the National Association of REALTORS who meet the specified educational and practical experience criteria. The National Association of Exclusive Buyer's Agents (www.exclusivebuyersagents.com) has a "find an agent" section. The group says its agents provide full fiduciary services to their clients and advocate the right of consumers to be fully represented when purchasing real estate.

Tell me more

The National Association of Exclusive Buyer's Agents suggests that all future home owners ask their agents the following questions before making their selection:

❏ How long have you been representing buyers as a buyer's agent?
❏ Do you, or the company you are with, take listings? Do you practice dual agency?

❏ What percentage of your personal business and what percentage of your company's business is representing buyers? Is the balance of that representing sellers?

❏ Will you try to sell me one of your listed properties before you show me listings from other real estate companies?

❏ Do you have information about FSBO properties?

❏ How many buyers have you successfully represented in the last six months? Can I have the names and phone numbers of three to six of your most recent buyer clients?

❏ What training have you taken that specifically relates to being a buyer's agent and representing buyers? Do you have any specific buyer's agent professional designations?

❏ Do you know the six fiduciary, client-level duties you would owe to me if I chose to hire you as my buyer's agent? (These duties are confidentiality, accountability, reasonable skill and care, undivided loyalty, obedience to lawful instructions, and full disclosure.)

❏ What is your commission? Or do you have hourly rates or a set fee?

❏ Will there be a written contract?

❏ Do you have a list of home inspectors, insurance agents, and reputable lenders for me to consider?

❏ What clauses will you incorporate in our offer to protect me as a buyer?

❏ How will you help me save money?

❏ Specifically, how will you protect my interests, and why should I hire you rather than another agent?

12. Can I find my home on the Internet?

The Internet has become a terrific starting point for folks like you who are looking for a home. In fact, in its 2003 Profile of Home Buyers and Sellers, the NAR found that 65 percent of home buyers used the Internet to start their home search, up from 2 percent in 1995. With the advent of virtual tours (where you can view an entire home, room by room, online), digital photography (still photos of the home), and search tools like the online MLS services that many brokerages offer on their Web sites, the Internet has become a consumer-friendly tool useful for culling out undesirable homes and pinpointing those that would make good candidates.

Tell me more

The truth is, while technology has put information and resources into the hands of more consumers, it hasn't really made the homebuying process itself that much easier. So while you might be able to narrow your choices down to six homes by previewing them on the Internet (instead of driving around the neighborhood on a Sunday with your real estate agent), you will still need to touch, smell, and feel a home before making the ultimate buying decision. Whether that means you'll have an agent, an attorney, or just your spouse by your side when you go into a house is your choice.

13. How do I start my Internet home search?

A good starting place for your Internet search is a national Web site like Realtor.com, which essentially "aggregates" listing information from agents across the country and makes a limited amount of that information available to potential buyers. Once you've narrowed down a few homes, you can contact directly the agents who have listed the home, or you can put your own agent on the case by handing over the MLS numbers or listing information on the specific properties.

Tell me more

If you're looking for an FSBO, try a Web site like BuyOwner.com, For SaleByOwner.com or Foxtons.com, where you can key in geographic preferences and home qualities to see what type of properties are being offered directly by owners in your region.

Realizing that home buyers are more sophisticated and accustomed to having information at their fingertips, most agents and sellers these days create Web sites that include basic information about the home (general location, asking price, square footage, number of bedrooms/baths, etc.), one or more still photos, and a virtual tour that will give you a 360-degree view of one or more rooms. Combined, these various tidbits of information can help you decide whether the home is worth seeing in person.

14. How long should I plan to live in my new home to make the investment worthwhile?

The market will dictate the purchase price and length of time to sell, and if you haven't been in the home very long, you could end up losing money on the deal in your urgency to sell. It's something to think about before you start your house hunt, since the mobility that renting provides can be an advantage when it comes to dealing with such issues.

The length of time you expect to own your home also affects your down-payment and closing strategies, as well as the type of mortgage you choose. For example, a fifteen-year mortgage will require larger monthly payments than a thirty-year loan, but you'll see your principal loan amount reduced sooner if you take the shorter-term loan. If you plan to stay in the house five years or less, you may want to consider an adjustable-rate mortgage (ARM)—which offers lower interest rates and helps the owner start paying off the loan principal balance sooner—but if you plan to live in your home for the next ten to twenty years, you may want to lock into a fixed-rate mortgage.

There are also prepayment penalties to watch out for (charged by the lender if the loan is paid off before maturity), and if you sell your home before the loan matures, you must also pay the remaining balance of the loan.

Tell me more

How long you plan to stay matters because real estate investments aren't liquid, and because they could be either easy or difficult to sell (depending on market conditions and other variables). It's best to choose a home in a location where you're going to stay a while. If something comes up (a family change, a job relocation, etc.), you can always put your home up for sale, but it's best not to count on a quick sale before you even get into your new house.

The longer you own a home, the more equity you establish in your property. Studies show that most people stay in their homes for five to seven years. For the first few years, however, nearly 100 percent of your mortgage payment will go toward interest. Mortgages are "front-loaded" on the interest side, which means lenders use your payments primarily to pay down interest before applying it to the principal amount. This is good if you're itemizing tax deductions, but bad if you're counting on a quick accumulation of equity during those early years.

Also remember that unexpected personal or family crises (medical emergency or a death in the family) or change in lifestyle (a new job in a new city) could force you to sell your home long before you had anticipated.

15. What is a starter home?

A starter home is a small, inexpensive home suitable for first-time home buyers. The home may be in move-in condition, or it may need some tender loving care to make it livable. Either way, these are generally single-family homes that are considered good starting points for families or individuals purchasing their first home. Find out what price points the starter homes in your region are demanding by looking through your local Sunday paper (look for adds that say things like "needs TLC" and "good starter home"), searching the Internet, or consulting with a local real estate professional.

The concept of the starter home is simple: You buy a small, inexpensive home (typically when you're single or recently married) with the intent of selling it within a few years. By that time, your income will have grown (allowing you to purchase a larger home), or you'll need more space for a growing family. The idea works well for some, who improve the home and within a few years end up making money on the sale and "moving up," and not so well for others, who outgrow the starter home too soon and end up losing money if the property hasn't appreciated.

Tell me more

According to 2003 NAR Profile of Home Buyers and Sellers, first-time buyers were less likely to buy a detached single-family home than were repeat buyers. Instead, they more frequently purchased lower-cost, "starter homes" such as townhouses, row houses, or condos. A greater proportion of new-home buyers (82 percent) than buyers of previously owned homes (78 percent) bought detached single-family homes.

Starter homes run the gamut from well-kept, cozy dwellings to fixer-uppers and everything in between. From modern to antiquated, some homes may need a lot of work and effort to make them livable, while others may be small, yet livable. Don't expect a lot of bells and whistles with these homes, which are often a good match for someone who is either handy with repairs and upgrades or willing to shell out a few bucks to have some-one else do the work.

Starter homes are generally priced anywhere from $40,000 to $120,000 and up, depending on where you're located in the country. It might be hard to find a starter home under $120,000 in a city like Miami, for example, but easy to find a $65,900 three-bedroom, two-bath home in Fargo, North Dakota. Prices on most of these homes have spiked in recent years, thanks to a new demand spurred on by the low mortgage interest rates of the 2000s, but there is still a category of homes that are thought of as perfect choices for first-time home buyers.

16. What should I consider when looking at starter homes?

If you're in the market for a starter home, ask yourself the following ques-tions during your review process:

- ❏ Am I generally pleased with the condition of the home?
- ❏ If I had to move into the home as-is, would it be livable?
- ❏ If not, can I make some repairs and upgrades (such as painting, removing or replacing wallpaper and carpeting) myself?
- ❏ Do I need to hire someone to help bring the house up to speed, and if so, can I afford the extra expense?
- ❏ Is the neighborhood safe?
- ❏ Is my family going to fit in with the neighborhood?
- ❏ Does the area offer the quality of schools that I'm looking for?
- ❏ Could I live in this home comfortably for three to five years, or will I grow out of it sooner?
- ❏ If a starter home isn't the right fit, can I afford the down payments, mortgage payments, repairs, maintenance, and taxes on a larger, more suitable dwelling?

Tell me more

Starter homes can be a perfect "starting" point for first-time home owners who are willing to put some elbow grease into repairs and customizations that will make the home ready to live in, or who don't mind sacrificing some square footage (or that two-car garage) in order to live within their means and ultimately save for a larger home sometime down the road.

17. How important is location in the homebuying process?

There's a saying in the real estate profession: location, location, location. As a new home buyer, you'll want to integrate those words into your search process because location will play an integral role in your selection. Going beyond the home itself, factors like area schools, neighborhoods, quality of life, surrounding businesses and developments, and roadways will also play an important part in your ultimate decision. Don't make the mistake of falling in love with a home that's built twenty feet away from a proposed power line, or a beautifully kept home in a neighborhood where the rest of the properties are run-down. Do your research, check out the specifics on location before making any buying decisions, and you won't be sorry.

Tell me more

Where your new home is located is probably more important than the home itself, since structures can be changed but the location—and its surroundings—cannot. Start from the top down during your selection process, looking first at the city or town, then at the communities, the neighborhoods and subdivisions, and ultimately the specific locations of the homes within those neighborhoods or subdivisions. Where your home is located can be just as important as its appearance and size. If you ignore location issues like proximity to a particular school district, a job, or a bus line, even the nicest home will lose its luster when you become dissatisfied with the surrounding neighborhood.

Once you've determined which city, town, or suburb you'd like to live in, you'll want to identify one or more neighborhoods that suit your tastes. Look at factors like crime rates, school quality, commuting time to and from work, and amenities offered by the neighborhood. Do you have a family with young children? Then you'll also want to make sure there are other children in the neighborhood. Just as you created your home "hot button" list, you can list all of the criteria that are important to you and focus only on neighborhoods that meet those criteria.

18. How do I determine whether a neighborhood is right for me?

One great way to experience a neighborhood before buying is by driving through it at different times of the day. If you're looking for evidence of other young families, for instance, drive around either after school or on weekends, when children are most likely to be out playing. If you're concerned about noise from a nearby intersection or other neighbors, cruise through late at night, watching and listening for any signs of disturbance that might end up being a nuisance.

Tell me more

You can use a similar drill for condos, town homes, co-ops, and other types of detached housing, with one advantage: Because the units are usually close together—and sometimes joined by a common area—you can more easily talk to a few current owners. When doing so, don't be afraid to ask how satisfied they are with their own home choice. Tell them that you're thinking about buying a home in the development and ask them some or all of the following questions to get a feel for the development. If any of the answers or comments send up red flags, dig a little deeper (perhaps with another owner) to find out if the complaints are valid and worth noting:

❑ How do you like living here?
❑ Have you run into any major problems or issues in the development or surrounding community?

❑ Do the residents tend to be loud, quiet, or in between?
❑ Are there children living in the development?
❑ Does the area have any major issues with crime?
❑ Is the condo management firm or homeowners association receptive to its residents who have problems or issues?
❑ Would you recommend this development to one of your friends or family?

When shopping for a home you'll also want to look at the positioning of the home. If you have small children, for example, then a cul-de-sac would be a perfect choice, even if the homes on that particular part of the street don't fit your perfect home profile. Think about it: Would you rather have a fireplace or peace of mind knowing that your child is riding a bike on a street where few cars drive through? Also, if you have a large extended family that owns more than two cars, you might want to avoid a corner lot with a small driveway, since parking those cars on the grass is probably not an option.

Last but not least, talk to someone or do a bit of research on the neighborhood and surrounding community. Find out if it's a part of the city or an unincorporated area of the county (the latter usually means lower property taxes and fewer regulations, but also fewer city services). Ask about future infrastructure projects (you don't want to find out a month after closing that a fifty-foot-high cell phone tower is being constructed ten feet from your property line), and any such projects that your condo or homeowners association might be ready to hand out hefty assessments for, like a $5,000 per-unit assessment for new roofs. All of these issues should be factored into your choice of location and used to help make the best decision.

When choosing a location, also remember that not everyone can afford the perfect home in the perfect neighborhood, but that compromising on both ends just might find you living in a nice home in a good neighborhood. In the long run, most buyers find it better to live in a less-than-ideal home in the right location, rather than the other way around.

19. How much home can I afford?

Just how much home you can afford relies on two factors: how much money you can borrow, and how much down payment you have available to put down on the home. Thanks to the Internet, you no longer have to sit down with a lender to get an idea of what you can afford, as there are several online resources where buyers can key in a few numbers and get an estimate of how much home they can afford.

Ginnie Mae (a corporation within HUD) has a homeownership mortgage calculator on its Web site at www.ginniemae.gov/index.asp. You key in your gross income and liabilities and the site will spit out a rough estimate of what you can afford. If you want a more detailed estimate, click on "detailed estimate" and key in more parameters to obtain a more precise calculation for your specific region. Bankrate Inc., an Internet consumer finance marketplace that owns and operates a portfolio of Internet-based personal finance channels, also has a good "How much house can you afford?" calculator online at www.bankrate.com/brm/calc/newhouse/cal culator.as.

Tell me more

Using the following parameters, the calculator will produce two estimates for you: affordable mortgage payment and affordable home amount.

- ❏ *Gross Monthly Income:* Wages, investments/dividends, alimony received, other income
- ❏ *New Home Info:* Down payment, loan term (use thirty years if you aren't sure), interest rate (use 6.5 percent if you aren't sure), homeowners insurance (estimate $800 to $2,000, depending on size of the home, location, and your own insurance record), and real estate taxes (check your local tax collector or property appraiser's Web site for last year's taxes assessed on a property that you might be interested in)
- ❏ *Monthly Expenses:* Car payment, alimony paid, credit card payment, other debts

A word of caution: While this process will give you an idea of what size home you can afford (provided you're forthcoming with the numbers), don't confuse it with a "preapproval" (see Question 26). A prequalification estimate basically states that you're qualified for a loan based on a few preliminary questions, but it doesn't commit a mortgage lender to approve the mortgage. The mortgage lender will still have to conduct a complete review of your financial situation, including your credit report, income, and employment history. The preapproval process is very thorough, with the lender doing much of the work needed for a full-fledged approval, but without your having to identify an exact property for purchase.

A lender's prequalification process will give you a ballpark estimate of how large a mortgage you can afford. It doesn't matter which lender you obtain this from, since nearly all of them use the same criteria when determining what size monthly mortgage payments, property tax bill, and homeowners insurance you can handle. This will give you a good idea of the maximum mortgage amount you can afford and will help you focus your house search on properties within your price range.

20. What if I can't find the home of my dreams?

If this is your first home, don't expect your efforts to produce the home you've dreamed of all your life. Even your second or third home may not meet those expectations, but that's really just part of the process. Once acclimated to how it works, the homebuying routine does get easier, since many of the fundamentals haven't changed in the last few decades. The first time out, for example, you may not realize just how important a good credit rating is to your getting the right loan at the right interest rate, but after owning a home for several years and making timely payments, that score will improve and the next time out you'll be that much closer to reaching your goals.

Tell me more

Unless money is no object and your choice of locations is completely flexible, the odds that you'll find the perfect home at the right price and in the right place are pretty slim. Add in that the home search can be a time-intensive process, and the idea of perfection slips a little further away. A big part of buying such a large investment—particularly one that's already standing and that's been lived in by someone else—is the need for concessions that result in a good purchase decision, and that don't necessarily address your every single want and need.

According to NAR, most buyers face budget limitations when shopping for a home. Oftentimes buyers must spend more money or be forced to compromise on their vision of a "dream home." In 2003, 65 percent of buyers reported compromising on at least one characteristic of their home purchase. Buyers were most likely to compromise on the size of the home they purchased (21 percent) or the lot size (18 percent). Buyers were less inclined to compromise on neighborhood quality (12 percent) and their budget for a home purchase (14 percent).

You might, for example, give up that spare bedroom in exchange for a larger backyard for your family to play in. Or, you could cross that in-ground pool off of your wish list and instead purchase a town home that offers a community pool for all owners (a great way to meet and mingle with new neighbors!). Instead of that lake-view condo, opt for a unit with a garden view and save a few hundred dollars a month on your mortgage payment. Avoid "keeping up with the Joneses" and instead balance your and/or your family's unique wants and needs.

As you make compromises, be sure to address all of the "hot buttons" that you listed earlier in this chapter. Keep the list handy and maintain a record of what you're giving up in exchange for what to determine if the concession is worth it. Who knows, you may ultimately find your own dream home in the most unlikely of places.

CHAPTER TWO

NAILING DOWN THE FINANCES

21. How much do homes cost?

Existing homes run the gamut from $40,000 (or less) condominiums to $1 million-plus single-family homes. New homes are more expensive, generally running anywhere from $125,000 and up, depending on location, size and amenities. We can narrow the ranges down to a more digestible number by looking at the National Association of REALTORS' (NAR's) latest statistics, which reported a national median existing home price (half of the homes sold for less, half sold for more) of $169,900 in 2003, an 8 percent increase over the 2002 median home price of $158,100. The national median new-home (newly constructed) sales price was $194,500 in 2003, up about 3.7 percent over 2002. NAR forecasted the median existing-home price to grow by 4.6 percent in 2004, while new homes were expected to increase by 5.1 percent.

Tell me more

Using NAR's statistics as a guide, it's clear that home buyers have been paying more and more for the same homes over the last few years, but the group predicted that the high level of appreciation would level off in 2004. The 8 percent increase across the board in 2003 was the strongest showing since 1980, but NAR expected the percentage to decrease to 4.6 percent for existing homes and 5.1 percent for new homes in 2004, which is good news for you.

Besides consulting with your local paper or online multiple listing service, you can compare home prices across the nation via indexes created by companies like Coldwell Banker, which publishes an annual Home Price Comparison Index (HPCI). You can access more detailed information at the firm's Web site at www.coldwellbanker.com/homepage.html—click on Home Price Comparison Index.

In 2003, Coldwell Banker Real Estate Corporation compared the price
of a 2,200-square-foot house with 4 bedrooms, 2½ bathrooms, a family
room, and a two-car garage in neighborhoods across the country to come
up with the following data:

Most expensive markets

City	Price
La Jolla, Calif.	$1,362,375
Palo Alto, Calif.	$1,179,000
Greenwich, Conn.	$1,170,600
Beverly Hills, Calif.	$1,097,250
San Francisco, Calif.	$971,750
New Canaan, Conn.	$963,750
Wellesley, Mass.	$959,048
Newport Beach, Calif.	$916,000
Kailua Kona, Hawaii	$906,250
Manhattan Beach, Calif.	$904,500

Least expensive markets

City	Price
Binghamton, N.Y.	$121,400
Killeen, Tex.	$127,175
Minot, N.D.	$129,075
Oklahoma City, Okla.	$132,670
Topeka, Kans.	$136,266
Tulsa, Okla.	$136,625
Aberdeen, S.D.	$138,000
Billings, Mont.	$138,725
Sioux City, Iowa	$139,500
Parkersburg, W.V.	$141,250

Source: Coldwell Banker Real Estate Corporation, 2003 Home Price Consumer Index

The cumulative national average sales price of all markets surveyed in
the Coldwell Banker® HPCI was $318,172, a 9 percent increase over 2002.
The study's most expensive market was La Jolla, California ($1,362,375),
and the most affordable market was Binghamton, New York ($121,400),
indicating a price difference of $1,240,975 for a similar 2,200-square-foot
home. Six of the country's ten most expensive markets were in California,
two were in Connecticut, and one each was in Hawaii and Massachusetts.

Geography aside, how much you pay for a home depends on the following factors:

❑ The specific community or neighborhood you've selected
❑ Size of the home
❑ Age (in years) of the home
❑ Amenities the home offers
❑ How eager the home owner is to move out (sometimes urgency can create a "fast sale" environment, which is good for you as the buyer)
❑ The price of "comparable" homes that have sold in the community/ area recently
❑ Any other positive (or negative) features of the home or surrounding area (such as sinkholes, proximity to a large highway, or other factors)

22. What is a mortgage?

A mortgage is a long-term loan that you obtain from a bank, mortgage broker, online lender, thrift, or other source (sometimes even the property seller) to cover the purchase price (excluding your down payment) of your home. In exchange, the lender holds the home and land as collateral. You sign documents at the closing table that give the lender a "lien" against your property. If you fail to make payments as promised, the lender has the right to take the home through a process known as foreclosure.

Large in size, mortgage loans are paid off over long periods, typically either fifteen or thirty years. Monthly payments chip away at the principal balance, but don't expect to see that principal balance number go down much during your first few years as a home owner, particularly if you're using a thirty-year mortgage. That's because for the first few years you will be paying down your interest and not much of your principal balance.

Tell me more

Where would we be without mortgages? For starters, there certainly wouldn't be very many home owners. The typical individual or family isn't able to cough up enough to cover the six-digit price tags of homes, which makes mortgages a basic necessity for home buyers. Today's lenders offer a very wide variety of mortgage options or "products" (as they call them) to meet the needs of the nation's wide and varied base of home buyers.

23. How do I determine how long the term of my mortgage should be?

You can basically break down mortgages into two sections: fifteen years or thirty years. Use an online mortgage loan calculator from a Web site like

QuickenLoans.com (go to mortgage calculators, then to homebuyer tools and monthly payment estimator) to figure out which will work best with your budget, based on the home price range that you're looking at.

Tell me more

Here are two comparisons:

> Total loan price (home price plus closing costs, less down payment): $150,000
> Length of loan: 30 years
> Interest rate: 6.5 percent
> Monthly payment: $949

> Total loan price (home price less down payment): $150,000
> Length of loan: 15 years
> Interest rate: 6.0 percent (shorter-term loans generally have lower interest rates)
> Monthly payment: $1,266

As you can see, the fifteen-year loan increases your monthly payment by $317, but the amount of interest saved over the life of the loan is a whopping $130,800, nearly the price of another home! Low interest rates have pushed some home owners to the fifteen-year option (a choice previously unattainable due to double-digit interest rates), although many still opt for the thirty-year loans to avoid higher monthly payments. It's a decision you'll have to weigh once you select a home and loan option.

24. Should I get a fixed-rate or an adjustable-rate mortgage?

Here's the difference between the two:

- ❑ *Fixed-Rate Mortgage:* Just what it sounds like, this option features an interest rate that is fixed at a certain percentage throughout the life of the loan. Typically, the longer the term of the loan, the lower the monthly payments will be. With a shorter term, you will have higher monthly payments; however, you will realize a savings in the amount of interest you will pay over the life of the loan. Fixed-rate mortgages are recommended to borrowers who:
  - Look for predictable payments, because the payment is the same each month over the entire life of the loan

- Are willing to pay a higher interest rate in return for protection against the possibility of rising interest rates
- Are interested in building equity in their property through monthly principal and interest payments

❑ *Adjustable-Rate Mortgages* (ARM): This type of mortgage provides an interest rate and payment that periodically adjusts based on the current interest rate environment. With an ARM, you can tap the benefits of lower interest rates and payments in a falling interest rate environment, and the initial interest rate on this type of loan is typically lower than the interest rate on a fixed-rate mortgage. ARMs are recommended for borrowers who:

- Seek extra borrowing power, based on a lower initial payment, than is typically available with a fixed-rate mortgage
- Want to take advantage of a lower monthly payment to save money
- Plan to refinance or sell their property in a few years

Tell me more

Your mortgage broker or lender can help you decide which option is best for your situation. Talk to one or more mortgage professionals, and check out the current mortgage interest rates (they're usually published in your local newspaper, or you can check an online source like HSH Associates at www.hsh.com/today.html) to use as a comparison.

25. What is a prequalification letter?

A lender's prequalification process will give you a ballpark estimate of how large a mortgage you can afford. It doesn't matter which lender you obtain this from since nearly all of them use the same criteria when determining what size monthly mortgage payments, property tax bill, and homeowners insurance you can handle. This will give you a good idea of the maximum mortgage amount you can afford and will help you focus your house search on properties within your price range.

Tell me more

Lenders, real estate agents, online financial Web sites, and other resources all use pretty much the same formula to figure out what priced home you can afford. You'll want to figure this out before you start house hunting, since your budget can have a significant impact on your new home's size, style, and age. The more amenities and square footage a home has and the newer it is, the more expensive it will be. By obtaining a mortgage prequalification letter prior to embarking on your house hunt, you'll have a much better idea of exactly what you can afford.

26. What is a preapproval?

A preapproval letter tells home sellers that you have the ability to qualify for a certain mortgage amount, as judged by your lender. The process helps the lender determine the size of mortgage that you qualify for and helps you decide the price ranges to spend your time looking at. Unlike a prequalification, the preapproval process is very thorough, with the lender doing most of the review work required for a full approval, with the exception of the appraisal and title search (which can't be completed until you've identified a home to buy).

Tell me more

Preapproval helps you to:

❏ Know how much you can borrow.
❏ Confirm your ability to qualify for a mortgage based on your credit, financial, and employment information.
❏ Strengthen your position to make an offer on a house. (A seller will be more willing to accept an offer if the buyer is preapproved.)

To become preapproved, you'll need to work with a mortgage lender who will review your credit history, earnings information, employment history and assets. You can get this done in person, or via telephone and/or fax and the Internet. Here are the basic items that the lender will want to see:

❏ A loan application
❏ Verification of your employment (pay stubs, W-2s, and/or tax returns if you are self-employed)
❏ Information concerning any other sources of income (such as alimony)
❏ Source of cash for your down payment and closing costs
❏ Authorization to have your credit checked

27. What is a loan application?

The loan application is a detailed form that lenders use to evaluate whether or not they can give you a loan, and if so, the amount of money they can lend you. Lender applications vary by company, but on the application you may be asked to provide all or some of the following:

- ❏ Bank account balances and account numbers, as well as bank branch address
- ❏ Information about where you work or what sources of income you have
- ❏ Outstanding debts (including loans and credit cards with names and addresses of creditors)

Tell me more

Once this information is provided, the lender will pore over your financial situation, based on that information, and suggest programs that most closely meet your needs. If your financial situation doesn't measure up, the lender may also suggest steps you can take (cleaning up your credit, paying down some of your monthly debt, for example) to get it into mortgage-worthy shape. If this happens, bear in mind that not all lenders are alike, and that some may be more willing to extend flexible programs to first-time home buyers while others may be more stringent with their criteria. If you run into issues working directly with a bank, for example, find a good mortgage broker (unlike banks, these folks have a knack for matching lenders with borrowers who need help getting their finances in order) and have that person work on the preapproval for you.

It's not a final loan commitment, but a preapproval letter does show that you've taken steps to get the ball rolling on the financing before spending time on your house hunt. It shows your financial strength and proves that you're not just out there "kicking tires" but that you have the wherewithal to follow through with a purchase. This information is important to owners since they do not want to accept an offer that is likely to fail because financing cannot be obtained. It also helps you, as the home buyer, to know exactly where you stand when it comes to how much you can pay for a home when you enter into a purchasing agreement.

28. What are lenders looking for?

Let's just say that if there are any financial skeletons in your closet, they'll come out during the homebuying process. When reviewing your application, lenders typically look at the "four Cs" of credit—capacity, credit history, capital, and collateral—so come prepared to discuss and/or show proof of everything from past bankruptcies to alimony payments to credit blemishes, and everything in between. The individual lender has its own requirements, but the process generally starts at the credit rating and works backward from there. The better your credit, the less "other" documentation you'll have to show.

At a minimum, you'll need to produce the same information you did for the preapproval (see Question 26), then sit back and wait while the lender sifts through it. Be prepared to come up with additional documentation, such as proof of additional income, statements that show certain accounts were "paid off" even though it doesn't reflect that on your credit report, and tax returns for the last two years if you're self-employed.

Tell me more

Every year, roughly 1.1 percent of all home mortgages go into foreclosure, according to the Mortgage Bankers Association of America's 2003 numbers. The rates are higher in individual states. Lenders are wise to the issue, so before giving you cash to buy your home, they must make sure that:

❏ First and foremost, you are financially capable of paying for the home, the homeowner's insurance, and property tax payments.

❏ Second, you are not a credit risk (based on your past credit history with other lenders/debtors).

To determine these things, lenders will examine the following key aspects of your finances:

❏ *Assets and Resources:* Anything of monetary value that you own, including real property, personal property, and enforceable claims against others (such as bank accounts, stocks, mutual funds)

❏ *Liabilities:* Your financial obligations, including long-term and short-term debt, as well as any other amounts that are owed to others (such as credit cards)

Here's a description of each of the "four Cs" of credit that lenders look at:

1. *Capacity:* A borrower's ability to repay a debt. To determine your capacity, a lender will look at two basic ratios: the housing-to-income ratio, and the total debt-to-income ratio. The first compares monthly mortgage expenses (payment of principal and interest, taxes, and insurance, also known as PITI) to your gross monthly income. If your mortgage payment is $1,000 per month, for example, and your income is $4,000, then the housing-to-income ratio is 25 percent (this ratio shouldn't exceed 28 to 32 percent but can

be higher with certain programs). The second ratio compares total monthly debt payments (including PITI and obligations like car payments and credit card payments) to monthly income. If your monthly debt payment is $1,200 and your income is $4,000, then the debt-to-income ratio is 30 percent (this ratio shouldn't exceed 38 to 45 percent but can be higher depending on the loan program).

2. *Credit history:* A measure of willingness to make timely payments on debts, as illustrated by the borrower's credit history. The lender will review one or more credit reports to determine whether you qualify for a loan, and ultimately what interest rate you will pay on that loan. (See Questions 30–32 for more information on credit histories and scoring.)

3. *Capital:* A measure of how much cash (or assets readily converted into cash, such as stocks, bonds, certificates of deposit) the borrower has to make a down payment; cover closing costs; and handle other incidental expenses, such as moving expenses, utilities, and necessities like furniture. Lenders like to see that after paying such expenses, borrowers retain enough cash to pay two months of mortgage payments.

4. *Collateral:* The value of any assets that you pledge as security for a debt. When you request a mortgage, for example, the value of the property serves as a guarantee that the lender will get its money back. As such, lenders will typically lend only a percentage of the total property value (loan-to-value or LTV ratio). To calculate this ratio, divide the loan amount by the property value—for example, if the loan amount is $100,000 and the property value is $130,000, the LTV is 77 percent.

29. What should I ask my mortgage lender?

As a borrower, you have the right to ask questions of any lender with whom you might do business. Before handing over your financials, ask the loan officer, mortgage broker, or online lender the following six questions:

1. Does the application fee include the credit report, or do I pay for that separately?

2. Approximately how much should I factor in for closing fees? (Your lender is required by law to give you a good-faith estimate when you apply for your loan, but your loan officer should also be able to provide an estimate of closing costs before you apply.)

3. How long have you been in the mortgage business? (Look for a lender with experience, who can walk you through the application process and help you work through any obstacles that might crop up.)
4. Can I get a preapproval letter to take with me on my house hunt?
5. Will I be able to lock in the interest rate at any time? (Interest rates change daily, and many lenders will give you the option of locking in a rate at any time.)
6. Will this loan have prepayment penalties? (Make sure that you can prepay your loan without incurring a penalty. There may come a time in the future when you will want to make additional payments to save money on interest.)

30. What is a credit report?

Credit ratings are very important to lenders because they show your overall financial health and package it neatly into a multipage report that reads something like a report card from grade school. Credit reports are pretty telling, but they're also not always 100 percent accurate, so be prepared to deal with any inaccuracies that may come up during the review process.

Credit-reporting agencies prepare the reports. There are three reporting agencies and they all have slightly different ways of determining your financial health although they are focused on the same task at hand. The three main reporting agencies are Equifax, Experian, and Trans Union. If you have concerns about your report and what lenders will see on it, it would be wise to order a copy of your credit report (typically for a nominal fee) via phone or on the Web from:

Equifax
www.equifax.com
(800) 685-1111

Experian
www.experian.com
(800) 682-7654

Trans Union
www.transunion.com
(800) 916-8800

Once you've filled out your loan application, the lender will order your "score," commonly known as a FICO score (for Fair Isaac & Co.), from one or more of the reporting agencies just listed. Lenders also use salary, length of employment, and other factors when making their decision, but the FICO score is one of the first places they look. Some lenders use one of the three scores while others select the "middle" score as a measure.

Tell me more

A credit score basically condenses your credit history into a single number, and while the credit bureaus don't reveal how these scores are computed, the scores themselves are calculated by using scoring models and mathematical tables that assign points for different pieces of information that best predict future credit performance.

Credit scores analyze various aspects of borrowers' credit history, including:

❑ Late payments
❑ The amount of time credit has been established
❑ The amount of credit used versus the amount of credit available
❑ Length of time at present residence
❑ Employment history
❑ Negative credit information (bankruptcies, credit card charge-offs, accounts that are in collections)

According to Fair Isaac & Co., the five factors that determine your credit score are:

1. *Payment History (approximately 35 percent of your score):* The factor that has the biggest impact on your score is whether you have paid past credit accounts on time. However, an overall good credit picture can outweigh a few late payments, and late payments will continue to have less impact over time.

2. *Amounts Owed (approximately 30 percent):* Having credit accounts and owing money doesn't mean you are a high-risk borrower. But owing a lot of money on numerous accounts can suggest that you are overextended and more likely to make some payments late or not at all. Part of the science of scoring is determining how much debt is too much for a given credit profile.

3. *Length of Credit History (approximately 15 percent):* In general, a longer credit history will improve your FICO score. Lenders want to see that you can responsibly manage your available credit over time. However, even people who have not been using credit very

long may get high scores, depending on how the rest of their credit report looks.

4. *New Credit (approximately 10 percent):* People today tend to have more credit and shop for credit more frequently. But opening several credit accounts in a short period of time can represent greater risk—especially for people with short credit histories. Requests for new credit can also represent greater risk. However, FICO scores are able to distinguish between a search for many new credit accounts and rate shopping. FICO scores generally do not associate shopping for the best rate on a loan with higher risk.

5. *Types of Credit in Use (approximately 10 percent):* Your FICO score will reflect your mix of credit cards, retail accounts, installment loans, finance company accounts, and mortgage loans. While a healthy mix will improve your score, it is not necessary to have one of each, and it is not a good idea to open credit accounts you don't intend to use. The credit mix usually won't be a key factor in determining your score—but it will be more important if your credit report doesn't have much other information on which to base a score.

31. What does a low credit score mean?

The importance of a good credit rating really can't be overstated during the mortgage lending process. While lenders have become more flexible with their loan programs, most still hold the credit rating as one of the key deciding factors in both lending money and determining interest rates. Credit ratings show your overall financial health.

When you or a lender receives your FICO score, up to four "score reasons" accompany that score and help explain the top reasons why your score was not higher. According to Fair Isaac & Co., these reasons are more useful than the score itself in helping you determine how you might improve your score over time, and whether your credit report might contain errors. However, if you already have a high score (for example, in the mid-700s or higher) some of the reasons may not be very helpful, as they may reference the factors that have the least impact on your score, such as length of credit history, new credit, and types of credit in use.

Tell me more

Here are the top ten most frequently given score reasons. (Note that the specific wording given by your lender may be different from the reasons shown in this list):

1. Serious delinquency
2. Serious delinquency, and public record or collection filed
3. Derogatory public record or collection filed
4. Time since delinquency too recent or unknown
5. Level of delinquency on accounts
6. Number of accounts with delinquency
7. Amount owed on accounts
8. Proportion of balances to credit limits on revolving accounts too high
9. Length of time accounts have been established
10. Too many accounts with balances

32. How do I improve my credit score?

Because most creditors only report to the bureaus once a month, improving a credit score doesn't happen overnight. However, there are a few steps you can take right now to start cleaning up your credit blemishes. Here they are:

❑ Pay your bills on time. Late payments and collections can have a serious impact on your score.

❑ Do not apply for credit frequently. Having a large number of "inquiries" on your credit report can worsen your score because it looks like you're being turned down for credit and "shopping around."

❑ Reduce your credit card balances. If you are "maxed out" on your credit cards, this will affect your credit score negatively.

❑ If you do have any "unpaid" debt that you now have the ability to pay off, either do so, or try to set up a "payment plan" or settlement option with the debtor.

❑ If you have limited credit, obtain additional credit. Not having sufficient credit can negatively impact your score. (Even if you don't like charging purchases, obtain a low-limit credit card, use it every month, and pay off the balance within thirty days.)

❑ When you do get your mortgage, be sure to always pay it on time. Late mortgage payments are one of the most significant blemishes that you can have on your report.

33. What are my down-payment options?

Generally, the down-payment requirements start at 3 percent of the purchase price and increase from there, depending on the price of the home and your own ability to come up with the cash. There are also a number of first-time homebuyer programs (designed to help buyers who haven't purchased or owned a home within the last three years) that require no down payment, as well as "gift" down-payment programs available from organizations like Nehemiah and Ameridream (see Question 34). When calculating your down-payment needs, don't neglect to factor any out-of-pocket closing costs (which can't be folded into your mortgage—see Question 36) into your up-front expenses.

If you're a first-time home buyer, saving up for a down payment can be a daunting task. In fact, it's one of the biggest obstacles to home ownership in this country, since the average mortgage payment on a first-time or starter home isn't much higher than a rental payment anyway. The good news is that lenders realize this and have made your options both flexible and extensive when it comes to offering mortgage programs that weren't available a few years ago.

Tell me more

If you don't have a down payment to buy a home, there may be other options available to you. Lenders offer an unprecedented range of loans with 100 percent (or sometimes more) financing options with very attractive rates and flexible credit and income guidelines. Thanks to these programs, the need to come up with a hefty down payment is no longer such an issue. Still, even 100 percent financing requires some financial commitment on the part of the borrower, like covering closing costs, the cost of an appraisal, and a home inspection.

Home buyers can also use "gift" money for down payments—something that was not allowed just a few years ago. While some lenders may view this attempt to help (by, say, a parent) as a signal of the borrower's indebtedness, it is becoming a more acceptable way of obtaining the funds necessary to obtain a loan. Lenders have different guidelines for accepting gift funds of less than 20 percent of the home's purchase price, so inquire before taking this route.

If coming up with a down payment is a sticky point for you, a mortgage broker or lender can point you in the right direction, particularly if you fall into one of these categories:

- ❏ You have a strong source of income, but not much savings.
- ❏ You prefer to keep your assets in higher-yielding investments.
- ❏ You have low-to-moderate income and minimal cash reserves.
- ❏ You are a first-time home buyer with high rent costs that eat up much of your cash.
- ❏ You are a move-up home buyer with minimal cash reserves.

34. What mortgage programs are available if I don't have the down payment?

Lenders today offer a variety of flexible mortgage programs. The most basic is the conventional mortgage, which has no security guarantees other than the value of the property. Such loans typically demand either a 20 percent down payment, or a lower amount combined with private mortgage insurance (PMI). Federal Housing Administration (FHA) loans and other programs guaranteed by the government do not require such insurance, which is offered by independent insurance companies to qualified borrowers with down payments of less than 20 percent of a purchase price. The cost of such insurance varies by lender and loan type but generally costs about seven-tenths of 1 percent of the total loan amount annually.

There are many other nonconventional options available to home buyers right now. One of the country's largest lenders, for example, offers the following programs with down payments as low as 3 percent:

❏ No Money Down Plus Program: Lets all qualified buyers finance the entire purchase price *plus* up to 3 percent of the closing costs. (No income limits.)
❏ 3 Percent Solution Program: Gives all qualified buyers the opportunity of putting only 3 percent down on a primary residence and taking advantage of flexible qualifying guidelines. (No income limits.)
❏ Easy-to-Own 3 Percent Down loan: Lets qualified low- to moderate-income borrowers put only 3 percent down and take advantage of flexible qualifying guidelines. (Limited to borrowers who fall within HUD median-income levels.)
❏ Easy-to-Own 5 Percent Down loan with 3/2 Option: Allows low- to moderate-income buyers to use their own funds for 3 percent of the down payment and get the remaining 2 percent as a gift, grant, or from an approved Down Payment Assistance Program. (Limited to borrowers who fall within Department of Housing and Urban Development [HUD] median-income levels.)
❏ FHA Mortgage: Allows all qualified buyers to take advantage of a low down payment with flexible qualifying guidelines, with loan limits set by area. (See Questions 40–44 for more homebuying assistance options.)

Tell me more

One issue to be aware of when you're obtaining a mortgage and are either short on cash or dealing with a poor credit rating are subprime loans. Some of these loans have fallen under considerable scrutiny lately because of a practice known as "predatory lending." Subprime involves lending to borrowers with blemished, less-than-perfect credit or insufficient credit history who typically would not qualify for loans in the conventional prime market.

To offset the increased risk, the lender charges higher interest rates on these loans; legitimate subprime lenders have played an important role in allowing access to home ownership (or home improvements) for many consumers who would not have qualified otherwise.

35. What should I keep in mind when looking for a subprime loan?

If your own situation requires a subprime loan, the Virginia Housing Development Agency suggests following these ten tips.

1. Ask questions.
2. Shop around.
3. Be an educated consumer.
4. Read before you sign.
5. Avoid balloon payments (a loan that starts with small payments at first, then culminates into one or more significantly large payments).
6. Avoid prepayment penalties.
7. Know your rights.
8. Don't be afraid to say no.
9. Be prepared—build your credit.
10. Be wary of targeted advertising.

Lastly, if you believe you've been victimized by predatory-lending practices, contact the Office of Consumer Affairs in your state to report the problem. You can find a state-by-state list of predatory-lending reporting bureaus at the HUD Web site: www.hud.gov/buying/localpredlend.cfm.

36. What are closing costs?

Closing costs (also known as settlement costs) are expenses above and beyond the price of the property that the buyers and sellers have to pay when transferring ownership of a property. That includes a loan origination fee, the cost of the title search ("title" is the legal term for one's ownership interest in land), notary fees, attorney's fee (if applicable), taxes, and the cost of the property survey. Your total closing costs will vary depending on your location, and either the lender or the real estate agent can provide estimates of closing costs on your mortgage.

Tell me more

When your mortgage is finalized, you as the buyer will have to pay closing costs. Most lenders will not roll the costs into the mortgage, so they're essentially "out-of-pocket" or "up-front" fees that will need to be covered. Along with the basic title, service, and lender fees, closing costs include payments in advance for such items as taxes, property insurance, and interest to the end of the month.

Certain closing costs, such as recording fees and taxes, title examination, and credit reports, may be paid by the seller, or they may be shared between the borrower and the seller, depending on the terms of the sales contract. The Real Estate Settlement Procedures Act (RESPA) requires that your lender give you an information booklet and a good-faith estimate on your closing costs within three days of receiving your written loan application. RESPA also requires that at closing or shortly afterward, you must receive a uniform settlement statement (USS), which is a permanent record of all the final settlement charges. You are entitled to review the settlement statement one business day before you close on your loan. Read more about RESPA in Chapter 8: The Home Buyer's Legal Rights.

37. How can I reduce my closing costs?

Closing costs are pretty straightforward, but there are certain ways that you can reduce your out-of-pocket expenses. You can ask the home seller to cover some of the costs, for example, since lenders allow the seller to credit the buyer up to 5 percent of the purchase price for nonrecurring closing costs. These are costs that are paid on a onetime basis such as escrow, title, and transfer fees. Bear in mind that you may have to pay a bit more for the home to compensate the seller for paying your closing costs, particularly in a "hot" market, where the seller could easily find buyers who can cover their own closing costs.

Tell me more

Here are a few other strategies for reducing and/or eliminating your up-front closing costs:

    ❑ *Ask your lender to pay your closing costs:* Because lenders make a fee on each loan they make, your willingness to take out a loan at higher-than-market interest rates could convince the lender to make extra up-front fees. Those fees can be used to pay your closing costs.

❑ *Finance your closing costs:* Some lenders will allow you to finance (via a credit card, or by rolling them into the loan). Ask your lender up front if either or both strategies are acceptable.

❑ *Secure a no-point, no-fee loan:* The lower the points (see glossary), the higher the interest rate—and subsequently, the higher the payments—on a mortgage. Securing a no-point, no-fee loan will lower your closing costs, but realize that there is always a trade-off between points paid and the mortgage's interest rate.

❑ *Negotiate with the service providers:* Most buyers won't argue with a $300 title search, but what they don't realize is that they have choices of appraiser, escrow company, and title company. Check that each of these providers' fees are competitive before doing business with them.

❑ *Defer closing costs by closing late in the month:* Opt for a closing date around the end of the month and you'll save money on up-front interest. When you close, lenders collect interest for the remainder of the month. With only a few days left in the month, you'll end up paying just a few days of interest up front.

To best educate yourself on closing costs and what's required of you financially at settlement, check out the HUD settlement statement online at www.hud.gov/offices/hsg/sfh/res/sfhrestc.cfm (click on "Specific Settlement Costs"). Here, HUD gives home buyers a comprehensive look at settlement costs and goes through an actual closing statement line by line. Familiarize yourself with the form, which is used on all mortgage transactions, and you'll be well prepared when you get to the closing table.

38. Can I get a mortgage online?

The online lending environment has become increasingly sophisticated, thanks to Web sites like LendingTree.com, Interest.com, Eloan.com, and 4LowRates.com, all of which serve as sales channels for the originating lenders, who subsequently lend you the money and to whom you will make your mortgage payments. Most of the major lenders (Wells Fargo, Countrywide, etc.) also offer an online application process, homebuyer educational information, and other resources online.

Whether you're using a traditional lender or an online marketplace, the loan process is fairly simple. I recently applied for and obtained a home equity line of credit from GMAC Financing. The process took about forty minutes: five minutes to fill out the online application; five minutes on the phone with a loan officer to guarantee that I was who I said I was; and about thirty minutes of gathering necessary paperwork, such as proof of homeowners insurance, and faxing it to GMAC. For a first mortgage, that means entering the required information and/or providing necessary documentation from the comfort of your own keyboard, then letting the online lender use that information to track down the right mortgage for you.

Tell me more

After completing the application form, LendingTree.com guarantees that you will receive up to four "real" loan offers within hours. The company says it's unique in that it spurs lenders to "compete" for your business, rather than your having to track down the lenders individually. Whether you choose to work with one of those lenders is up to you, but the process will give you a good idea of what type of mortgage product will be best for you.

   With online security issues like credit card fraud and identity theft at the forefront of consumers' minds right now, it would be wise to inquire about the online lending firm's information protection and security processes before sending sensitive financial data (particularly social security numbers, driver's license numbers, and other personal information) through cyberspace. Lending Tree, for example, has reserved a Web page for explaining its security process, information protection, and other privacy issues at www.lendingtree.com/stm/aboutlt/privacy/security.asp. Interest .com has a similar site at www.interest.com/privacystatement.html. Make sure your online lender has taken similar measures, and ask questions if you have any specific concerns about these issues.

39. What information must I give to obtain a mortgage online?

Each online lender has different application requirements. A visit to Lend ingTree.com, one of the Internet's better known lenders, for example, revealed a checklist of items to bring with you when you're ready to sign up:

❑ *Social Security Number of All Borrowers:* Lenders use your social security number to access your credit record, which contains information about your income, debts, and credit payment history.

❑ *Current Mailing Address and Number of Years You've Lived at This Address:* This information will be compared against your credit

record to determine if your rent or mortgage payments have been
made on time each month.

❑ *Property Type of the Home You Are Purchasing:* Lenders need to
know what type of home you are purchasing because your home
becomes the collateral for your mortgage in the event that you default on the loan.

❑ *Purchase Price, Down Payment Amount, and Amount You Wish to
Finance:* This combined information helps lenders determine the
type of mortgage that may be best for your needs.

❑ *Employment Information:* Lenders normally like to see that you have
been with the same employer for a few years, or at least in the same
line of work, to demonstrate career stability.

❑ *Total Monthly Income and Debt Payments:* Your income and debt
payments illustrate your debt-to-income ratio, which is the amount
of money you owe each month compared to the amount of money
you make. This ratio helps lenders understand your total financial
situation.

❑ *Total Liquid Assets:* Lenders are interested in the amount and value
of any assets you may have to help them judge your ability to make
loan payments from available cash.

40. What government resources are available for home buyers?

A number of government-sponsored and -supported organizations offer a
plethora of resources, opportunities, and programs for home buyers, particularly first-time buyers and those that fall into very specific categories,
like veterans, who have access to Veteran's Administration mortgage programs. Programs developed by community development departments (at
the local level) and the Department of Housing and Community Affairs (at
the state level) assist home buyers with flexible lending programs; housing
options; and other resources, such as counseling.

Tell me more

At the national level, in December 2003 President George W. Bush signed
into law the American Dream Downpayment Initiative, which is expected
to help more Americans enjoy greater access to more housing opportunities. The legislation will provide an average of $5,000 in grants to approxi-
mately 40,000 lower-income families in 2004 and 2005 to help them pay
down-payment and closing costs on their first homes. Grants are made to

state and local governments through the U.S. Department of Housing and Urban Development's HOME Investment Partnership program. The program launched in spring 2004 and information about it is available at HUD's Web site: www.hud.gov.

Through the Fair and Accurate Credit Transactions Act of 2003, the government is also helping individuals with credit-reporting issues. Under this legislation, consumers will receive one free annual credit report; full disclosure of their numerical credit score and the factors influencing that score; notice of any negative impact on their credit score caused by multiple shopping inquiries; notification when negative information is added to their credit files; prompt investigation and correction of inaccurate credit information; and new tools to combat identity theft such as placing a fraud alert in their credit file. The legislation also calls for federal regulators to conduct a study of the effects of consumers' credit scores and credit-based insurance scores on the availability and affordability of homeowners insurance.

The three most popular homebuyer programs offered by or supported by the government are Veterans Administration Loan Program, Fannie Mae's Community Home Buyer's Program, and FHA loans.

41. What is a Veterans Administration loan?

Veterans Administration (VA) loans are available to qualified veterans, reservists, and active servicemen and women; these loans allow you to secure a mortgage up to a specified amount with no down payment and with flexible qualifying guidelines. The loans typically offer lower interest rates than you would find on any other mortgage. An application, a veteran's certificate of eligibility, and a VA-assigned appraisal are required.

Tell me more

To obtain a VA loan, the law requires that:

- ❑ The applicant be an eligible veteran who has available entitlement
- ❑ The loan be for an eligible purpose (such as the purchase of a primary home)
- ❑ The veteran occupy or intend to occupy the property as a home within a reasonable period of time after closing the loan
- ❑ The veteran be a satisfactory credit risk
- ❑ The income of the veteran and/or spouse be stable and sufficient to meet the mortgage payments, cover the costs of owning a home,

take care of other obligations and expenses, and have enough left over for family support

Find out more about VA loans at the VA's Home Loan Guaranty Web site: www.homeloans.va.gov.

42. What is Fannie Mae's Community Home Buyer's Program?

This is an income-based community lending model, under which mortgage insurers and Fannie Mae, the nation's largest supplier of home mortgage funds, offer flexible underwriting guidelines to increase a low- or moderate-income family's buying power, and to decrease the total amount of cash needed to purchase a home. Borrowers who participate in this model are required to attend prepurchase homebuyer education sessions. With this program, you can use a greater portion of your monthly income toward housing costs compared to other standard mortgage products.

The program also

- ❑ Requires a 5 percent down payment
- ❑ Does not require one month's mortgage payment (or cash reserves) in your savings account at closing time
- ❑ Provides expanded debt-to-income ratios (you can use up to 33 percent of your gross monthly income for housing expenses each month, rather than the standard 28 percent, and 38 percent for your total monthly debt expenses, instead of the standard 36 percent

Tell me more

To be eligible for Fannie Mae's Community Home Buyer's Program, you must attend a homebuyer education session offered or approved by your lender. You can't earn more than your area's median income (this varies by your location), and the loan can be used to buy single-family, principal residences, including condos, planned unit developments, and manufactured housing. Learn more about Fannie Mae's program at the group's Web site: www.fanniemae.com.

43. What is a Federal Housing Administration (FHA) loan?

FHA loans are a popular choice for home buyers, although the program isn't reserved only for first-time buyers. A wholly owned government corporation, the FHA has been around since 1934, with the goal of improving housing standards and conditions and providing adequate home financing through insurance of mortgages. Its loans feature reduced down-payment standards, lower mortgage insurance charges, and an approval process that's more relaxed than conventional mortgage loans.

Tell me more

The FHA loan program requires only 3 percent down and is typically more forgiving of past credit issues, but it requires that borrowers not have a bankruptcy discharged within the last two years; that they not have a foreclosure within the last three years; and that any outstanding collection amounts, judgments, or charge-offs be paid in full before closing. The advantages of using an FHA loan include the following:

❑ A lower down payment is required.
❑ FHA loans are assumable (transferable to a new buyer) with a qualified borrower.
❑ Higher qualifying ratios of 29 percent for housing and 41 percent for total indebtedness are allowed on existing construction; 31 percent for housing and 43 percent for total indebtedness are allowed on new construction.
❑ The underwriting (approval) standards are more flexible.
❑ Gift funds for down payment and closing costs are allowed.
❑ The up-front mortgage insurance premium can be financed.
❑ Less cash is required out of pocket.
❑ The down-payment requirement (as low as 3 percent and never more than 5 percent) is the lowest of any nonsubsidized financing program.
❑ Nonoccupant coborrowers are allowed for qualifying purposes.
❑ The seller is allowed to pay prepaid expenses (closing costs) and can pay up to 6 percent of the purchase price toward closing costs and discount points.
❑ Charges on conventional loans such as tax service fees, underwriting fees, copy fees, and courier fees are not allowed to be charged to the buyer.

Find out more about how FHA loans work from your lender or mortgage broker, or visit HUD's Office of Housing Web site at www.hud.gov/offices/hsg/index.cfm.

44. What homebuyer programs are available in my region?

There are a number of homebuyer programs available at the state, regional, and community level. In southwest Florida, for example, the Pinellas

County Community Development Department (PCCDD) is just one group that helps match up buyers with homes and financing. To promote home ownership in the region, the PCCDD offers the following services (see www.pinellascounty.org):

❏ *Low-Interest Mortgages:* The purpose of the low-interest loan program is to preserve the existing housing stock and encourage neighborhood improvement efforts. The program provides home repair loans to low-income and moderate-income home owners at interest rates ranging from 0 to 5 percent, depending on household income and family size.

❏ *First-Time Homebuyer Program:* The Housing Finance Authority provides financing for the rehabilitation, construction, and/or purchase of new and existing housing for moderate-, middle-, and lower-income families.

❏ *Down-Payment Assistance:* This program assists low- and moderate-income households to purchase homes that will serve as their principal residence. It provides financial assistance in the form of interest-free second mortgages with repayments deferred for up to five years.

❏ *Special Lender Programs:* Low-, moderate-, and middle-income buyers who have the desire and capacity for home ownership often lack the financial resources to purchase housing that meets their needs. According to the PCCDD, such individuals and families may be qualified for one of the programs offered by local governments or nonprofit corporations.

Tell me more

In Los Angeles, the Community Development Commission offers similar services, targeted at helping first-time home buyers through its Home Ownership Program (HOP), which provides loans of up to $60,000 (or 25 percent of the home purchase price) in designated target areas of the city, or $50,000 (or 20 percent of the purchase price) in nontarget areas. The loans are "shared equity loans" with no monthly payments and no interest. There are income guidelines to meet, and all information is on the city's Web site at www.lacdc.org/programs/homebuyer/ownership/index.shtm.

Whether you're looking for first-time homebuyer counseling programs, down-payment assistance, or low- to zero-interest loans, a phone call to your city or county offices should be able to get you pointed in the right direction. You can also use a search engine like Google.com to find such programs. Try combining your city or county name with words like "first-time homebuyer program" or "homebuyer assistance" for the best results.

45. What is seller financing?

When a property owner agrees to payment of a portion of a home's purchase price over time, with the debt to the seller registered on the title as a mortgage, it's known as seller financing, a vendor take-back mortgage, or a purchase-money mortgage. This is a home-financing strategy in which you, the buyer, borrow from the seller instead of—or in addition to—a bank or traditional lender. Seller financing is usually used when a buyer can't qualify for a bank loan for the full amount, and when the seller is willing to gain a sales commitment, but is not as concerned with getting the full sales proceeds immediately.

Tell me more

In a seller-financed real estate transaction, a seller agrees to lend money to the buyer to purchase and close on the property. The seller is basically assuming the role of banker, and as such carries back the loan. As a buyer, you negotiate a down payment with the seller, then send regular, monthly payments to that person over the life of the loan (as negotiated). This financing option is flexible in that sellers and/or buyers can determine the structure of the loan, repayment period, interest rate, late charge provision, and other variables. The necessary paperwork is prepared by the title or escrow company after the terms are worked out between the buyer and the seller.

46. Is seller financing a good thing?

Depending on your financial situation, there are both pros and cons of using seller financing. Here are the positives that you can expect from this financing strategy:

❑ *Easier Qualification:* Buyers who don't meet the sometimes rigid requirements necessary to qualify for a conventional mortgage can use seller financing as an option. While conventional lenders put a lot of weight on credit ratings, for example, a low credit score doesn't always mean the borrower is a credit risk. A past bankruptcy, a job layoff that resulted in a few bills left unpaid several years ago, or a divorce can all have adverse effects on a person's FICO score. If you have experienced such challenges, seller financing can give you the opportunity to purchase a home.

❑ *Flexibility:* Unlike a typical mortgage, seller financing can be conducted on terms that are completely negotiable between the two parties. There may or may not be a credit check, and the down payment will be negotiable, as will the length and structure of the loan. If you know that your financial picture is going to improve over the next three years, for example, you might negotiate a small down payment, low monthly payments for the first five years, then a larger balloon payment down the road. Who knows? By then you may be able to finance the rest of the purchase through a traditional lender at a favorable rate.

❑ *Cost Savings:* Bank loan origination fees can be hefty, but seller financing basically eliminates such fees, which can save you 4 to 10 percent of the total loan price. You can also save on monthly mortgage insurance fees and additional closing costs, like loan fees (points). As for the interest rate, it will likely be higher than current market rates (sellers are looking for a return similar to what they would get from investing the sale's proceeds).

❑ *Time Savings:* Seller-financed transactions can close quickly, as long as both parties agree to the terms. Such transactions eliminate the bureaucracy and paperwork that lenders require, making the path to the closing table that much shorter.

Tell me more

There are also downsides with seller financing, the most obvious being the fact that the seller is taking a chance by extending a hefty dose of credit to a borrower whom other lenders have turned down. Buyers also have to be aware of certain challenges of seller financing. Before getting too involved in the process, ask yourself:

❑ *Does the property have significant defects?* Sellers who know their properties won't qualify for conventional financing (say, because of active termite problems, which a lender's termite inspection would reveal) are quick to offer financing. To protect yourself, conduct inspections and have professional inspectors do the same before committing.

❑ *Is the property overpriced?* A lender won't finance a home unless an appraiser determines that it's worth at least the asking price. Don't overpay for a home just to get seller financing. If you're unsure about property values in the area, talk to a real estate professional about having a CMA (comparative market analysis) done on the home to determine its fair market value. You can also get a rough idea of a home's value at a Web site like www.gethomevalues.com.

❑ *Are the monthly payments too high?* Conventional loans are based upon monthly payments over fifteen or thirty years. Don't fall for a seller-financed sale that involves high monthly payments over a short time, as you could quickly find yourself in over your head. Instead, make sure the payments are appropriate for your financial situation.

❑ *Does the seller expect a balloon payment?* This is a lump sum amount that will come due at some point during the regular course of payments. While right now it may not seem like much of an issue to sign up for a balloon payment of $10,000 or $20,000 in five years, think carefully before committing to such a financing arrangement. It may sound good right now, but five years down the road it may not be easy to come up with the hefty sum.

Weigh out the pros and cons of seller financing and do your homework before dealing one-on-one with a home owner who is eager to finance your buy. Look at property prices and as an added precaution, ask for references (they'll be holding your title and taking payments from you, after all) and obtain legal counsel to ensure that the investment you're making is both solid and beneficial for you as the buyer.

47. What is PITI?

You'll probably hear this term used more than once during your homebuying venture, and it stands for principal, interest, taxes, and insurance. Every loan includes principal and interest payments, and those labeled "PITI" also include taxes and insurance (homeowners insurance and PMI, if applicable).

Property taxes and homeowners insurance payments can be paid in an annual lump sum. PITI means that these payments are instead spread out over the year and included in each mortgage payment. So if your mortgage payment is $600 (P and I), and your annual tax payment and homeowners insurance fees are $2,500 total, then your monthly mortgage payment will be about $808.

Tell me more

Because mortgages are such large loans, paid off over a period of fifteen to thirty years, the monthly payments comprise all or some of the following five components:

1. Principal: The actual loan balance
2. Interest: The interest you owe on that balance
3. PMI
4. Real estate taxes: Assessed by different government agencies to pay for school construction, fire department service, and other facilities
5. Property insurance: Insurance coverage against theft, fire, hurricanes, and other disasters

At a minimum, your mortgage will cover #1 and #2, with #3 depending on the type of mortgage that you've taken out. Lenders typically require this insurance if the loan exceeds 80 percent of the home's value (in other words, if your down payment was less than 20 percent of the purchase price).

With PITI, you essentially "escrow" your tax and insurance payments (meaning that the amounts are tacked on to your monthly mortgage payment, so that they're covered when the tax or insurance bill comes in). You can also opt to pay the latter in full when they come due, rather than in monthly installments to the escrow account, which is also known as an "impound" account.

If you choose to have your property taxes and insurance included in your monthly payment, you will also need a certain amount of "reserves" of these monthly costs to be deposited with the lender at close of escrow. Whether you get a PITI loan is a purely personal decision, based on your own financial situation. Property taxes are usually billed once a year, and insurance varies from monthly to yearly.

If you would rather manage these bills on your own, opt for the lower monthly mortgage payment. If you know that you will have difficulty coming up with the extra money to cover such costs, which can be significant (depending on the price of the home), you will probably be better off paying PITI throughout the year and not having to worry about it when the bills come due.

CHAPTER THREE

THE HOUSE HUNT

48. What should I do before searching for a home?

Before you start your home search, make sure you have your ducks in a row, both on the financing side and in terms of your own wants and needs. Use this checklist as a guide:

- ❑ Get your financial house in order first (see Chapter 2 for in-depth information on how to do this). That includes determining what your budget will comfortably allow and sticking to it and getting preapproved for a mortgage.
- ❑ Familiarize yourself with the different housing types available to help narrow your search.
- ❑ Determine your minimum requirements, as well as any desired additional features.
- ❑ Clearly outline any items that you *don't* want in a house.
- ❑ Determine the desired location (close to schools, work, public transportation, and other amenities or infrastructure).
- ❑ Familiarize yourself with the mortgage process.
- ❑ If you're using a real estate agent, select one with whom you feel comfortable and who understands your needs.
- ❑ Check listings and prices throughout the United States on the Internet.
- ❑ Tap resources like friends, relatives, a good real estate agent, home advertisements in the newspaper, home magazines, foreclosure databases, and listings of homes for sale by owner (FSBO).
- ❑ Use a scorecard to compare homes (see Question 58).
- ❑ Familiarize yourself with the home inspection process that you will need to conduct in a short period of time on all homes (see Question 58) that you look at.

❑ Through it all, maintain your perspective, keep a critical eye open, and try to keep emotions out of the process.

49. How do I start the house-hunting process?

If you didn't jot down notes about your wants, needs, and desires in Chapter 1, flip back and do that before you go any farther (see Question 6). Having these house-hunting parameters in hand while you are touring homes will keep your search focused and grounded and will help you avoid getting too emotional or caught up in the process. Approach the market from a pragmatic standpoint, and act like an investor—no matter how much actual "money" you're investing in this home—who is most interested in getting the best return for her money, not the fanciest house on the block.

Ask any successful home buyer about his own search process and he will probably tell you that the combination approach worked best. That means using a mix of local newspaper advertisements, yard signs, online for-sale ads, online multiple listing service (MLS) systems, the services of a professional real estate agent, and a sprinkle of your own knowledge of "what you want" to find the right home, rather than just expecting a single channel to produce the home of your dreams.

Tell me more

Once you've determined that you're financially ready to buy a home, it's time to start looking for the right one. Some people may already have a community or specific neighborhood in mind, while others may not have narrowed down that part of their search. For the latter, a good first step is to simply drive around in your city, county, or community of choice and envision yourself living in the homes that you pass by. Ask yourself if you'd rather live in the city, the country, or a suburban area, whether you'd like to have neighbors "close by" or farther away, and whether you would prefer a single-family home, or one of the many multifamily options available on the market today (see Chapter 4: Multifamily Housing Options).

Here are a few key first steps that you can take when whittling down your options to locate the right home:

❑ *Find the prime location:* Ask yourself: How far am I willing to commute to my job? How are the local schools, shopping centers, public transportation, and other public amenities? Does the neighborhood or community offer amenities that will either fit with or improve my lifestyle? (Schools are usually a large factor for buyers, and you can get information about school systems by contacting the city or county school board or the local schools themselves. Your real estate agent may also be knowledgeable about schools in the area.)

❑ *Educate yourself:* The more research you do prior to buying your home, the better off you'll be. Learn all you can about the community that you've chosen, ask about the typical tax obligations and insurance requirements (a property in a flood zone, for example, will require flood insurance coverage), contact real estate agents, and drive through your selected neighborhoods to get a true feel for them.

❑ *Get preapproved for a mortgage:* If you haven't done this already, see Question 26 for more information.

❑ *Get detail oriented:* Once you've located desirable neighborhoods, start your search. View as many homes as you can and jot down notes about each as you go through them. At the end of the day, review the notes and cross off any homes that don't meet your criteria, and come up with any additional questions about those that looked like good prospects.

By pinpointing a location, educating yourself, and getting your finances on the table before embarking on your house hunt, you'll have a much better chance of finding the appropriate home without losing too much hair in the process. First-time home buyers, in particular, should follow these early steps as the process doesn't change much as you purchase homes throughout your lifetime. Once you've been through it once, you'll know exactly what goes into the house hunt and be able to replicate your success as you move up into larger homes, or into new geographies.

50. What resources can I tap to help with my house hunt?

Home buyers generally use a number of different sources of information in their home search, with the majority of them using the services of a real estate agent to locate the home that they ultimately purchase. In 2003, for example, the National Association of REALTORS (NAR) reported that 41 percent of all buyers stated that they first learned about the home they purchased through an agent. With the advent of the Internet, an increasing number of home buyers are finding their homes on the Internet, then turning to an agent to seal the deal.

In 2003, NAR says, 11 percent of buyers first found their home on the Internet—up from 8 percent in 2001 and an increase from less than 1 percent in 1995. Many buyers search the Internet in addition to relying on an agent, so that while an agent searches for homes for his buyer, that buyer is doing his or her own ferreting around for the right home. NAR reports that yard signs (16 percent) remained the second most common way that buyers found out about their homes, followed by newspaper advertisements (7 percent), friend, neighbor, or relative referrals (7 percent), and builders (7 percent). Least helpful to buyers were home books and magazines (just 1 percent found their homes this way, presumably because of the timeliness issue involved with hard-copy publications).

Tell me more

Potential buyers have many information sources at their disposal as they search for a home. Still, NAR reports that buyers rely on their agents more than any other source for home search information. In 2003, for example, 86 percent of buyers consulted an agent to some degree in their home search—up from 79 percent in 2001. Here are a few local resources that can be particularly helpful to home buyers looking for specific information:

- ❑ *Community Resources:* Contact your local chamber of commerce for promotional literature, or talk to your real estate agent about welcome kits, maps, and other information. You may also want to visit a local library, which can be an excellent source for information on local events and resources, and librarians who are probably familiar with the community.
- ❑ *Home Prices in Certain Areas:* A real estate agent can give you a ballpark figure by showing you comparable listings (known simply as "comps"). Agents have access to comparable sales maintained on a database. If you have a specific property in mind, check out your local property tax or tax appraiser's Web site for similar data on specific properties.
- ❑ *Property Taxes:* The total amount of the previous year's property taxes is usually included in the listing information located in the MLS. You can also ask the seller for a tax receipt or contact the local assessor's office. Remember that tax rates can change from year to year.

As a buyer, you have a broad range of resources, professionals, and educational sources available to help with your house hunt. Even though the Internet is gaining in popularity, yard signs and open houses (see Question 61) remain popular "traditional" resources that can help you identify what homes are for sale in a certain neighborhood. (When the home across the street from mine went up for sale recently, no fewer than ten cars a day stopped in front of the property as their drivers and passengers jotted down the listing real estate agent's name and number.)

During your search, you'll also find a number of FSBO properties for sale. On these, you'll deal directly with the property owner (unless you have a buyer's agent, in which case he or she will handle it). Other good sources of house-hunting information include the local newspaper, which typically features an expanded real estate section on Sundays. Internet Web sites like Realtor.com, BuyOwner.com (for FSBOs), Yahoo! Real Estate at www .realestate.yahoo.com, and MSN House and Home http://houseandhome .msn.com all feature homes for sale, searchable by geographic region, price, and other criteria.

One word of caution for buyers, particularly those who are looking in "hot" markets, where homes that are priced right sell quickly: Don't get your hopes up too high until you determine that the home is still available. Most online real estate sites have vastly improved their updating capabilities but early on were criticized for updating only weekly and posting outdated listings that—by the time the buyers contacted their local real estate agent—were already sold or under contract.

Be particularly aware of this if you're looking for a home in an area that is currently a "seller's market," where the best homes sell fast and multiple offers are common. If there are more buyers than homes for sale in your area, the days a home is on the market may shorten to a week or even less than a day. In fact, homes may sell before they're even registered in the MLS, since agents have a certain grace period between the time they list the home and the time they submit it to the MLS. If you fall in love with a home that someone has made an offer on, take heart: In a multiple offer situation, the seller is not under any obligation to negotiate with the first buyer who submits an offer.

51. What should I keep track of when looking at homes?

One of the best ways to keep track of the various homes that you'll look at during the home search process is to simply jot down notes as you preview the properties, or immediately afterward. It might seem time-consuming at first, but having those records will pay off in the long run, particularly when it comes time to make your final decision.

If you're in the middle of an intensive home search, you're bound to forget a good portion of the information you learn along the way. As you cross that twentieth threshold, for example, expect to have already forgotten the total square footage of home number two, or the color of the pool deck on home number ten. In today's information age, there are a number of tools that you can use to keep track of the information and make it readily available, should you need it. Even if you're working with a buyer's agent who will keep track of the most vital housing information, it's advisable to retain your own notes to pore over when the home sellers aren't standing over you and when you're not packed into a car driving around neighborhoods.

Tell me more

The Government National Mortgage Association (Ginnie Mae) suggests using this homebuyer checklist during your house hunt:

Ginnie Mae's Homebuyer Checklist

Basic Information
Home address _____
General description _____
Asking price _____
Taxes _____
Total sq. footage _____ Lot size _____
Age _____ No. of beds/baths _____

Interior
Rooms/sizes & features
Living room _____
Kitchen _____
Dining room _____
Master bedroom _____
Bedroom 2 _____
Additional bedrooms _____
Bathroom(s) _____
Closets _____
Basement/attic _____
Laundry area _____
Storage _____
Other _____

Appliances/condition & comments
Stove/oven _____
Refrigerator _____
Dishwasher _____
Garbage disposal _____

HVAC
Heat type _____

Forced air, heat pump, baseboard, radiators, etc. _____
System age/condition _____
Heat source _____
Electric, gas, oil _____
Air-conditioning type _____

Exterior
Condition _____
Surface (wood, stucco, brick, siding, etc.) _____
Comments _____
Gutters _____
Yard
Comments _____
Natural features _____
Landscaping _____

Additional features
Porch, deck, patio, etc. _____
Garage/carport _____
Neighborhood _____

Location/commute
Close to _____
Work _____
Schools or day care _____
Other _____
Water source (city or well) _____
Sewer or septic _____
Trash pickup _____

Emergency services
Police station _____
Fire station _____
Hospital _____
Comments and questions
_____
_____
_____
_____

If you're not too keen on using such a comprehensive checklist for every home you look at, try this shorter, more concise worksheet when previewing homes, and make any additional notes on the bottom of the page:

1. Your first impression of property: (good, average, or poor?)
2. Location is convenient to: (circle those that apply) employment/ transportation/schools/shopping/recreation
3. Do floor plan, layout, and outdoor area suit your family needs?
4. Will your furniture and appliances fit?
5. Is the house in keeping with the general neighborhood area?
6. Are neighborhood real estate values rising, or at least constant?
7. Does the property represent good resale value?
8. Do zoning bylaws protect values and prevent undesirable change?
9. Is the tax rate reasonable?
10. Are projected improvements likely to increase taxes?
11. Condition of house: construction (good, average, poor)
12. Condition of house: plumbing
13. Condition of house: electrical system
14. Condition of house: heating
15. Condition of house: evidence of seepage or shifting?
16. Landscaping: (good, average, poor)
17. Annual heating cost $
18. Annual property tax payment $

Whether you use Ginnie Mae's lengthy list or a shorter format, the key is to find something that you're comfortable using and that will truly help you weed out the less appealing properties after a day or more of looking at various homes. Caught up in the showing process, you may forget an important aspect—positive or negative—that could play an integral role in your house hunt. These are the same oversights that come back to haunt you when you take over ownership of the home. Transparent issues like zoning restrictions (Will I be able to add a room in five years?), resale expectations (Will I get my money out of the home and possibly pocket some profit if I sell it in three years?), and the neighboring homes (Does my neighbor do proper upkeep on his property?) are especially critical to note, since such problems aren't visible to the naked eye.

To reduce future problems with your home (I say reduce because there's no such thing as a perfect home or neighborhood, and there will always be some issues to grapple with as a home owner), take good notes during this exploratory process and compare homes to find one or more that make the best fit. You'll be glad you did!

52. What is the multiple listing service (MLS)?

As you go about your home search, you'll probably hear the three letters "MLS" a lot. Created and managed by real estate professionals, the MLS is a proprietary database that serves as a gathering point for all property listings in a certain geographic region. Each home "listing" includes extensive information (not always available to the general public on a Web site, for example) about the home, the property, and its surroundings.

To gain access to the MLS, you must be a member of the local Board of REALTORS, which means the service is most available to real estate agents. Because of this, the MLS also covers issues like how commissions are to be split and other information regarding the relations between brokers and agents.

Tell me more

The MLS is more of an issue for home sellers, and less of one for you, the buyer. Without a listing in the MLS, for example, a home doesn't get the kind of exposure that it needs to sell within a desirable time frame and at the right price. There are exceptions to the rule, of course. We once put out an "FSBO" yard sign and sold our home within an hour to a neighbor, but most real estate agents will tell you that we probably "left money on the table" by doing so.

53. How can I access the MLS?

There was a time when the MLS was a highly secretive system accessible only to real estate agents, but as a home buyer in the 2000s, you'll be among the early users of online MLS systems designed specifically for home buyers who start their searches on the Web. For buyers, the MLS provides a concise, comprehensive look at all of the homes that are listed for sale with brokers in a specific area.

Tell me more

You can gain access to at least a portion of that information by logging onto a local agent's or broker's Web site and clicking on a link that might say, "See All Properties Listed in Your MLS Area." After inputting a few parameters, you'll get an eyeful of the properties, their prices, sizes, and general location. To get more specific information—like address, property taxes, and other key criteria—you will have to deal with an agent who can access the entire MLS.

Because real estate agents have all the access they need to their own MLS systems, they are your first stop on the road to getting all of the listings. However, if you're not interested in working with an agent, or if you'd rather do some intensive research before calling one, then the online MLS system is a good first step. Remember, however, that when you surrender your personal information, it is going to immediately be turned into a "lead" for an agent, so expect a phone call, an e-mail, or both, from an agent who would like to work with you on the house hunt.

54. What is a virtual office Web site (VOW)?

You can gain more specific information in another way: by providing a bit of your own information to a real estate broker (including an online broker like eRealty, Inc., at www.erealty.com), through a system known as a virtual office Web site (or VOW, for short). These systems literally include "all of the information" available through the regional MLS systems, and can be accessed by consumers who give up some personal information (name, address, phone, homebuyer preferences or criteria, for example), essentially becoming "clients" of that online or traditional broker.

Tell me more

On eRealty, for example, you will first select your geographic region. At press time, the company offered listings in eleven different states. Click on Falls Church, Virginia, and you'll get a Web page where you can click on "view eRealty homes" under the "Buying a Home" header. The link will give you a listing of homes for sale by eRealty agents, in descending order by price. At the top of the page, however, you'll see these words: "There are X number of properties available in the local Multiple Listing Service (MLS). Register now to see them all." This is where you sign up for what the company calls a "free account," by providing the following information—through a system known as a VOW:

- ❑ First name
- ❑ Last name
- ❑ Valid e-mail address
- ❑ Phone number
- ❑ Preferred contact time
- ❑ eRealty password (which you create)

Through the registration process you will also tell the company how you heard about it, whether you currently own or rent, whether you're interested in selling, where you're looking to buy and/or sell, and any comments for the eRealty real estate agent who will receive your "lead" and follow up on it with a phone call to you. The company also asks you to agree to its terms of use before accessing "all the data," which it defines as "gaining access to the private password-protected, Intranet area of the eRealty Web site."

55. Are MLS postings accurate and up-to-date?

The information shared through the MLS is generally considered to be the most updated available, as many such systems have taken to updating their systems as often as every fifteen minutes. When they first emerged in the late 1990s, online brokerages got a lot of flak for not keeping their systems updated, but many have since improved their systems to reflect what's currently available in the market. Before you get too excited over a great-priced home with an attractive virtual tour, however, it's wise to double-check to see if it's still on the market. Also know that you won't find any FSBO properties in the MLS, as most owners either create their own online presence or sign up for a service like BuyOwner.com, which maintains its own database of listings online.

Tell me more

As you look at MLS listings, remember that they were prepared by the seller and/or that person's real estate agent, so the information could be inaccurate. Before making any final decisions on your home choice, be sure to verify any such information with another, more reliable source. The best approach is to mix the MLS information with other sources, such as guidance from a real estate agent, information gathered from yard signs and newspaper ads, and other sources to round out your home search.

56. What are the different types of real estate agents?

Consumer demands and industry changes have led the real estate industry to break out of its traditional mold of only representing the seller in a transaction, and into a more flexible way of doing business. There are traditional agents, dual agents, transaction facilitators, and buyer's agents (a category further segmented into "designated buyer agent" and "buyer agent" working for a traditional company), with the last three comprising the "new" type of agent on the market today.

Tell me more

Here's a breakdown on the various types of real estate agents working in your local market right now. Keep in mind that some real estate agents perform a mix of services for both home buyers and sellers (listing a property one day, representing a buyer on another property the next, etc.). Because their roles tend to cross over, agents are required to disclose their roles via an agency relationship disclosure statement, which you will probably be asked to sign before they start working for you:

❑ *Traditional Real Estate Agent:* This agent represents the seller all of the time and does not represent buyers. Most agents have broken out of this mold since the opportunities to represent buyers are usually more abundant, and because the listing is usually considered the "holy grail" of the industry, since it is common knowledge that listings basically "sell themselves" while buyers need attention and a multitude of services in order to get a sale closed.

❑ *Dual Agent:* This type of agent represents both the seller and the buyer at the same time and is legally required to disclose that "dual" relationship to both parties since a conflict of interest could occur. If this occurs and you have not already agreed to a dual agency relationship in your (written or oral) buyer agency agreement, your buyer's agent will ask you to sign a separate agreement or document permitting him to act as agent for both you and the seller. The general consensus is that it's difficult for a dual agent to advance the interests of both the buyer and seller, so you might want to avoid this situation. The dual agent owes each party the same duties, yet buyers and sellers can prohibit dual agents from divulging certain confidential information about them to the other party. Some companies also offer a form of dual agency called "designated agency," in which one agent represents the seller and another agent represents the buyer. This option (when available) may allow each "designated agent" to more fully represent each party.

❑ *Transaction Facilitator:* This agent represents neither the buyer nor the seller and typically handles the paperwork and filing necessary to see the transaction through to a close.

❑ *Buyer's Agents:* Such agents sometimes represent the seller, and sometimes the buyer. They are traditional agents who have embraced the fact that buyers also need representation, yet they do not limit themselves to only working with buyers. If your agent is a designated buyer agent, then that person can represent buyer or seller in a specific transaction.

57. How do I decide which type of agent to use?

When choosing an agent to work with you'll want to first set up an in-person (if possible) interview with a handful of agents. During those interviews, ask the following nine questions and use the information gathered to make an educated decision:

1. Are you a full-time real estate agent? If not, when will you be available to work with me? (Part-time agents may not be willing or able to give you the full attention that you need.)
2. How many transactions do you close a year?
3. What is your average annual sales volume? (Active real estate agents generally sell $1.5 million in properties annually.)
4. Are you a Realtor, a broker, or an agent? Are you licensed to sell real estate? (This is a must for all professionals who facilitate real estate transactions between buyers and sellers.)
5. How long have you been conducting business in the area, and how familiar are you with the region, its communities, amenities, transportation, and other features?
6. Will you provide me with your e-mail address, fax, and cell phone numbers in the event that I need your help while you're away from the office?
7. Do you have access to the MLS?
8. Will you represent me or the seller in the transaction?
9. Would you work as a buyer's agent, seller's agent, or dual agent? How will your fee be handled? Will I have to sign a buyer's agreement?

Also ask the agent for references of several people who have bought their homes from him or her during the past three months. When calling those referrals, ask if the buyers—in particular—were satisfied with the agent's performance. Find out what they liked and did not like about the real estate agent, then use that information to determine whether that agent will be a good fit for your own needs.

Tell me more

If you are unsure of whether you need a real estate agent to handle your home purchase, the Department of Housing and Urban Development (HUD) says, "Using a real estate agent is a very good idea." That's because the details involved in home buying, particularly the financial ones, can be overwhelming. A good real estate professional can guide you through the entire process and make the experience much easier. Additionally, that professional will be well acquainted with all the important things you'll want to know about a neighborhood you may be considering, such as:

- ❏ The quality of schools
- ❏ The number of children in the area
- ❏ The safety of the neighborhood
- ❏ Traffic volume
- ❏ Community amenities

The real estate agent can also help you figure out the price range you can afford and search the classified ads and MLS for homes you'll want to see. "With immediate access to homes as soon as they're put on the market, the broker can save you hours of wasted driving-around time," says HUD. And when it comes time to make an offer on a home, the broker can point out ways to structure your deal to save you money by explaining the advantages and disadvantages of different types of mortgages. A good agent will also guide you through the paperwork and be there for some hand-holding at the closing table, where you'll sign the final papers and leave with the keys to your new home tightly clenched in your fist.

58. What should I look for when previewing homes?

It's easy to get caught up in the home-previewing process. Sellers tend to keep their properties in perfect, "showing shape," complete with that apple-pie-baking-in-the-oven smell (it's true—agents often suggest owners bake a pie before an open house), neatly manicured lawn, and spotless kitchen. Homes for sale usually look great, which makes it very hard to use a critical eye when looking at them. Buyers often lose sight of the fact that there might be structural problems or defects that they'll have to contend with later.

To avoid falling into this trap, have a good idea of exactly what you should be looking for *before* entering the home. Determine on your own, with your family or with your significant other, just which elements of the home each of you will check out during the tour and stick with the plan, no matter how terrific the home looks to the naked eye.

Tell me more

All homes are complex, no matter how big or small, old or new. In every home there are internal heating and cooling systems, electrical components, hot water heaters, plumbing fixtures, and myriad other issues that are hard to assess for the average home buyer. Realize that you're not going to catch every single flaw or defect on your first run through a home, although there are a few key areas that every home buyer should look at before making a decision. Once you've decided on a home, you will also want a professional home inspector to conduct a more thorough review of the home (see Question 60).

Here are the most crucial areas of a home that you should look at, ask questions about, and review critically on your first visit to a home:

Interior
_____

- ❏ Windows, doors, and door frames
- ❏ Flooring
- ❏ Ceilings
- ❏ Cabinets and counters
- ❏ Fireplace
- ❏ Basement
- ❏ Attic

Exterior
_____

- ❏ Maintenance
- ❏ Color and quality
- ❏ Porch and deck
- ❏ Gutters and roof
- ❏ Foundation
- ❏ Doors and windows

Surroundings
_____

- ❏ View and boundaries
- ❏ Driveways and walkways
- ❏ Bushes, trees, and grass
- ❏ Neighboring homes (and how they're kept and maintained)

59. What should I ask if the house needs work?

If your first impression of these different aspects of the home is either good or "workable" (meaning you have the time and money needed to correct any flaws), HUD suggests asking yourself these five questions before coming back for a second showing (see Question 62) and prior to making an offer on the home:

1. Is the asking price in line with prices of similar homes in the area?
2. Is the home in good condition, or will I have to spend a substantial amount of money making it the way I want it?

3. How long has the home been on the market? (If it's been for sale for a while, the seller may be more eager to accept a lower offer.)
4. How large a mortgage will be required? (Make sure you really can afford whatever offer you make.)
5. How much do I really want this home? (HUD says the closer you are to the asking price, the more likely it is that your offer will be accepted. In some cases, you may even want to offer more than the asking price, if you know you are competing with others for the house.)

Tell me more

At this point, you'll either be ready to move on to the next house on your list or to come back for a more thorough second showing, during which you'll have a good idea of certain areas that need more attention prior to making a decision.

60. What should I look for in a newly constructed home?

New homes are a bit different than their "existing" counterparts. Everything in them is so shiny and new, and it's much easier to overlook structural defects and other problems in the dwellings. Making it particularly difficult is the fact that you will have either a model home or someone else's home (which you accessed through a builder referral) to look at, not your actual home.

Fortunately, there are ways to ensure that your new home doesn't become a money pit. From checking builder references to hiring independent home inspectors who will monitor the entire business process to clearly communicating your wants and needs to the builder, there are myriad steps you can take to educate yourself on the new-home buying process.

Tell me more

For starters, make sure the builder is properly licensed and insured. Do this by checking with your state's Construction Industry Licensing Board and by asking to see the builder's certificate of insurance. Next, ask for a list of customer references and call them. If possible, try to visit at least one home (not the builder's model) to look for any structural problems or defects that might end up in your own home.

During that visit, ask yourself:

❏ Do the walls meet in the appropriate places?
❏ Are the walls straight?
❏ Are there any noticeable major blemishes?
❏ Does it look as if the home was built with quality workmanship?

As you move through the home, open and close doors to make sure they operate correctly, and check out the workmanship and operability of cabinets. Don't be afraid to ask the home owners if they received good service from the builder after the sale because any builder will tell you that there is "no such thing as a perfect home." The builder who is responsive when it comes to follow-up work is the one you want to work with. Also in the realm of after-sale service is the home warranty—an area that you should discuss with your prospective builder. Most will offer a one-year warranty at minimum, or an insured warranty that protects against major structural defects and is transferable to the new owner, should you decide to sell before it expires (typically ten years). Ask about the warranty, study the contract, familiarize yourself with it, and then ask questions.

For more insurance, check to see if the builder is a member of the local home builders association. The National Association of Home Builders lists its local affiliates online at this Web site: www.nahb.org/local_association_search_form.aspx. This extra measure of protection is important because membership in an industry group typically indicates a true interest in keeping up with codes, regulations, and industry trends. You can also contact your local consumer affairs department or Better Business Bureau to see if any complaints have been filed against the company. Bear in mind that complaints lodged by home owners aren't necessarily valid and are often resolved quickly.

When you're shopping for a new home, it's important to realize that while model homes may look snazzy, they're not always a good benchmark from which to measure. That's because the models typically go up first, with subsequent structures benefiting from any modifications or changes that were made as construction progresses. If you're purchasing a home that's not built, you may also want to enlist the help of an American Society of Home Inspectors–certified new home inspector who, for a flat fee, will monitor the home's various stages of construction to ensure that everything is being handled correctly.

61. What is an open house?

Drive around on a Sunday afternoon and you're bound to see "open house" signs strategically placed near the road, pointing you to homes that are for sale and "open" for all prospective buyers to walk through freely without the assistance of a real estate agent. There will be a listing agent and possibly other licensed agents on hand, but you as a buyer are free to inspect these homes without your own agent. You will also see FSBOs holding their own open houses, without the help of an agent. Regardless of the format, the basic goal is the same: to get potential buyers into the home to look around and possibly come back for a second, private showing or even make an offer on the home.

Tell me more

Open houses are a great tool for buyers, particularly for those who haven't yet settled on a particular neighborhood or community. Getting into homes without having to set up showing appointments and get preapproved by a mortgage lender is a terrific way to see specific homes in certain areas and get a handle on the general condition, interior design, and exterior qualities of homes. Depending on how busy the open house is, you may not have the opportunity to ask important questions of the owner or agent, so save them for a an "official" showing at a later date. If the home is in a highly desirable neighborhood and the open house is packed with people, try to get that showing scheduled as soon as possible.

And if the home is listed with a real estate agency, don't expect the home owner to be on hand as real estate professionals generally handle the showings, open houses, and negotiations for their sellers.

To find open houses, start with your local newspaper. Many agents advertise their open houses, the hours they will be held, the prices and features, and the addresses for the homes. Agents and/or sellers will usually put a sign in the ground (one near the road, another in front of the home) a few days before the open house, announcing the event and the times. Keep your eyes peeled for these indicators as you drive through communities where you think you might like to live.

Because open houses are usually held between 11 A.M. and 4 P.M. on Sundays, you might want to plan your day to include a few open houses. Create a route that allows you thirty to sixty minutes at each home, sign in on the home's guest list (used by the agents for follow-up, and to show owners how much traffic came through during the event) and use the time to get a relaxed, no-pressure perspective on homes that you might like to purchase.

62. What is a second showing?

Everyone knows you can't possibly check out an entire home in an hour or two, which is why agents and sellers offer second—and sometimes even third or fourth—showings to prospective buyers. If you're working with a real estate agent, she may schedule your first showings just twenty minutes apart in order to get in as many homes as possible on a weekend afternoon. It won't take you long (fifteen minutes maximum) to determine whether the home is a possibility, and if it's worth a second showing, which is typically longer and more involved than the first run-through.

Tell me more

The goal of the second showing is to make sure that all the things you liked about the home on the first time out are still appealing and alluring. If this isn't the case, then you'll probably want to cross the home off your list and move on. If you do still like the home, this showing is where you should take a closer look at the structure and mechanical systems. Ask a lot of questions and, if working with an agent, request that the home owner be on hand to respond to queries that the agent may not be able to answer. (Be prepared for resistance on this one, as most agents prefer to keep buyers and sellers apart until they reach the closing table.)

Even if you're going to hire a home inspector to do a professional home inspection before buying, the second showing is a great time to examine a few physical aspects of the home. Try to schedule your second showing at a different time of day from your first showing. If you saw the home on a Sunday morning, for example, schedule the second look for a Tuesday evening, so you can get a better feel for the neighborhood and the home's surroundings.

63. What should I look for during the second showing?

As you go through the home for a second time, use this laundry list of questions for each area of the home:

The Exterior

- ❏ Is the home in good shape?
- ❏ Does it look sound?
- ❏ Are the lines of the home straight?
- ❏ Does the roof sag? (Walk across the street and look at it from a distance.)
- ❏ On brick homes, is the mortar between the bricks cracked?
- ❏ Is the paint in good shape, or is it peeling?
- ❏ Is the aluminum siding dented, or is it in good shape?
- ❏ Is the sidewalk cracked around the house?
- ❏ Does the sidewalk pitch in toward the home (a problem that could lead to basement leaks) or slope away from it?

The Roof

- ❑ Are the shingles curling or lifting?
- ❑ How old is the roof? (A new roof should last between fifteen and twenty-five years.)
- ❑ Have there been any problems with it? (Ask the agent or owner.)
- ❑ Are there any signs of leakage (discolored paint near the ceiling, for example) in the home?

Windows and Door Frames

- ❑ Are they in good shape?
- ❑ Are there storm windows?
- ❑ Has the caulk dried out and pulled away?
- ❑ Are the windows or door frames cracked?
- ❑ Can you feel air blowing in around the windows?
- ❑ Are the frames square?
- ❑ Are there cracks in the plaster above the door frames?

The Interior

- ❑ Does the home look sound and sturdy?
- ❑ Is the house clean and well kept?
- ❑ Do the wood floors creak when you walk on them?
- ❑ Are they pitched in any one direction?
- ❑ Are the stairs shaky?
- ❑ Is the kitchen or bath linoleum tile peeling or bubbled?
- ❑ Is the plaster cracked?
- ❑ Is the paint or wallpaper peeling?
- ❑ Are the walls and ceiling straight?
- ❑ Do doors and drawers open easily?

Basement

- ❑ Are there cracks in the walls or foundation?
- ❑ Does it smell damp or musty? (Most unfinished basements do, by their very nature.)
- ❑ Does the basement leak?
- ❑ Is the house in a flood zone?

Attic or Crawl Space

- ❑ Is the area insulated?
- ❑ Is there a fan?

❑ Are there air leaks?
❑ Is there poor ventilation?
❑ Is there any sign of water leaks or insect damage (rotting wood beams, for example)?

The Mechanics

❑ How old are the hot water heater and furnace systems?
❑ Is there a central air-conditioning system or are there window units?
❑ Do the window units work, and do they come with the home?
❑ What are the typical heating, electricity, and water bills? (Ask the owner or the agent.)

Plumbing and Electricity

❑ When you turn on the faucets, showers, and bathtubs, do they all work?
❑ Do they all drain well?
❑ How is the water pressure?
❑ Does the water have an odor?
❑ Is the home on the city water system, or does it have its own well?
❑ Do the lights work?
❑ Are there enough electrical outlets and telephone jacks?

Tell me more

Once you've gone through this checklist, ask if it's okay to plunk yourself down on the couch and try to imagine yourself living, sleeping, and playing in the home. Ask yourself the following more personal questions:

❑ Does it feel right?
❑ Will my furniture and "stuff" fit well in the home?
❑ Is this a place I'd like to come home to after work?
❑ Will I enjoy spending weekends in the home, or in the pool or back-yard?
❑ Will my family and/or friends also enjoy the home?
❑ Do I feel comfortable here?

Depending on whether your answers are mostly positive, mostly nega-tive, or a mix of the two, you'll either want to sleep on it, cross the home off your prospective list, make an offer (see Chapter 5), or even ask for a third or fourth showing.

64. How long will it take to find my home?

In 2003, the typical home buyer searched for a home for eight weeks before making a purchase, viewing about fifteen homes during the process, according to the HUD Home Scorecard, which shares this sage advice with home buyers: "There isn't a set number of houses you should see before you decide. Visit as many as it takes to find the one you want. On average, home buyers see fifteen houses before choosing one. Just be sure to communicate often with your real estate agent (or the seller, depending on whom you're working with) about everything you're looking for. It will help avoid wasting your time."

Tell me more

Wouldn't it be great if buying a home were like buying a used car? You'd visit a car lot on a Sunday afternoon, drive a few models that catch your eye, and select one. If you don't like any, a short skip and a hop over to the next car lot is sure to reveal at least one that meets your criteria. After an hour or so of waiting while the finance folks approve your loan and draw up the paperwork, you're driving off in your new wheels.

Unfortunately, home shopping is not as easy, or as clear-cut, as automobile shopping. A five-minute drive in a used car will reveal whether the brakes work properly, the gears shift correctly, and the interior is to your liking. When shopping for a home, even a one-hour tour won't turn up all defects and your likes and dislikes. Approach the process with a critical eye and be willing to spend some time (at least the average of eight weeks, sometimes longer) to find the right one. There are always more newspapers to look at, more homebuyer magazines to peruse, more yard signs to follow up on, and more listings to look at with real estate agents, so unless you're in a time crunch to get into a home, the best bet is to just take your time and wait for the right home to come along.

That said, there are slightly different rules for certain home buyers. Here are a few exceptions to the rule:

❑ *New-Home Buyers:* New-home buyers are able to pick from a selection of new neighborhoods in their target area, then drill down to a certain model, ask for customizations, and be done with their search. That's not to say the process can't take as long as the existing home search, but there are some "constants" in the new-home buying process (namely, that the construction and main systems in the home are new and covered by a warranty) that can make the road a bit shorter.

❑ *Buyers on a Budget:* Buyers who are on a strict budget are somewhat limited in their home selection and therefore have less to choose from. It doesn't sound like a desirable situation to be in, but it does cut down the number of homes that you would qualify for, and therefore can make the house hunt shorter (or longer, depending on how discerning you are).

❑ *Buyers in a Hot Market:* Here's where things get sticky. No matter how much money you have to spend or how much time you have to complete your house hunt, all bets are off if you're in a real estate market where home-listing inventories are low and demand is high. Certain areas of California are currently a perfect example of this, particularly for buyers in search of affordably priced homes (the median home price in the state in 2003 was about $410,000, according to the California Association of REALTORS). In such a market, you'll be forced to make decisions more quickly (no third and fourth showings lest you risk losing the home to another buyer) and spend less time on the house hunt.

Regardless of what type of market you're operating in, how big or small your budget is, or how quickly you need to get into your new home, it's important not to rush this decision, as it's probably the biggest financial commitment you'll make in your lifetime. If you find yourself in an uncomfortable situation (being pressured to make a decision or risk losing the home, for example) that doesn't feel quite right, your best move may be to back away from the deal and sleep on it for a night or two, talk it over with your real estate agent, attorney and/or family, and come back to the situation with an educated, fresh view. If the deal is still there when you return, then it may be time to make a decision. If not, then move on to the next opportunity.

PART II

THE HOMEBUYING PROCESS

CHAPTER FOUR

MULTIFAMILY HOUSING OPTIONS

65. What is a town house?

A town house (also called a town home) is basically a row house located on a small lot with other similar units. In fact, a town house is what used to be called a "row house" in cities five decades ago. Town house owners generally share an interior wall with one or more other units. Title to the unit and the land under it is vested in you, the individual owner, with a fractional interest in common areas (if applicable). Most town houses also have a homeowners association, which levies fees and uses the funds to maintain common areas (roofs, fences, landscaping, etc.) of the properties.

Generally two-story units, town houses are one step away from the single-family home, in terms of both price and living space and amenities. (A one-story version of the town house is usually called a villa.) Town houses typically have their own private entrance, parking right in front of the unit or in a garage, and amenities that you wouldn't always find in a single-family home, such as community pools, exercise rooms, and tennis courts. These units also do not require the same upkeep and maintenance that a single-family home owner has to worry about.

Tell me more

If mowing lawns, repairing wood fences, and painting exteriors aren't your thing, then a town house might be a good choice for you. Known for their low-maintenance lifestyles, town house buyers become the exclusive owners of the structure and the property it's located on, but they don't always have to handle all of the repairs and maintenance that goes with it. Property boundaries distinguish your property from that of your neighbors, but to the naked eye the lines are blurred, thanks to the uniformity of the complex and the proximity of the dwellings to one another.

One of the most attractive qualities of the town house is price. Overlooking the fact that your living space may include a shared wall, a smaller garage, and a more community-like living environment, town houses are close to a single-family home, yet they're usually more affordable than the average home. In the Tampa Bay area of Florida in 2003, for example, the average price of a new town house was $140,000, while the average price of a new single-family home was $201,000.

As the buyer of an attached dwelling like a town house, you will obtain exclusive ownership rights to the interior space of the particular unit. In addition, you also own the common area—grounds, fences, shared walls, and facilities—with other owners in town houses (the same holds true for condominiums). Such housing developments are also known as PUDs, or planned unit developments. Like single-family residences and unlike condos, town houses include the land they occupy (if the land is not owned individually, then the property is considered a condominium).

One key point to remember when purchasing a town house is the fact that as a new owner, you automatically become part of the homeowners association, to which you pay dues on a monthly, biannual, quarterly, or annual basis. Those dues usually cover the cost of upkeep, maintenance, and insurance of the complex's common areas. If you're looking at town houses, it's important to ask exactly what is covered before making your purchase decision. Some of the funds may go to a reserve account, used to cover major expenses (such as a new brick fence around the entire complex or roof replacement), and others may go for services like cable television service, garbage collection, and water.

Buying a town house involves some of the same issues that are involved in buying a detached home, so look back at Chapter 3 for house-hunting tips that you can use when going through these units in search of the right one. Look for a unit that minimally meets your current housing needs (or that includes some "room to grow"), that is within your price range (as determined by your preapproval), and that is reasonably priced. Most important, be sure to find out if the unit is indeed a town house, versus a condo, as the latter can also be a two-story unit with an attached garage. Ask questions, and find out if your purchase includes ownership of the land and common areas. If it does, then it is indeed a town house. If not, then it's a condominium.

66. What is a condominium?

Another popular multifamily housing option is the condominium, or condo. When you purchase a condo, you hold the deed for the unit, take out a mortgage, pay property tax on the unit plus a percentage of the common areas, and a monthly maintenance fee. Condominiums are typically "stacked" on top of one another, although some have multiple floors and look more like town houses, complete with garages.

With a condo, a board of directors governs the complex with the owner having one vote. The condominium owner has a fee-simple absolute unrestricted ownership and is characterized by the individual ownership of living units and the joint (as a group) ownership of the common elements of the project.

Tell me more

Condos have gained in popularity over the last few years, mostly due to increases in land costs in certain areas of the country, which—along with the low mortgage interest rate environment—has driven up the cost of single-family homes. Condos are much like apartments in their appearance, and they can run the gamut from low-rise complexes of several units to high-rises with hundreds of units.

When you own a condo, you own the interior walls, floors, ceilings, and everything located between these boundaries. Once outside the unit, the ownership is shared in common with the other unit owners. This includes the exterior walls of the building, the roof, sidewalks, pool/spa areas, landscapes, and other elements. Condominiums are formed by executing and recording a "declaration of condominium" by the complex's owner or developer. Also part of the filing are the articles of incorporation and bylaws for the election of the governing board.

With a condo, the common areas are maintained by a homeowners association, which handles the daily responsibilities of maintenance, repair, and cleaning. The expenses of maintaining and operating the building are paid by the unit owners in the form of fees and assessments, both of which are levied and collected by the homeowners association. What you'll pay in association fees is usually determined by the size of the unit. The owner of a one-bedroom unit, for example, would pay less than the owner of a three-bedroom unit in the same condominium complex.

You may sell your condominium, but the directors of the association must give advance approval to the purchaser. Most condominiums restrict or control leasing, and it is very important that you make yourself aware of these policies before buying if you are purchasing as an investment.

67. What are the pros and cons of condo ownership?

If you're considering a condo purchase, realize that there are some key pros and cons of this housing choice. They are:

Pros

- ❑ There is little or no exterior maintenance
- ❑ Amenities like pools, spas, tennis courts, and playgrounds are included but are not your responsibility to maintain on a day-to-day basis.
- ❑ Condos are often located in populated areas near employment centers, shopping, and community services.
- ❑ This housing choice is attractive for those on limited budgets or for first-time home buyers.

Cons

- ❑ A part of your monthly housing obligation will include homeowners association fees (these are factored in when your lender considers your financing application).
- ❑ There are limitations on ownership in that your "property" is limited to the interior walls and their contents.
- ❑ As a condo owner, you will share one or more walls, a ceiling, and a floor with your neighbors.
- ❑ You will have less privacy than you would in a single-family home.
- ❑ Condos can take longer to resell than single-family homes.

Here are some of the key questions to ask about the condo or town house on your first trip to the property:

- ❑ What are the monthly or quarterly assessments that I must pay (with the understanding that this may increase in the future)?
- ❑ What are the restrictions on my right to sell, lease, or mortgage my unit?
- ❑ What are the restrictions on the age of children who may use the pool, beach, or other facilities?
- ❑ What are my obligations in terms of the maintenance of windows, screens, air conditioners, and plumbing?
- ❑ Are there any mandatory club memberships or recreation facility leases involved with this condo?
- ❑ What pet restrictions are in place?
- ❑ Are there restrictions on parking certain vehicles or boats?
- ❑ Are there rules governing the types of drapes, window hangings, or floor-coverage materials that I can use?
- ❑ Are there limitations on the use of recreational facilities, or any noise ordinances (such as the playing of music) that I should be aware of?

If you're satisfied with the answers and interested in digging further, use these queries, which are more detailed:

❑ What does the association's insurance cover and what do I have to insure?

❑ How is the association organized?

❑ How are voting percentages determined, and what will my percentage be?

❑ How are association fees charged, and is there a limit on the number of fee increases that the association can implement in a given period of time?

❑ How are decisions made? (Important decisions, such as the erection of a new brick wall typically require a majority vote of all owners.)

❑ Who actually runs the association? Is it the members through their board of directors or a professional manager or management company?

❑ Is there pending litigation—or has there been litigation against the complex? (This is particularly important, especially in terms of issues like shoddy construction and defects. If a condo seems underpriced, for example, it could be because the owner wants to get out of the legal wrangling.)

❑ Are there any liens against the property itself?

❑ How financially stable is the association? Are owners paying their dues and adding to the association's reserve fund (a portion of monthly fees that the association saves to pay various expenses)?

❑ Can I have a copy of the articles of incorporation and a current financial statement to review?

❑ Do you have a copy of the minutes from the last few homeowners association meetings that I can review? (If time permits, find out when the next meeting is and attend, just to see for yourself how the complex is governed. If the meeting leaves a bad taste in your mouth, you may want to do a similar check on other condos or town houses in the area to find one that's more suitable.)

If after weighing the pros and cons and investigating the requirements and obligations of your target property, you feel that a condo is the right choice, realize that many before have discovered such properties to be an excellent choice for those who don't have time for the maintenance of the home and yard. Factor in the amenities that most complexes offer their residents, and it's easy to see why condo ownership has become a popular option for home buyers.

68. How do I finance a condo or town house?

Financing on multifamily housing is basically the same as that on single-family homes, although (depending on your area) condos and town houses are generally thought to be a more affordable option, particularly for first-time buyers who may not be financially ready to purchase a single-family home. A waterfront condo many not fall into that category, of course, but a three-bedroom town house will typically cost less than a three-bedroom home of the same age and quality in the same geographic area.

Some lenders have restrictions on types of condos approved for Federal Housing Administration (FHA) financing, and others may charge a slightly higher interest rate depending on the owner-occupancy rate of the development, since lenders want to be assured that the development is financially sound. The higher the investor-owner rate—or the higher the number of buyers who rent their units instead of occupying them—the riskier the development is financially. It's all about stability: Renters are transient in nature, so those owners who "rent" rather than occupy are more likely to default on their mortgages.

Tell me more

Because financing a multifamily property is much like buying a single-family home, you can find all of the details on this part of the homebuying process in Chapter 2. The difference with condos and town houses lies in the way the ownership is structured, since you don't always own the land under the unit and because there are other variables involved, such as ownership and homeowners associations.

When you own a condo or town house, property taxes are paid on the unit and your share of the land and common facilities.

69. How do I insure a condo or town house?

Town houses are generally insured by their individual owners—just like single-family homes—but condo insurance is typically handled much differently. Your condo association probably has a master policy that insures all the property and common areas that are collectively owned by the unit owners. These policies usually cover the actual structure of your home, which means you don't have to purchase this coverage separately. That's good news for most, since homeowners insurance rates have skyrocketed over the last few years.

Tell me more

What a condo association's policy doesn't cover is your personal property and (sometimes) the improvements or custom work on your unit. To protect your new investment, you'll want to obtain a separate policy that covers at least:

❑ Your personal property, up to the limits you wish to purchase

Plus all or some of the following, depending on your needs:

❑ The replacement cost of your residential unit and certain permanent attachments
❑ Coverage for loss of use (reimbursing you for expenses for loss of use of your home caused by certain events or perils)
❑ Medical expenses
❑ Liability exposures (protecting you against certain risks, such as bodily injury or property damage)
❑ Expense of loss assessment by the association against the unit owners
❑ Protection from damages resulting from freezing of plumbing, vandalism, and other causes

Before making a purchase decision, be sure to factor in the additional association fees, possibility of assessments (additional fees levied on owners to cover large projects) in the near future, property tax liabilities, and included insurance coverage; then figure out how much extra you'll have to pay to cover the rest of your personal property and liabilities. With a firm handle on exactly how much your condo will cost, you'll be able to make a much better purchasing decision.

70. What is a homeowners association?

This is where the purchase of condos, town houses, and cooperatives becomes much different from that of single-family homes. While the latter may be located in a neighborhood with a homeowners association—and while home owners may pay fees for certain upkeep and maintenance—associations that govern condos and town houses tend to be much more active and involved. These organizations are made up of unit owners within the development who govern relations between the owners and administer the rules, bylaws, and covenants of the complex.

Before you buy a condo or town house, find out everything you can about the homeowners association, bylaws, and other factors that will govern everything from the number of people and pets in your home to the way you change or modify the unit's interior.

Tell me more

The land and all common facilities in the condominium such as swimming pools, tennis courts, lobbies, meeting rooms, elevators, as well as the walls, roofs, plumbing, and wiring are typically owned and operated by the owners through their elected representatives (directors). This joint ownership and operation means that no individual owner has control over the management and decision-making process, and that owners must cooperate with one another as a group (called the condominium association). All owners must abide by the rules and regulations required when so many people are living so closely together.

Before you buy into a multifamily community, investigate how the community is organized and how it operates. Owners of town houses, patio homes, twin homes, and condominiums large and small are members of an association, with certain rights and obligations. Rights include voting on association business, and obligations might include service on the association's board or committees.

All attached housing complexes are governed by what are known as covenants, conditions, and restrictions (CC&R) that restrict ownership rights. The CC&R could include restrictions on remodeling, renting, and parking, while others prohibit pets. It's important that you read and understand the complex's CC&R before making your buying decision. Since attorneys usually draw up these documents, they may not be easy to read or understand. For help, ask an attorney with expertise in multifamily housing to review them with you.

One of the best ways to find out about the homeowners association, the complex itself, and whether things are being run in a favorable manner is by talking with the current owners themselves. If you do decide to buy, you'll be sharing walls and some common living space with these folks anyway, so why not take the time to research the resident mix before making your final decision? Walk around the property, talk to owners, and spend some time in the common areas (elevators are great places to start conversations) to get a feel for your future home before you buy.

71. What is a condo conversion?

A condo conversion is a change of title from a single owner of an entire project or building (such as an apartment complex) to multiple owners of individual units. Not all rental apartments can be easily converted into condominiums. Typically, real estate developers look for buildings in fair or good condition that require little investment (on their part) in repairs, compounded by the ability to sell the units at a price that reflects a monthly mortgage payment equal to the cost of a month's rent, after factoring in mortgage, taxes, insurance, and maintenance fees.

Because most of the units were occupied by renters prior to the conversion, these condos tend to sell quickly as those renters scramble to purchase the homes that they're already living in. However, there are also opportunities for new home buyers to come in, check out the complex, and purchase one of the newly converted units.

Tell me more

Condo conversions were popular in the late 1970s and early 1980s, when high interest rates and rising single-family home prices drove demand for condos. Wanting to build equity but unable to afford single-family homes, buyers opted for condos to fill their needs. A large number of units were converted, but as buyers sprawled out to the suburbs in the late 1980s and early 1990s, the demand for such conversions waned.

Now they're back with a vengeance. Condo conversions are all the rage right now as vacancy rates on apartments rise and homeownership rates increase, spurred on by low interest rates that often leave owners paying less than renters. The double whammy has pushed some apartment owners—and even a few hotels—to "convert" into condominiums. The trend is prevalent in urban and downtown areas, where the physical structures are already in place and demand for downtown living close to work and amenities is high.

If you have your eye on a recently converted condo in your area, follow the same guidelines that you would use when dealing with any other multi-family housing option. Ask the same questions, check out the resident mix, and have a home inspector give the property a once-over to make sure there are no defects or construction issues that could become problems for you down the road. Do your due diligence—checking the accuracy of information contained in company documents—on the condo's ownership, and consult with a lawyer if you need help poring over the legalese.

72. What is a co-op?

Cooperatives are an animal all their own, which is why I've devoted a few separate questions in this chapter solely to what are more commonly known as "co-ops." Co-ops can comprise almost any type of housing, from high-rise apartment buildings to garden-style units, to town houses, single-family homes, and even senior housing. To the naked eye, a co-op looks like any other home. That's because the uniqueness of the co-op is not in the physical structure itself, but rather in the way that the properties are owned and governed. Other types of housing co-ops include mobile-home park co-ops, which own the land, utilities, and community facilities while members own the individual "mobile homes."

For the most part, co-ops are incorporated and a board of directors governs the complex with the owner of each individual unit having one vote. The owner has no deed, and instead holds stock and a proprietary lease that has a term of ten to fifty years, renewable automatically or at the discretion of the shareholders. Mortgage, property tax, and maintenance fees are paid on a pro rata basis (proportionately according to an exactly calculable factor) by the owner according to the percentage of the overall size of the unit.

Tell me more

Particularly popular in areas of high density and high land values, such as New York City, co-ops are similar to condominiums, but without the exclusive ownership rights. Instead of owning the three-dimensional space and the interest in the "common elements" of the condo project, you own shares of a corporation that owns the entire project. You're also a tenant of this corporation with respect to the unit you occupy within the project.

Unlike a condominium, where you can own a unit provided you have the money to do so, a co-op requires that new owners be voted upon and "approved" by the board of directors before being allowed to buy shares in the corporation. As a co-op buyer, you'll likely be asked by the board of directors to provide a financial statement and references and to participate in an interview.

One of the drawbacks of co-op ownership is the fact that the bylaws and rules and regulations limit what you can—or cannot—physically change about the unit that you're living in. Be prepared for restrictions on loud music, rental regulations, and limitations on selling your shares before first making them available to the co-op itself for repurchase. The co-op can impose such limitations because the corporation or association owns the title to the real estate, and residents simply purchase stock in the corporation, which entitles them to occupy a unit in the building or property owned by the cooperative. While you don't technically "own" your unit, you do have the absolute right to occupy that unit for as long as you own the stock.

Housing cooperatives are quite common in certain parts of the country such as New York City, Washington, D.C., and Chicago, according to the

National Association of Housing Cooperatives (NAHC) but can be more challenging to find in other areas. A local real estate professional may also be able to offer assistance, or you can consult your local yellow pages under the "apartments" header. The NAHC's Web site lists a number of its members online at www.coophousing.org/finding_co-ops.shtml.

73. Why is co-op ownership unique?

Their unique ownership structure makes co-op purchases a bit more intricate than any other type of residential property. Qualifying and choosing the right co-op requires due diligence and consideration of all financial and related documents governing both the project and the corporation that runs it. Here's a tip: Approach it as if you were buying a business, since that's essentially what you're doing. That means that in addition to checking out the property itself, you'll want to do your homework on the corporation itself to avoid any nasty surprises down the road. Those who have never purchased a business, or who don't understand co-op ownership legalese, will probably want to enlist the services of an attorney or accountant to assist with this process.

Tell me more

Also different about co-ops is the way in which you accumulate equity, which depends on what type of cooperative you buy into: a market-rate housing cooperative, a limited-equity housing cooperative, or a leasing cooperative. Here's how they differ:

❑ *Market-Rate Housing Co-op:* This most closely mimics other types of real estate in that you're able to purchase or sell your share(s) in the corporation at the going market price. With this type of co-op, the purchase prices and equity accumulation are similar to that of a condo or single-family home ownership in that your equity equals the difference between the market value of the shares and the total outstanding balance of your share loan.

❑ *Limited-Equity Housing Co-op (LEC):* These units may be subsidized by low-interest mortgages, grants, and favorable tax status and are often designed to provide affordable housing to lower- and middle-income families. There are restrictions on how much co-op members may ask for their units, with those restrictions imposed because the co-op's members benefit from below-market interest rate mortgage loans, grants, real estate tax abatement, or other features that make the housing more "affordable" to both the initial

and future residents for a specified period of time, according to the
NAHC.

❏ *Leasing or "Zero-Equity" Co-op:* In some circumstances, the cooperative corporation will lease property from a nonprofit organization, with the members of the corporation essentially acting as
tenants. The cooperative corporation leases the property from an
outside investor (often a nonprofit corporation that is set up specifically for this purpose), according to the NAHC.

74. What should I consider before purchasing a co-op?

When purchasing a cooperative, most people focus on location, size, amenities, and price. Understandably so, since those are the basic criteria that
most home buyers use during the home search process. To complete this
process, turn to Chapter 3 for information on exactly what to look for and
what to look out for. Then sharpen your pencil and get ready to dig a little
deeper into the inner workings of the co-op.

The NAHC advises potential buyers to remember that they are buying
a share of a corporation that owns real estate, which means "you will want
to find out about the financial health of the corporation." You will also want
a clear understanding of what your financial obligations to the cooperative
will be. Be sure to find out what all the rules and regulations of the community are. Here are some sample questions to ask before making your investment:

❏ *What is the share price?* A share is the proportion of the cooperative
that each member owns, and it represents the proportionate amount
that each member invested in the co-op when the co-op was started.
A certificate, often called a stock or membership certificate, documents the purchase price and membership in the cooperative.

❏ *Where can I obtain share loan financing?* A share loan is a loan
obtained to purchase a share in a housing co-op secured by the
shares and occupancy rights (cooperative interest). A member can
get an individual loan for that amount from a bank or other lending
institution, just as when an individual is buying a house.

❏ *How much are the monthly carrying charges?* The monthly carrying
charges or monthly maintenance fee is the member/shareholder's
proportionate share of the cooperative's operating expenses, reserve
funding, property taxes, and mortgage payments.

❏ *What is the underlying mortgage?* This is the overall mortgage on
the entire property, as paid for by the corporation.

❑ *What is your pet policy?*

❑ *What is your subletting policy?* A sublease is a lease between a current co-op shareholder and another person. According to the NAHC, most co-ops restrict subleasing and require subleases to be approved by the board.

❑ *What is the policy for making alterations to my unit?*

Tell me more

Before you buy into a co-op, you'll also want to review your rights and responsibilities, as outlined in the cooperative's documents, which typically include the articles of incorporation, bylaws, proprietary lease or occupancy agreement, subscription agreement, and house rules, according to the NAHC, which has a comprehensive co-op glossary posted on its Web site at www.coophousing.org/glossary.html. As a shareholder, you have a right to elect board members, to remove board members, and to amend the bylaws. You also have the responsibility to pay your monthly charges on time as well as follow all other rules and regulations of the cooperative.

As you shop around for a co-op, bear in mind that these entities are known to be highly selective in approving shareowners, since most communities are seeking members who can not only meet their financial obligations but who share a similar lifestyle and will abide by the rules of the corporation. But that doesn't mean they can discriminate. In keeping with the Fair Housing Act, it is illegal for a co-op to discriminate on the basis of race, color, religion, sex, family status, national origin, or disability. If you suspect discrimination of any sort during your hunt for the right co-op, visit the Department of Housing and Urban Development's (HUD's) Web site at www.hud.gov/complaints/housediscrim.cfm to learn more and fill out a housing discrimination complaint form.

75. How do I finance the purchase of co-op shares?

Because co-op owners don't directly own real estate, getting the financing together to purchase co-op shares is different from taking out a mortgage loan on a condo, town house, or single-family home. If you decide that a co-op is the right housing choice for your situation, you'll be taking out what is known as a "share loan" and using it to purchase shares of a corporation, rather than real estate. Much like a mortgage, the share loan provides you with funds to buy the share or shares from the seller. In turn, you make monthly payments to the lender on that share loan and monthly maintenance fees (carrying charges) directly to the co-op.

Tell me more

As a buyer of shares or a membership in a co-op housing corporation, which in turn owns or leases the real estate, you pay for a share or shares of that corporation. According to the NAHC, the purchase price of that share varies, depending on location, size of the unit itself, whether the co-op limits resale prices, and whether it has an underlying mortgage for the entire property. Once the price is determined and accepted, you'll either pay cash for the shares or obtain a share loan (usually from a lender that specializes in them) and fork over a down payment, much as you would with a traditional mortgage.

In addition to that monthly payment, you'll also pay a monthly carrying charge (often called a monthly maintenance fee) to the corporation, which covers your proportionate share of operating and maintaining the cooperative. The fee covers some or all of the following: blanket mortgage payments, property taxes, management fees, maintenance costs, insurance premiums, utilities, and contributions to reserve funds.

According to the National Cooperative Bank, which finances co-ops nationwide, such entities exist not to generate a profit for themselves or outside investors, but rather to provide goods and services at the lowest possible cost. Net margins (the excess of income over expenses in the cooperative) if any, are distributed to patrons in proportion to their use of the cooperative in the form of patronage dividends.

Once a year, a formal accounting determines a cooperative's income and expenses. Income remaining after deducting all expenses (net margin) is then distributed in proportion to patronage. In other words, the income in excess of expenses generated by a member's use of the cooperative is refunded to them. This is called a patronage refund, and the bank says the refund is an important source of financing for cooperatives. Members usually elect to leave a portion of the refund in the cooperative to help keep its operations on solid financial ground.

Setting up your financing on a co-op will take a bit of research to find the right lender, since not all banks offer financing for co-ops. To get funded, you'll need to fill out a share loan application and go through the typical approval process used by lenders (see Question 28). Check out the NAHC's Web site at www.coophousing.org for a list of lenders who specialize in co-ops.

CHAPTER FIVE

MAKE YOUR OFFER AND
NEGOTIATE CONTRACT TERMS

76. What is an offer?

When you find the house that meets all of your criteria and falls into your predetermined price range, the next step is to make an offer, then haggle over the details until both parties (in this case, the buyer and seller) come to an acceptable agreement. Realize that in a hot market a seller may have several offers on the table to consider at once, so making an offer doesn't necessarily mean the home will be yours. In a buyer's market, however, where properties aren't as easy to sell because of variables like higher mortgage interest rates or economic uneasiness, the chances that you can come to terms after making an initial offer are usually very good.

Tell me more

The actual offer-and-acceptance process is defined as the act of discussing an issue between two or more parties with competing interests with the aim of coming to an agreement. Every home seller starts at an asking price that's a certain percentage higher than what he thinks the home will actually fetch on the market. A home that's valued at $150,000, for example, may be listed on the multiple listing service for $159,900, often with real estate fees and other closing costs in mind. When you come on the scene, ready to make an offer, you'll need to investigate the local market and/or use the services of a real estate professional to come up with an appropriate amount to offer.

Once made, an offer may be accepted any time prior to being rescinded (to remove the validity of authority of something). Once accepted, the offer and acceptance form a legally binding contract. The key to getting to that point is not to go too high or too low when making your offer, and to ask for just enough concessions (if necessary) to make the seller feel as if she's getting a good deal. Lowball the offer, for example, and you may offend the seller. Go too high and you'll overshoot the seller's low point (the lowest possible price she'll take on the property) and end up leaving too much money on the table.

77. How do I make sure my offer is appropriate?

One simple way to make sure your offer is appropriate is by using one of the many home value estimators now available online. Check out House-Value, for example (www.housevalues.com), which is a free service that helps you determine the value of a house. Many of the nation's tax collectors and/or county appraisers have their home sales data posted online (key your county's name and the words "tax appraiser" or "tax collector" into a search engine to see if yours is online), searchable by property address and even by the owner's name.

Tell me more

The Department of Housing and Urban Development (HUD) advises buyers to "make a point" of asking any involved real estate agents to keep your discussions and information confidential. Listen to your real estate agent's advice, HUD says, but follow your own instincts on deciding a fair price. The group says calculating your offer should include the following factors:

- ❑ The prices for which homes in the area are selling
- ❑ The home's condition
- ❑ How long the home has been on the market
- ❑ The financing terms
- ❑ The seller's individual situation

By the time you're ready to make an offer, you should have a good idea of what the home is worth and what you can afford. And, HUD suggests, be prepared for give-and-take negotiation, which is very common when buying a home. The buyer and seller may often go back and forth until they can agree on a price.

When making an offer, remember to focus on the actual selling price, as opposed to the asking price that the seller has advertised. Also keep in mind that tax values are not a good indicator of what a home is worth, since most are based on sales that took place two to three years ago. In today's market, where some areas are experiencing 15 to 20 percent annual property appreciation rates, the tax collector's data may be outdated.

When comparing homes that sold recently to the one on which you're interested in making an offer, keep in mind the following basis of comparison:

❏ Total square footage under roof
❏ Age (in years) of the home
❏ Total lot size
❏ Number of bedrooms and bathrooms
❏ Size of garage (two car? three car?)
❏ Whether it has amenities like a pool, patio, or fireplace
❏ Whether kitchens and bathrooms are updated, new, or original

If the house next door to your desired dwelling sold for $200,000 two months ago, for example, but is 500-square-feet smaller than the one on which you're making an offer, expect the value on your target home to be higher. However, if the home you're interested in is the same size and age of one two doors down that sold two months ago for $50,000 less than your seller's asking price, it should send up a red flag and drive you to do more research and ask more questions before making an offer.

Should you decide to make an offer on a home, don't expect the real estate agent who is representing the seller to be too much help in the process, since his fiduciary duty is to the home seller, not to you. Retaining a buyer's agent, however, can be a good strategy for anyone who hasn't navigated the process before and who is unsure of home values.

The buyer's agent will run comparable sales data for you (looking at the prices of a few homes that have sold in the neighborhood and surrounding areas in the last year) and walk you through the offer process. Such professionals can be particularly helpful if you're working with a for sale by owner (FSBO) property, as they have access to the necessary forms, documents, and ancillary services (local appraisers, title companies, etc.) that you'll need to close the deal.

78. What is earnest money?

Once you've made your offer, you'll be asked to come up with what is known as "earnest money" to show just how serious you are about buying the home. This deposit money is given to the seller (or her real estate agent or attorney) and applied against the down payment. If the sale does not go through, the earnest money will be forfeited or lost unless the binder or offer to purchase expressly provides that it is refundable.

If you cannot get a mortgage, for example, the earnest money will be returned in full if the offer stated such a contingency (see Question 83). If you decide for some reason that you want another home, however, you could end up forfeiting your earnest money in full.

Tell me more

Earnest money is a sum paid by a potential purchaser as proof of her intention to complete the purchase transaction. Held in trust, usually by the listing agent (or directly by the seller in an FSBO situation), the money basically shows that you indeed intend to purchase the home, and that you're not wasting the seller's time since he or she will be forced to take the home off the market as soon as it's under contract.

79. How much earnest money do I need?

So now you're probably wondering, just how much earnest money is enough? It depends. The higher the amount, the more convinced a seller will be to take your offer. This is a strategy that is often used in hot markets where homes priced right sell in less than a week. In a more typical market, a minimal amount that lets sellers know you're serious—without putting significant funds at risk—should suffice.

Generally, you'll want to make your deposit 1 or 2 percent of your offered price. So if you're offering $235,000, your earnest money deposit should be $4,700 or less. (I myself once purchased a $92,500 home with a $1,000 deposit, then purchased a $269,900 home two years later with a $3,000 deposit—both of which were closer to 1 percent than 2.) To be perfectly candid, your goal as a buyer in most market conditions is to fork over the smallest amount of earnest money possible, plain and simple.

Tell me more

As mentioned earlier, there are exceptions to the rule if you're operating with few cash constraints in a market where piggyback offers and multiple offers are the norm. (Piggyback offers are those made after your offer was made and accepted—if your deal falls through, that buyer will have next dibs on the house.) In such cases, a hefty earnest money deposit could catch the seller's eye and lead him to select your offer, even if it's not the highest one in front of him.

Once your offer is accepted, your earnest money check will be cashed and deposited with the listing broker, a title company, or an attorney. These earnest money funds are held in a separate escrow account reserved only for earnest money deposits. They do not draw interest, and on closing day, the total amount of your earnest money is credited to you as a portion of your down payment.

80. What is a counteroffer?

If the seller doesn't jump at the offer you've made, expect to get a counteroffer back that's a bit different from what you've offered. The owner can either accept your offer as it stands, reject it outright, or respond with a counteroffer that may change certain terms of the original offer. By law, making a counteroffer entails rejection of the original offer, which means you can then counteroffer back by making changes to the owner's counteroffer. This process will continue until both parties are satisfied with the terms of the contract and the offering price.

Tell me more

As the name implies, counteroffers are replies to original offers. Much as you would verbalize a counterpoint to another person's statement, the counteroffer is a response to an original offer. The negotiating involved with offers and counteroffers isn't limited only to monetary values. For example, you ask that the buyer leave the portable microwave with the home. The seller declines and counters back to the buyer with the portable microwave crossed off from the personal property section of the contract. By doing this, the seller has made a counteroffer.

81. How do I make an offer?

When you make an offer (in the form of a sales and purchase agreement, covered in the next question) the contract will stipulate how much time the seller has to respond to your offer. Generally, you will allow at least forty-eight hours but not too much more because allowing too much time gives the seller the opportunity to shop other buyers. You (or the agent or attorney representing you) will present the contract to the seller, who must pick one of three options upon reading it:

1. Accept your offer as is, at which point the contract becomes binding for both parties.
2. Reject your offer, which makes the contract nonbinding. At that point, the seller may entertain competing offers.
3. Change the terms of the contract, and then counteroffer the original contract.

If the latter occurs, be prepared for either an entirely new document, a marked up or altered version of the original document, or addenda to the original contract. (At this point, you can accept the seller's counteroffer or walk away from the deal and get your earnest money back.) You can also counter that counteroffer by simply changing the terms of the seller's counteroffer. This can kick off a series of such exchanges, with most offers reached on the second or third round of counteroffers.

Tell me more

Once both parties agree to the terms and sale price stated in the contract, the terms of the contract are binding on both parties. If, after that point, you change your mind for any reason and breach the terms of the contract, the seller has the right to declare the contract null and void and retain your earnest money. You may also be liable for any other financial damage suffered by the seller and the seller's agent. If the seller fails for any reason to complete the sale of his home according to the terms stated in the contract, the earnest money will be returned to you and the seller may be liable for any financial damage.

82. What does a real estate contract include?

A real estate contract (also known as a sales and purchase agreement) is a legally binding agreement (oral or written) between two or more persons regarding the exchange of real estate. The purchase offer that you submit to the seller, if and when accepted, becomes a binding sales contract known by most as a purchase and sales agreement, which will serve as a blueprint for the final sale of the property.

Tell me more

A real estate contract generally includes (but is not limited to) the following information. Be sure to review every line item before you sign the contract because once it leaves your hands and is presented to the seller, you will be legally bound by its terms (if the seller accepts the contract without any changes).

- ❏ The buyer's and seller's names and contact information
- ❏ Address and legal description of the property
- ❏ Sales price
- ❏ Personal property that will be included in the sale, such as kitchen appliances, window drapes, and light fixtures

❏ Amount of earnest money deposit accompanying the offer

❏ Any mortgage contingencies (see Question 83)

❏ Closing date

❏ Method by which real estate taxes, fuel, rents, water bills, and/or utilities will be adjusted (prorated) between the buyer and seller

❏ A resale certificate or condominium documents for common interest properties such as condominiums

❏ A seller's disclosure form, stating what—if any—defects or problems the seller is aware of

❏ Other requirements (which vary by state), such as lead paint disclosure, dual agency disclosure statements, and other documents

❏ A provision that the buyer may make a final walk-through inspection of the property just before the closing (this generally means within forty-eight hours of closing, although I've completed such walk-throughs an hour before heading to the closing table)

❏ A time limit (generally a short period of time, such as thirty days) after which the offer will expire

You may also want to request a home warranty provision in the contract to protect against costly repairs for one year after the sale. The warranty usually covers the plumbing, electric, built-in appliances, heating, and air-conditioning units. Sellers are not obligated to offer a home warranty, but feel free to ask for it as part of your contract. The cost to the seller is minimal, but the warranty can be worth the price of the home, so ask the seller to add a warranty provision as part of the sale terms. If a furnace, air condenser, or refrigerator breaks within the next twelve months, you'll be covered—the home warranty company, typically an insurance company, will pay for the repairs.

Also include in your contract provisions stating that everything should be in working order on the settlement date, that all personal items that belong to the seller should be removed from the house and property, and that the house should be thoroughly cleaned before taking possession. When drawing up the contract, you may also want certain items to remain in the home after closing, including:

❏ Window draperies

❏ Shower curtains

❏ Wall ornaments

❏ Yard decorations

❏ Home appliances

❑ Home furniture
❑ Building sheds
❑ Shelving

Specify exactly what you would like included, and write down model numbers (a digital camera can come in handy on more general items) to prevent the seller from replacing the item with an inferior substitute. I know real estate agents who have purchased new washing machines and dryers for buyers whose sellers replaced the desired models (seen during the initial tours of the home) with old, rusted-out versions before closing day.

When all of the terms of the sales contract are agreed to, the document is signed or "executed" by the seller(s) and buyer(s) and used as a cornerstone for the rest of the sale process. You and the seller will retain executed copies of the contract, which then becomes a part of the sales file, retained by the real estate agent or the home owner or attorney, in the case of an FSBO.

83. What contingencies should be included in an offer?

Once your offer is accepted and the contract(s) signed, a number of wheels are put into motion, some of which can affect whether you make it to the closing table for that particular home. Most of these variables are addressed as "contingencies" in your initial offer, and they should all be included to ensure a win-win situation for both parties. The most-used contingencies include the financing or mortgage contingency, the home inspection contingency, the contingency on the sale of a home, and the clear title contingency.

If you need to take out a mortgage, for example, the seller will generally give you a set amount of time to do so or risk having the house put back on the market. If you are going to have a home inspection completed (it's highly advisable), then the offer should also include a certain time frame in which to get that inspection completed.

Tell me more

There are myriad contingencies that can be included in a real estate contract, but here we discuss a few of the most popular ones. Each individual deal is different, so if you feel there is a need for more such contingencies, by all means discuss them with your real estate agent or attorney to figure out how to best deal with them.

❑ *Financing or Mortgage Contingency:* Unless you're a cash buyer, you'll definitely want a financial contingency included with your offer, which when accepted will be presented to buyer and seller in the form of a contract. If you have a financial supplement that states that your earnest money is totally refundable if the offer is not accepted or if some condition in the contract is not satisfied (such as not being able to obtain a mortgage), you'll get your earnest money back.

The mortgage contingency includes the amount of the mortgage, interest rate, term, commitment date for the written approval, and type of financing (conventional or government-insured loan). Most buyers will require this mortgage contingency, and most also realize that it can take anywhere from two to four weeks for the lender to approve their mortgage (I've had contracts where the length of time was as short as ten days in a situation where a number of buyers were vying for the home).

❏ *Home Inspection Contingency:* If for nothing else than peace of mind, you'll want to include an inspection contingency in the contract. I always use home inspectors, even on homes that are sold "as is," just to be sure that there aren't any hidden defects that could come back to haunt me in a year or two. You'll want to do the same, and include your intentions and a time line in the contract.

❏ *Contingency of the Sale of Home:* Another common contingency involves the sale of the buyer's present home, also known as a "Hubbard Agreement." Sellers generally dislike these types of contingencies, since it's hard for them to gauge when your home will sell and when their home will be off their hands. If you're operating in a market that's not so hot, or if the seller is not anxious to sell and move out, then such a contingency could be acceptable. Most of these contingencies are also conditional upon the buyer's home inspection and mortgage contingencies and tend to extend to a period of anywhere between thirty and sixty days from the date of the purchase contract.

❏ *Clear Title Contingency:* This is a built-in contingency, as sellers have to provide clear title to the buyer, or the lender will not finance a loan. Banks won't touch properties that have liens or obligations against them, and a contingency outlines this requirement in the contract. If it's not met, you will be able to get your earnest money back and recommence your house hunt.

The most common of these contingencies is the one that deals with financing, since the average home buyer can't afford to fork over cash for a six-figure purchase. Make sure the purchase and sale agreement includes a provision stating that your earnest money deposit will be refunded if the sale has to be cancelled because you are unable to get a mortgage loan. For example, your agreement of sale could allow the purchase to be cancelled if you cannot obtain a mortgage at or below an interest rate you specify in the agreement and with a certain percentage down. The agreement will also specify how many days you have to apply for the mortgage and at what point the seller may demand that you waive the financing contingency. Your real estate agent should provide you with a timetable of when these critical deadlines will occur.

Other, lesser-used contingencies include one that states that you will buy the home only if you receive the job offer that allows you to relocate into the area and purchase the home. Not all of these contingencies will be acceptable to the seller (or to you), so it's up to you, your agent or attorney, the seller, and his agent or attorney to determine which contingencies will be included and honored in the contract.

As an added layer of protection, you may also want to include—as part of your formal purchase offer—a provision that holds the seller responsible for paying you rent should he not move out on or prior to the agreed-upon date. This allows you, for example, to use the money you receive to pay your own rent if you are leasing your current residence.

84. Do I need an attorney?

This is a hotly debated topic, and one that has even made it to the various state supreme courts over the last few years. That's because most attorneys and state bar associations (and some Realtor organizations) feel that it's in the consumer's best interest to have legal representation at the closing table. On the other side of the argument are those consumers who either don't want to shell out the extra expense for an attorney or feel they can handle the transaction on their own or with the help of a good real estate professional.

In certain states, attorneys are required to perform closings. In others, a title company will generally handle the closing process. You'll want to check on exactly what your state requires prior to making your decision.

Tell me more

Buying a home will probably be one of the largest and most important financial transactions you'll ever have to make, so you'll want to make sure your paperwork and contracts are in order prior to signing contracts to purchase the home. One way to do this is by hiring a real estate attorney, who will protect your interests and help you resolve potential legal problems before executing any legally binding contracts.

If you'd rather not pay for an attorney's services, if you feel that you can competently handle this process on your own, and if your state doesn't require attorneys at the closing table, then you certainly don't need to bring an attorney into the transaction. If, however, you feel rushed to sign documents that you don't understand—or if the language in the contract looks like Greek to you—then you'll want to request the extra time necessary to consult with a lawyer who is well versed in real estate law.

Once the initial purchase documents have been reviewed, accepted, and/or amended, the attorney will handle various tasks, such as preparing and/or approving the contract, examining documents, and supervising the transaction closing process. There are a number of documents to prepare in any real estate transaction, and the attorney can evaluate and explain each document to you as it surfaces. The deed, bill of sale, mortgage, promissory note, title commitment, and closing statement are a few of the key documents that the attorney will go over prior to closing.

Determining the condition of the seller's title to the property is a key area that attorneys focus on during the home purchase process. That means figuring out if the seller is indeed the legal owner of the property and whether there are any unpaid liens against the home. Such liens must be settled before the property title can be legally transferred to the new owner. Attorneys will also keep an eye out for any restrictions or easements (such as a utility easement, which allows certain utilities to use that portion of the land when necessary) on the property, as well as any unpaid property taxes or assessments.

Most of the above will take place long before you reach the closing table, where you and your attorney will sit together and review and sign all documents pertaining to your purchase. It can be particularly helpful to have legal representation during closing, where your attorney can help clear up any remaining questions or financial matters related to the transaction. Post sale, the attorney will also take care of final details, such as recording the deed to your new home.

85. Why set an exact closing date?

Of everything that needs to be done to purchase a home, choosing a closing date probably sounds like one of the easier decisions you'll have to make. In reality, there are several advantages to closing during certain times of the month (or even certain times of the year) rather than others. Closing at the end of the month, for example, could result in less interest and principal paid at the closing table, since lenders invoice such fees in arrears. You can also reduce your up-front tax costs, since the property taxes on your new home will be prorated at closing.

Generally, closings take place thirty to sixty days following the date that the purchase contract is signed by all parties, but realistic considerations usually determine how long it will really take to close. Most home purchase contracts include contingencies that must be satisfied before the closing (see Question 83), with the most common being the contingency for buyer's financing, inspections of the property, and examination of title to the property.

Tell me more

You must include a closing date as part of your original offer to purchase real estate. Doing so ensures that both you and the seller can start making plans to move, and that the latter can start making plans to purchase or rent her next dwelling. Transactions generally close on the right transaction date, but last-minute issues sometimes can delay such target dates by a day or two. While the closing date is normally filled in when the offer to purchase is made by the buyer, realize that once your offer is presented to the seller, he or she may choose to change this date before accepting your offer.

Be prepared for a possible delay by giving your landlord notice that you're moving out and that you may need a few day's flexibility. That way, if the purchase closes a few days late, you won't end up staying in a hotel while your possessions languish in ministorage. If you already own a home, make sure you allow enough time to sell your current house if you are using the proceeds from your sale on your new home.

Your purchase contract will list settlement and possession dates and times, but the rule of thumb is this: Once closing is over, you walk away with the keys to your new home. Settlement date is when you close on the contract and both parties fulfill the contract terms. Occupancy date is the date when the buyer can move into the home. Some contract terms may allow the seller to stay in the home after possession date, but that's something you will have worked out with the seller long before coming to the closing table. For example, the seller may request more time to move out of the house and in exchange will generally pay the buyer a rental fee.

When selecting a closing or settlement date, consider a few factors that could either save you money or end up costing you more money at the closing table. Mortgage interest and principal payments are paid in arrears, which means that if your closing takes place on February 10, your first monthly payment would begin to accrue on March 1 and would be payable at the beginning of February. That means you'll be required to prepay the interest from February 10 through the end of the month. Do the math, and you'll see that you'll actually pay less at the closing table if you close on the first of the month, rather than in the middle of the month.

Taxes are another consideration, since the property taxes on your new home will be prorated at closing and your portion will be allowed to be deducted as an expense for income tax purposes. Your escrow officer will calculate the tax prorations by dividing the taxes between you and the seller, based on your state's due date for the property taxes. If the seller has paid the property taxes beyond the date of closing, the seller will be credited for this expense. If the taxes have not yet been paid, the amount owed will be charged to you and added to your closing costs. Your lender may also ask that the taxes be paid in full at closing, or may simply collect enough to cover the taxes until the next pay period.

86. Does it matter what time of the month I choose to close?

If you're purchasing your home at the end of the year, there are a few more issues to take into consideration if you're trying to determine whether to close in late December or early January. In some states, the homestead exemption is one of the most obvious reasons to make sure your loan closes on or before December 31. In Florida, for example, state law provides the home owner a $25,000 exemption from real estate tax assessment, so if a home is assessed at a market value of $250,000, the exemption dictates that the property taxes be computed on $225,000.

Obtaining homestead status on a property not only saves the home owner on his or her real estate tax assessments, but it also caps the amount that the property can be reassessed annually. Additionally, it provides the home owner with asset protection—for the home—against third-party creditors. The catch is that to be entitled to a homestead exemption for assessment purposes for the prior year, you must be a record titleholder as of January 1 of the current year.

Tell me more

There are also tax implications to closing by the end of the year versus the following January. For example, if you have a choice between a late-December closing and an early January closing, closing in December may allow you an income tax deduction in the current tax year rather than waiting a full year to take the deduction. New home buyers should reference IRS Publication 530, Tax Information for First-Time Homeowners (available online at www.irs.gov) for information on whether points paid at closing are deductible in the year paid, or whether they need to be spread out over the life of the mortgage.

The IRS allows home owners to deduct from their federal income taxes the mortgage interest paid, thus giving home owners the opportunity to deduct more than the standard deduction. When you purchase a home, you're also allowed to deduct any origination points (1 percent of the loan amount) paid for the new loan. Home buyers may also want to boost their deduction by prepaying their first month's interest at the closing table. If a mortgage costs $1,200 per month, for example, the lion's share of that amount will be deductible interest anyway. By paying that first payment in 2004, you'll be boosting your tax deduction when it comes time to file on April 15, 2005.

Closing by December 31 will also give you the option of deducting your discount points (which are considered prepaid interest) and the closing interest accumulated from the day of the closing through the end of the month. You can also deduct a number of charges that appear on the settlement statement. Consult with a financial adviser or an accountant to determine which charges are deductible completely, which are not, and which need to be deducted over the life of the loan.

87. How can I come out a winner in the negotiation process?

Some people are born negotiators, while others go through life accepting the prices put before them and never asking for discounts or concessions when making a purchase. Then there's the rest of us: the people who will negotiate in certain circumstances, such as when buying a home. As you've already learned, the "asking price" of a home is nearly always set higher than what the seller expects to get from the home, thus leaving room for negotiations not only on price, but also on other areas. Everything from the closing date to the curtains to the contingencies is completely negotiable, so sharpen your pencils and dig in.

Negotiating is common during the homebuying process, based on the fact that most sellers don't actually expect to walk away from the deal with the full asking price in their pocket. According to Freddie Mac's "Route to Homeownership" guide, the haggling process comprises several stages:

❑ Initial asking price, or list price, by the seller
❑ Initial purchase offer with contingencies including inspection and financing
❑ Acceptance of offer or a counteroffer by the seller

The counteroffer process can take some time as you and the seller find a mutually agreeable price and begin the home inspection and financing phases. If you included an inspection or appraisal contingency and if either reveals serious defects, you will likely want to submit a new counteroffer.

Remember that, like any negotiation, the seller will probably ask for more and then be prepared to lower the price. At the same time, however, the seller will also be expecting you, as the buyer, to offer less than you are willing to pay.

Tell me more

Nowhere is the old saying "everything is negotiable" more applicable than in the homebuying and home-selling process. Price, terms, contract dates, exclusions, inclusions, disclaimers, and just about everything else in the contract is completely negotiable. It's also a two-way street: You can ask for anything you want, and the seller can turn you down on any points on which she sees fit to do so.

There are a few strategies you can use to make sure that you come out a winner in the negotiating process. For starters, remember that you are the customer in the transaction and that the seller is the vendor who must make the offer appealing to you as a potential buyer. The seller is competing against many others like him in the marketplace, whereas you have a world of housing options to choose from. You've selected his home, and now it's time to negotiate for the best possible deal.

Strengthen your bargaining position by first looking at comparable homes in the market and using the information garnered when negotiating. Was another home in the next neighborhood a little newer and larger, yet priced a little lower? Mention it to the seller or the seller's real estate agent and decide if a lower offer is warranted. Try your best to keep emotions out of the process (no matter *how* badly you want this particular home!) and treat it like a business negotiation. Savvy sellers know when their homes have struck a chord in a potential buyer, and they'll use that information to their advantage.

Make your initial offer lower than you think you should. This gives the seller some room to negotiate, without putting you at a disadvantage for the remainder of the negotiation. It also lowers the seller's expectations and could set the tone for the rest of the negotiating process. At worst, you can always come back later with a higher, more reasonable offer, but keep in mind that in a hot seller's market you may not get the chance.

If your original offer is answered by a counteroffer, consider it carefully and decide which of the various concessions you can live with. If the offering carries on for more than one round, you might want to ask the seller flat out for her "final offer," which will give you a new playing field to work on when accepting or rejecting the offer. This is basically known as finding the seller's "bottom line," and it doesn't mean you can't test it further by firing back a counteroffer.

88. What other items are negotiable?

Remember that while price is important, you can make up some lost ground on the price side by asking for and agreeing to other trade-offs and concessions, such as seller financing, home warranties, seller-paid closing items, and various other seller concessions. Also keep in mind that the longer the negotiation process takes, the more likely it is that the outcome will be successful. The last thing any buyer or seller wants to do is allocate time and energy to a lengthy negotiating process, only to have the deal fall through and have to start from scratch with a new home, or with a new buyer, as in the case of the seller.

Tell me more

Here are a few more key points to consider when negotiating:

❑ Include time limits in all offers and counteroffers, preferably a day or two.

❑ Find out how long the home has been on the market. If it's been more than a few months, your bargaining position will probably be stronger.

❑ Use closing costs as a bargaining chip. Motivated sellers frequently pay some or all of a buyer's closing costs (see Question 89) to ensure a smooth sale.

❑ Try to learn whether the seller has any deadlines, such as job relocation, divorce, or purchase of a replacement home. Such time constraints could work to your advantage.

❑ Keep your cool and try not to appear too anxious. Act as if you've done this a hundred times before (even if you're a first-time home buyer!) and keep your emotions in check throughout the process.

❑ Try lowballing (making an offer considerably below asking price) on your initial offer, but realize that if you're in a hot market such offers could offend the seller. This strategy works best when you are truly prepared to walk away from the home if the price doesn't fall within your desired negotiating range.

❑ Be confident in your ability to negotiate in your best interest, even if it's not in your nature to do so. As a buyer, you have a wide range of homes to select from on the market and your seller only holds one of them. Stay strong and powerful without offending and you'll be sure to get what you want.

89. Why would a seller pay my closing costs?

Closing costs are about 3 percent of a home's purchase price, which means your up-front costs on a $200,000 home will be about $6,000. If this is a big pill for you to swallow, you may want to consider asking the seller to cover all or some of those expenses, sometimes in exchange for a slightly higher sales price. Often, these costs can be "financed into" the home by negotiating for the seller to pay all closing costs and allowable points on the loan. From the seller's point of view, this is the equivalent of reducing the purchase price by the given amount.

Tell me more

Asking a seller to foot the bill on your home's closing costs might sound absurd to some, but the practice is actually quite common, particularly in areas where homes spend more time on the market than they would in hotter, seller's markets. The practice is perfectly legal (although there are limits on just how much a seller can contribute) and is often used by first-time buyers who have solid incomes and credit histories, but who simply don't have the cash reserves needed to come up with a down payment.

The seller also has her own closing costs to cover, but one way to make the coverage of *your* closing costs a win-win situation for both you and the seller is by offering "full price" for the home, which basically means that you increase your offer to offset the closing costs that the seller is being asked to pay. Keep in mind that the seller will still have to cover items such as agent commissions and property taxes based on the higher purchase price, with the only risk being the fact that the bank's appraisal may not come in at the higher price. In other words, the lender won't finance the home at a price that's higher than fair market value in the neighborhood.

When a seller agrees to cover a portion or all of your closing costs, you'll need to disclose such an arrangement on what is known as a "HUD" statement, for Form HUD-1, which clearly spells out who is paying what amount of money for what, and to whom. Different types of loans have varying limits for seller contributions. Here are the restrictions on the three most popular loan types:

1. On Veteran's Administration loans, the seller is able to contribute up to 4 percent of the sale price toward buyer costs, plus discount points.

2. On Federal Housing Administration loans, the seller can contribute 6 percent, although the buyer is required to have at least a 3 percent personal contribution (in any combination of down payment and closing costs) in the home.

3. On conventional loans, the maximum seller contribution is 3 percent if the down-payment amount is less than 10 percent of the home's sale price. If the down payment is 10 to 24 percent, then that seller limit rises to 6 percent. For down payments of 25 percent or more, the seller's contribution can be as high as 9 percent of the sales price.

If the lack of a down payment and/or closing costs is preventing you from purchasing a home, there are also numerous other programs available, particularly for first-time home buyers (those who haven't purchased a home in the last three years). Check with your local government office for details on such programs, or check out national organizations like The Nehemiah Program (www.getdownpayment.com) or AmeriDream, Inc. (www.ameridream.com). The former offers gift funds from 1 to 6 percent of the final contract sales price, or flat gift amounts up to 6 percent of the sales price, toward down payment and closing costs, while the latter provides down-payment gifts based on a percentage of the purchase price of the home, typically 2 to 6 percent of the home's purchase price.

90. What is a seller disclosure?

Nearly all states require sellers of residential properties to fill out and sign what is known as a "seller's disclosure" prior to selling their homes. Requirements vary, but generally the state legislature outlines exactly what needs to be shown on the form. The document is not a warranty, but a disclosure that the seller must fill out and give to you, the buyer, or risk terminating an otherwise binding contract. This is where the seller is asked to reveal his or her knowledge of the property's condition, any possible defects in the home's major systems, or any ownership issues that may come up during title and deed searches.

Tell me more

The State of California was one of the first to require a seller disclosure statement, also known as the "Real Estate Transfer Disclosure Statement," or TDS. The seller's disclosure statement that the current home owner is legally required to fill out in most states usually comprises these four sections:

1. Appliances/systems/services
2. Property conditions, improvements, and additional information
3. Other items
4. Ownership information and state equalized value

Within each of these four sections, the home seller is required to disclose what he knows about the condition of the items listed. If a negative condition exists, he also has to explain what he knows about the item. The seller is required to reveal everything that might be of concern to a potential buyer, including the physical condition of the home's structure, appliances, and various systems; any environmental issues; and any issues concerning parking situations, easements, shared fences, or driveways.

Here are a few of the other items that generally appear on a seller's disclosure form (you will find a sample form in the appendix):

❑ Presence of roof leaks (now or in the past)
❑ Evidence of water in the basement or crawl space
❑ Condition and type of insulation
❑ Condition of the well and septic (including when the septic system was last pumped)
❑ Electrical problems
❑ Age and type of plumbing, heating system, and water heater
❑ Pest infestation from termites, carpenter ants, and other home-destroying insects
❑ Presence of hazardous materials like asbestos, radon gas, fuel tanks, formaldehyde, or lead-based paint
❑ Any encroachments, easements, zoning violations, or nonconforming use issues
❑ Evidence of settling, flooding, drainage, or grading problems
❑ Outstanding assessments or fees
❑ Pending or continuing litigation that could affect the buyer
❑ Whether the property (or any part of it) is a designated wetland
❑ Presence of underground fuel or storage tanks
❑ Whether the property is in a restricted parking area
❑ Any leases, encumbrances, or reservations (such as mineral or timber rights)
❑ Whether the property is currently being used as a rental
❑ Whether any fences, walls, drives, landscaping, or other features are shared with a neighboring property

❑ Presence of common areas, such as tennis courts, swimming pools, walkways, or recreation areas

❑ Structural modifications, repairs, or alterations that were made to the property without building permits or licensed contractors

❑ Length of time that the seller has owned and/or lived in the home

Remember that those problems that the seller has resolved herself—such as repairing a roof to stop a leak—must also be disclosed on the disclosure form. Sellers need not "guess" on this very important document, so if someone doesn't know the age of the air-conditioning unit, she will probably put "I don't know" in the box. This situation is common in homes where the seller may have owned or inherited the home but never lived in it.

As a buyer, you need to realize that while a seller's disclosure form was created with your best interest in mind, it is not an end all for determining whether the home is structurally sound. The average seller doesn't have expertise in engineering or construction and therefore is not required to inspect inaccessible areas such as complex operating systems within the home. He must, however, disclose everything he is aware of. The seller's disclosure statement is not a substitute for a home inspection, which you should have conducted before purchasing the home.

91. What does "as is" mean?

If you're buying a home that's being sold "as is," then you're accepting the property in its current condition and releasing the seller from any liability for problems discovered before or after closing. On such purchases, a statement in the agreement of purchase and sale will confirm that you, the buyer, accept the property and all chattels (everything that's attached to the property) included in the purchase in the condition in which it was found at the time that the agreement was signed.

You can still conduct a thorough home inspection on an as-is property, but the seller is not responsible for fixing anything that might come up during the inspection. Recall that you can also include a "home inspection" contingency in your offer and the subsequent contract, which will allow you a certain amount of time to do the inspection and cancel the contract.

Tell me more

Buying a home that's being offered "as is" means that while the seller is obligated by law to disclose all known defects in the property to prospective buyers, he doesn't have to pay for the repairs. So let's say you buy a home with a faltering air-conditioning unit. As long as the as-is seller discloses her knowledge of the problem on the disclosure form—and as long as you accept the fact that at some point the unit will probably need replacing, at your own expense—then she is not obligated to pay for its repair or replacement.

If it sounds like a risky proposition, your homebuying instincts are both sharpened and on high alert. Whenever you make a purchase as large as a home, you'll want some guarantee that your new acquisition won't quickly turn into a money pit. I've bought homes with standard contracts and with as-is contracts and have also sold them both ways and have never run into any major problems with either. I must say, however, that the as-is property required some updating and upgrading about one year after purchase that the other homes did not. The home inspection turned up nothing major at the time of purchase (a few electrical outlets that needed covers, for example). However, we bought the home at about $30,000 below the appraised value (after some tough negotiating), so we still came out ahead after a kitchen remodel and some ceiling repairs.

As you can see, there are a few key financial benefits to buying as is. Because many prospective buyers will be wary of as-is sales because there will probably be repair costs (compounded by any defects that the seller may have "overlooked" on the disclosure form), you as an interested buyer will have a strong bargaining position. That's because most buyers believe an as-is home seller might be hiding undisclosed defects that will become obvious after the purchase. If that occurs, the seller can be liable for the repairs, though proving that he or she actually knew about the defect could be tricky.

Choose your home carefully, ask for a home inspection (even if you know the owner isn't going to remedy any of the problems), and use the fact that many buyers would steer away from such properties as an advantage during the negotiation process.

PUT THE HOMEBUYING
GEARS IN MOTION

92. I've signed a contract. What now?

Let's just say that if the fun hasn't begun already, it will start now. For the next thirty to sixty days (or whatever time frame you put between contract signing and closing), the gears will be in motion, getting everything ready for the big day when you take possession of your new home. There will be appraisals and surveys to order, title searches and inspections to conduct, and lenders to meet with.

At the same time, you'll be making arrangements for your own move, informing your landlord about your expected departure, or putting your current home on the market to sell. This will be a time of excitement as well as stress, so just take it in stride and try not to get too overwhelmed. In just a few months you'll have your feet up on the coffee table in your new abode, and you'll be happy that you decided to embark on this journey.

Tell me more

The most important task that you'll need to tackle right now is finalizing your mortgage—a topic that has its own chapter (see Chapter 7: Sealing the Deal). And while the financial aspect of your purchase transaction is very important, so are the various additional steps that must be taken to ensure a smooth closing.

If you and/or the home seller are working with a real estate agent, it will make a big difference in the amount of work you'll be doing over the next one to two months. I've done it both ways, and both strategies have their pluses and minuses. The good news for buyers is that you probably won't be affected by the downside (namely, the commission that must be paid to the agent at the closing table) anyway. However, in today's changing real estate industry, there are a number of different business models that brokers are using, some of which do demand funds from the buyer's side of the transaction. (Inquire about any such fees before getting into a relationship with an agent.)

Since it's in the agent's best interest to be sure a deal makes it to the closing table, she will predictably handle—or orchestrate—much of what goes on behind the scenes between contract signing and closing. During this time, you may be asked to produce documents, review home inspection reports, or take other important steps, but for the most part your agent will handle the myriad tasks that must be checked off prior to closing. You'll be in close contact with your agent (or attorney) during this time as all parties anticipate the scheduled closing date.

During the interim, several key tasks will be completed. Here are the major steps, but remember that every sale is different and yours may require a different approach. All of the concepts mentioned below (with the exception of the financing) are detailed further along in this chapter:

- ❏ You will apply for financing.
- ❏ The lender will order an appraisal and termite inspection.
- ❏ The lender will also order a property survey to be completed.
- ❏ You or your agent will arrange for a home inspection, and, based on the report, you will decide if you are indeed going to purchase the home (if you included a home inspection contingency in the contract).
- ❏ By this time, you will find out if you have been approved for financing, thus fulfilling the "mortgage contingency" clause in the contract and locking in your interest rate.
- ❏ You will learn whether the home you're purchasing has "clear title" or if any liens or debts need to be cleared up prior to closing.
- ❏ You and/or your lender will conduct any further tests required, such as radon gas and lead paint testing.

93. What documents will a lender ask for?

In order to fully assist you, your lender is going to need to reference some important documents. You might want to start with your W-2 forms and federal tax returns for the past two years, year-to-date pay stubs, documentation of additional income, investment records, debt/creditor records, and cancelled mortgage/rent checks.

Tell me more

Listed below are some documents that may be required during the mortgage application process (some loan programs may require additional information). To get the ball rolling and make the entire application process much smoother, you can get a jump start on organizing them before you speak with your mortgage professional. Remember to make a copy of everything and to keep the original documents in a safe place:

❏ *Employment Information:* In order to verify your employment, your lender may require the names, addresses, and telephone numbers of all your employers for the last two years. If you are self-employed, your business records and tax returns for the last three years may be requested.

❏ *W-2 Forms:* Your W-2 form is sent from your employer and used to file your income taxes. Generally, you will need to produce your W-2s for the past two years.

❏ *Pay Stubs and Additional Income:* It is important to save your pay stubs for at least a thirty-day period before your mortgage application. Documentation of additional income information, such as social security, pension, interest or dividends, rental income, child support, alimony, and self-employment income may also be requested.

❏ *Federal Income Tax Returns:* If you are self-employed, or if more than 25 percent of your income comes from commission, overtime, or bonuses, you may need to provide complete copies of the federal income tax returns you filed for the two most recent years.

❏ *Account Statements:* You may need to provide statements from all of your accounts (checking, savings, mutual funds, money markets, certificates of deposits, 401k, or other retirement accounts) for the last two months to verify the funds available for your down payment.

❏ *Current Debts:* Be prepared to provide the account numbers, current balances, and minimum monthly payments of all credit accounts, such as loans, credit cards, child support, and other payments you make each month.

94. What is a home appraisal?

A residential property appraisal helps establish a home's market value, or the likely sales price that the property would fetch if offered in a competitive real estate market. Whenever someone uses a home or other type of real estate as security for a loan, the lender will order an appraisal to be conducted by a licensed appraisal professional. This step is critical from the lender's perspective because it ensures that the property will sell for at least the amount they are investing in it. It's also important for you, the buyer, because it shows you in black and white that the price you're paying is indeed in line with the fair market value.

The Federal Housing Administration cautions that market value should not be confused with asking price, offering price, or sales price. Asking price is what a seller indicates as a fair and reasonable offer for a home. A seller is free to set whatever asking price he chooses. An offering price, on the other hand, is a number that the buyer feels is a fair and reasonable offer for a home. This may be an accurate reflection of the true market value of a home or an attempt by the buyer to purchase the property at a considerable discount. The sales price is what the buyer and seller actually agree upon through negotiations; it generally lies somewhere between the asking price and the offering price.

Tell me more

Appraisers are licensed by their respective states after completing course work and/or a job internship that helps them become familiar with their local real estate markets. The appraisal process itself begins with a thorough inspection of the property being appraised to determine the true status of that property. The appraiser will look at features like number of bedrooms and bathrooms to ensure that they really exist and are in good condition.

The inspection often includes photographs of the property, ensuring the proper square footage and conveying the layout of the property. Most important, the appraiser looks for any obvious features—or defects—that would affect the value of the house.

95. How is a home appraised?

As an objective third party with no financial or other connection to the transaction, the appraiser will then use one of two formulas to come up with a residential property's appraised value. They are:

1. *The Sales Comparison Approach:* Using this method, the appraiser will estimate the property's market value by comparing it to similar properties that have sold in the neighborhood or surrounding area. The properties, which are called comparables or simply "comps," give the appraiser a benchmark to measure against to come up with a fair price. The appraiser will generally identify three to five properties that have sold within the last six months, noting any dissimilar features and making adjustments as necessary to come up with an adjusted value as follows:

Sales Price of Comp + or − Adjustments = Adjusted Value

2. *The Cost Approach:* The appraiser estimates the current market value of the home by estimating the cost of reconstructing the home (to include any improvements) plus the value of the land minus the estimated depreciation (loss in value due to physical deterioration, etc.) of the home since the home was first built. The idea is that the savvy buyer will not pay more for a house than the cost of reconstructing a substitute house on a similar lot in a similar condition. The formula is calculated as follows:

Cost of Reconstruction − Depreciation + Value for Land = Property Value

After combining information from one or more approaches and the on-site inspection, the appraiser will come up with an estimated market value for the property, which is most commonly reported on a uniform residential appraisal report (URAR). This "appraised value" will be used as a guideline for your lender. The buyer generally pays for the appraisal at closing, with most costing $250 to $400 for a single-family home.

96. How can an appraisal affect my ability to obtain a mortgage?

For a lender to loan money on a property, that property must be appraised at a value that falls within a certain percentage of the sales price. The reasoning is fairly simple: A bank won't lend $150,000 on a home that's only worth $120,000 because the odds that it will recoup its total investment should you allow the property to be foreclosed on will be slim.

The fact that lenders put so much weight on the appraisal process should give you (or your real estate agent) more reason to do your initial market research carefully and thoroughly. You don't want to go through all of the motions of shopping for a home and making an offer only to have a low appraisal force you to go back and renegotiate with the seller for a lower price (which of course can work in your favor, if the appraisal is indeed on target).

97. The appraisal was very different from the asking price—why?

Appraisals don't typically come in lower than the contract's purchase price, but when they do, it's usually because someone overestimated what the home is actually worth. If this happens to you, you gain bargaining power when you go back to the negotiating table with the seller. Because the appraisal affects your ability to get a mortgage, you'll also have the option of cancelling the deal, as long as you included a mortgage contingency in the contract.

Tell me more

You should also know that there are other reasons why problems crop up with the appraisal process. It could be that the appraiser isn't as knowledgeable about local property values as he should be, for example. Such a professional may not find the best possible "comps" in the area, or he may be new to the business or just not accustomed to handling appraisals in your region. Because the lender "orders" the appraisal, you probably won't have much choice of who appraises the home.

If you have reason to believe that the appraiser may be incorrect, let the mortgage lender know, request a copy of the appraisal (which will be included in your packet of closing documents), and back up your assertions with any comps or market information that will help the lender understand where you're coming from. Sometimes, you can also have a reappraisal done without an additional charge. On this part of the deal, however, the onus is ultimately on the seller to make sure the home is in good condition and presented in a way that will help the appraiser determine a value that is neither too high nor too low, but right on target.

98. What is a property survey?

Conducted by a professional surveyor, a survey determines whether the home you're buying is within property borders, whether any easements exist that could affect legal title, and if any encroachments exist on the property by neighbors (such as the neighbor who builds a fence two feet too far south and ends up "encroaching" on your property).

Chances are good that your lender will want a property survey conducted to determine the precise boundaries of the property you're buying. Expect to pay $150 to $300 for the survey, with that cost added to your closing obligations and the actual survey included in your packet of closing documents. Check with the home seller regarding the survey that was conducted when she bought the home. If it's less than six months old, your lender may be able to use that one at no cost to you. If it's older, then you might be able to save a few dollars by requesting an "update" from the professional who surveyed the property previously.

A drawing or map showing the precise legal boundaries of a property, the location of improvements, easements, rights-of-way, encroachments, and other physical features, confirms that the property's boundaries are correctly described in the purchase and sale agreement. Also called a plot plan, the survey may show that a neighbor's fence is located on the seller's property, or it may indicate the existence of more serious violations. These violations must be addressed before the lender will proceed.

Tell me more

If nothing else, a survey gives you, the buyer, a clear idea of exactly what you own and what you don't. Here are a few of the key areas that a property survey will determine:

- ❏ *Boundary Lines:* This is the main reason that a survey is conducted—to determine the location of boundary lines and other lines of occupancy or possession. You will need this information when you decide to erect a fence, put in a pool, or even pave your driveway. While a well-intentioned home owner or neighbor can easily make mistakes when pointing out property lines and easements (places where you don't want to put permanent structures, since the city government, utilities, or other factions can use that part of the land as needed), the surveyor will not. The boundary line certifications that he lays out in the survey report will confirm the legal description of the property you're buying.
- ❏ *Rights-of-Way, Easements, Encroachments, and Roads:* A survey reveals all conditions imposed by law that are then used to create a property's title report and other documents. If your city government has a 15-foot by 70-foot easement on the back of your property, for example, that strip of land can be taken by the city for use at any time. You may also share certain property elements with your neighbor, all of which will be reflected on the survey.
- ❏ *Access, Ingress, and Egress:* At a minimum, your survey will show whether there is physical vehicular ingress and egress to an open public street. If applicable, it will also reveal access for a particular purpose, such as emergency vehicles like fire trucks.
- ❏ *Bodies of Water:* If your home is near a visible body of water such as a pond, river, or lake, it will be reflected on the survey.
- ❏ *Existing Improvements:* The surveyor will certify that the buildings and other improvements, repairs, and changes made to your property that are in place when he surveys the property are in compliance with zoning laws and restrictions that deal with height, size, building

lines, and setbacks. This is good for the new-home buyer, who doesn't want to find out a year later that a shed built on the property is in violation of local zoning laws.

❑ *Telephone, Electricity, Cables, and Water:* The survey will also show the existence of underground cables and drains and other utility-supplied information. This information will be particularly useful should you decide to do any excavating or construction on the home.

❑ *Zoning Classification:* It is pretty easy to see if your property is zoned residential, but you may not know how specific zoning restrictions can affect the way in which you use your property. On your survey, the zoning portion will report the property's zoning jurisdiction and classification.

One more note about surveys. When you do get your hands on the hard copy, keep it in a safe place along with your other house documents. If you want to make any additions or changes to the structure itself or property itself—or if you have a neighbor who is getting overzealous about where his property lines are—the survey will come in handy.

99. Do I need a professional home inspector?

Unless you're a professional contractor or an engineer, you'll definitely want to spring $200 to $400 for a professional home inspection, which will be billed as a closing cost on your settlement or paid for up front, depending on your preferences and the inspector's policies.

Because most lenders do not require home inspections, it's up to you to decide whether you want one or not.

There was a time when real estate agents looked at inspectors as "deal breakers" because they always seemed to find defects or problems that stalled the trip to the closing table. Thanks to increased litigation and media attention regarding issues like toxic mold and dishonest property disclosures, most agents will now advise you to seek out a home inspector to give your home a once-over before finalizing your purchase contract.

Tell me more

Home inspectors are professionals who go over the home with a fine-tooth comb looking for defects, problems, and damage that could end up costing you money in the long run. Don't expect them to catch everything, but do expect them to uncover structural and operational issues not visible to the naked eye. If a problem or a symptom of a problem is found, the home inspector will include a description of the problem in a written report and may recommend further evaluation. The home inspector will supply this report to you for review.

A home inspection is particularly important for buyers, and the reasoning is simple: Emotion often affects the buyer and makes it hard to imagine any problems with a new home. By bringing in an objective third party, you can find out all of the possible problems before moving in. If you have a home inspection contingency in your contract, you can also back out of the contract if the home inspection turns up any costly repairs that the seller is not obligated to fix prior to selling the home.

A home inspection report is a lengthy, complex document that's carefully prepared by an inspector who scours the property looking for problems as minor as a missing electrical outlet cover or as complex as a malfunctioning furnace and everything in between. A home inspector's report will review the condition of the home's heating system, central air-conditioning system, interior plumbing and electrical systems; the roof, attic, and visible insulation; walls, ceilings, floors, windows, and doors; and the foundation, basement, and visible structure. Some inspectors will also offer additional services not included in a typical home inspection, such as mold, radon, and water testing.

As you can see, good home inspectors are both thorough and meticulous, but what you should also know is that just about anyone can call themselves a home inspector. Very few states offer licensing programs for home inspectors (although more and more are either imposing the requirement or considering such action). A good place to start your search for an inspector is at the American Society of Home Inspectors' (ASHI) Web site at www.ashi.org. Members of the organization must abide by standards of practice and a code of ethics set forth by the national organization.

ASHI also points to the experiences of and referrals from friends and neighbors as one of the best ways to find a home inspector. Someone who has used a home inspection service and is satisfied with the level of customer service and professionalism of that service will likely recommend a qualified professional. In addition, names of inspectors in your area can be found by searching ASHI's online database in the local yellow pages, where many advertise under "Building Inspection Service" or "Home Inspection Service." Real estate professionals are generally familiar with the inspection services in your area and can provide a list of qualified professionals.

100. What is generally included in an inspection report?

In the report, the inspector will cover the "main" areas of the home, then detail which components of those areas have been tested. He will also include several sentences/recommendations regarding those various areas and even recommend safety and/or care tips for appliances, flooring, roof, etc.

Tell me more

Here's a sampling of the various categories and specific areas/systems that you'll find on a typical inspection report:

General Information

- ❏ Structure:
- ❏ Year built:
- ❏ Weather conditions on the day of the inspection:
- ❏ Temperature:
- ❏ Recent weather conditions:
- ❏ Inspection attendees:
- ❏ Home occupied or vacant:

Area: Main house

- ❏ Foundation:
- ❏ Floor structure:
- ❏ Exterior walls:
- ❏ Roof structure:
- ❏ Foundation:
- ❏ Exterior walls:
- ❏ Roof structure:

Area: Roof

- ❏ Type of roof:
- ❏ Roof covering:
- ❏ Type of roof flashings:
- ❏ Gutters:
- ❏ Method of roof inspection:

Area: Siding and Trim

- ❏ Primary siding:
- ❏ Other siding:
- ❏ Soffits and fascia:

Area: Garage or Carport

- ❏ Garage attached or unattached to house:
- ❏ Garage doors:

Area: Grounds and Outside

- ❏ Porches:
- ❏ Entry driveway:
- ❏ Walkways:

Area: Windows and Doors

- ❏ Exterior doors:
- ❏ Interior doors:
- ❏ Windows:

Area: Basement and/or Crawl Space

- ❏ Type:
- ❏ How it was examined:
- ❏ Ventilation:
- ❏ Insulation:

Area: Attic

- ❏ How it was inspected:
- ❏ Insulation type:
- ❏ Insulation depth:
- ❏ Estimated r-value (measurement of the amount of insulation):
- ❏ Ventilation:

System: Electrical

- ❏ Service size:
- ❏ Main distribution panel:
- ❏ Subpanels:
- ❏ Service grounding connections:
- ❏ Wiring type:
- ❏ Wiring methods:
- ❏ Outlets:
- ❏ Smoke detectors:

System: Heating, Ventilation, and Air Conditioning (HVAC)

- ❏ Location of HVAC equipment:
- ❏ Heating type:
- ❏ Estimated age:
- ❏ Air filter location:
- ❏ Supply air ductwork:

System: Plumbing

- ❏ Main water valve location:
- ❏ Service pipe to house:
- ❏ Interior supply piping (where visible):
- ❏ Interior drain/waste/vent piping (where visible):
- ❏ Water heater:
- ❏ Fuel shutoff valve:

Area: Interior

- ❏ Wall and ceiling materials:
- ❏ Floor surfaces:
- ❏ Wall/ceiling finishes:
- ❏ Appliances:
- ❏ Other tests conducted (such as radon, termite):

101. How can I ensure an accurate, productive home inspection?

Being on site when the home inspector scours your new home is a great way to get to know the dwelling in an up-close-and-personal manner. If you're there while the inspection is going on, the professional home inspector can explain in person and answer any questions you may have (instead of having to call him up later and get explanations via phone). If it looks as if toxic mold is growing up the wall behind the air-conditioning unit, for example, he can point it out to you. Being there is a great way to learn about your new acquisition even if no problems are found. While you're there, however, make sure you give the home inspector time and space to concentrate and focus so he can do the best possible job for you.

Tell me more

Ed Frank, president of InspectAmerica Engineering, P.C. in White Plains, New York, is a nationally known licensed professional engineer (PE) who has thirty years of experience conducting engineering inspections for home buyers. He's been through a lot of inspections and has worked with a lot of buyers, some of whom went on to become happy home owners and others who used his inspections when asking for repair concessions from sellers or walking away from deals completely.

Frank advises home buyers to take these steps before and during the home-inspection process:

- ❑ *Select a home-inspection company with top credentials:* You have a goal, you want to be well informed, and you want to make a wise investment. Choose a home-inspection company that understands your needs and will work with you to help you meet your goals. Choosing a home-inspection company that is licensed to practice engineering is a wise choice. If you want your home inspection conducted by a licensed PE, be sure that your home inspection report will be stamped with the home inspector's licensed PE seal. The practice of engineering is state regulated and licensed; the PE seal on the home inspection report is the key to your protection. The practice of engineering is regulated in all states, whereas the business of home inspection is unregulated in about half of the states (as mentioned previously, anyone can be a home inspector).

- ❑ *Don't pay twice for a home inspection:* Consumers who retain the services of a home inspector who is not a PE may be faced with paying a second home inspection fee if the home inspector uncovers a problem, such as a structural defect, that requires the opinion of a licensed professional engineer.

- ❑ *Obtain a written home-inspection report:* Be sure that your home inspection report will be a detailed written report, not a handwritten checklist that is given to you at the conclusion of the home inspection. A checklist may be void of details and may not provide all of the information and engineering advice you need.

- ❑ *Inquire about important professional affiliations:* Make sure that the home inspection company you retain has professional affiliations, such as NABIE (National Association of Building Inspection Engineers) and NSPE (National Society of Professional Engineers). Unlike home inspection trade societies, NABIE and NSPE accept only licensed PEs as members. Members of NABIE need to meet tough entrance requirements, are highly qualified in the home-inspection profession, and adhere to a strict code of ethics.

- ❑ *Don't be confused by home inspector "certifications":* These certifications are offered by, or sold by, trade societies or companies, or obtained via home-inspection home-study courses. Such certifications are available to anybody—a high school diploma is not a requirement and certifications can be readily purchased.

❑ *Attend the home inspection:* Expect to spend about two hours with the inspector. One picture is worth a thousand words, and you'll gain a unique perspective on the home and its systems.

❑ *Make sure the home inspector is well equipped:* The home-inspection engineer should be fully equipped with necessary engineering tools including electrical testers, a fuel gas and carbon monoxide detector, a moisture meter, a ladder, an inspection mirror, a flashlight, a level, and other home-inspection tools.

❑ *Follow the inspector around and ask questions:* No questions are foolish. Learn as much as you can from the home inspector during the home inspection.

❑ *Consider optional tests:* Where applicable, they can include testing underground storage tanks, testing paint for lead, testing drinking water for lead, testing well-supplied drinking water for bacteria, testing for radon gas in the air, and testing for urea formaldehyde foam insulation.

❑ *Obtain a full oral report from the home inspector at the time of the home inspection:* The home-inspection engineering report should be available the next working day after the home inspection but a full oral report should be obtained at the conclusion of the home inspection.

102. What is a termite inspection?

As a protective measure, an increasing number of lending institutions require that homes be inspected for damage from termites or other wood-destroying insects before closing the sale of the home. Depending on which state you're in and what local codes are in place, the termite inspection report is known as an NPCA-1, wood-destroying insect infestation inspection report (WDIIR), and covers termites, carpenter ants, carpenter bees, and reinfesting wood-boring beetles.

This inspection report is prepared by a licensed pest control business that informs the lending institution and buyer about termite damage (past or present) or the presence of the destructive insects. This inspection is done for a nominal fee that can be as low as $35 or as high as $75, depending on the company, the size of the home, and the scope of the inspection. The fee will show up on your settlement statement at closing, or you can pay in full at the time of the inspection (because the fee is nominal, some inspectors will not wait until closing for payment).

Tell me more

The WDIIR consists of two pages, the first of which provides basic information about the inspection such as the address of the property, and answers these general questions:

- ❏ Are there any obstructions or areas inaccessible to inspection?
- ❏ Is there any visible evidence of infestation or previous treatment?
- ❏ If damage is present, who will correct it?

The report will also include a description of the terms, conditions, and limitations of the inspection. The second page of the report delves into more detail, pinpointing specific areas of concern, such as locations of previous termite treatment (a possible warning sign that the home had termites at one time) and areas of the home that the inspector can't access (such as small crawl spaces). Also on page two is a space for the inspector to draw the structure with these details included.

If the inspection report shows an active colony of any wood-destroying insect, the seller is responsible for the treatment and/or repairs. Depending on the wording in your purchase contract, the infestation will need to be treated and the repairs done prior to settlement. Generally there is a limit of 2 percent of the purchase price to cover treatment and repairs, or $2,000 on a $100,000 home, but check with your agent, attorney, or contract for details on your specific situation.

When an inspection is satisfactory, the inspector will issue a termite certificate that is valid for thirty days. For this reason, most lenders order the termite inspection fairly close to the closing date (to avoid having to reinspect if closing is more than thirty days away).

The termite inspection itself includes a visual survey of the home's interior and exterior, as well as any outbuildings and fences (inspections on the last two elements are generally not required by the lender, but it can provide more peace of mind knowing that the fences aren't rotting from termite damage). The average termite or pest inspection takes approximately thirty to forty-five minutes for a thorough inspection, depending on the size and condition of the home and property.

103. What is radon?

Radon is a colorless, odorless, tasteless, radioactive gas that has been found in homes nationwide. Produced by a natural breakdown of uranium in soil, rock, and water, radon moves up through the ground and into the air that we breathe. It also gets into homes through cracks and other holes in the foundation, or through well water. A home will essentially "trap" radon, thus making the living area dangerous for those inside who are breathing the radon-contaminated air. The Environmental Protection Agency (EPA) reports that radon is the second leading cause of lung cancer, second only to cigarette smoke.

As a home buyer, you may or may not have to worry about radon gas issues. Some home owners go about their business for decades, blissfully unaware of the hazards associated with the radioactive gas. Other homes in areas where radon is known to be prevalent will need to be tested and repaired before you move in.

Tell me more

According to the EPA, nearly one out of every fifteen homes in the United States has an elevated radon level (4 pCi/L or more), resulting mostly from radon's presence in surrounding soil or in well water. The gas enters a home through small spaces and openings like cracks in concrete, floor drains, joints, and pores in hollow block walls. If the home has a well, the likelihood of radon can be particularly high. The gas breaks down into radioactive particles that remain in the air and that can be damage the delicate tissue of the lungs. A home can be old or new, drafty or well sealed, and still have a radon problem.

That's the bad news. The good news is that fixing a radon problem isn't as costly and time-consuming as one might assume. You and/or the home seller will need to test for the gas, then have special ventilation added in the foundation and basement. If you suspect a radon problem, first consult with your local, county, or state government agency for recommendations of qualified radon-reduction contractors. The federal government has created a national hotline at (800) SOS-RADON, and all states have a radon office designed to help the public deal with radon issues. The EPA has a list of those offices posted on its Web site at www.epa.gov/iaq/whereyoulive .html.

104. Should I have the house tested for radon?

If you are thinking of buying a home, you may decide to accept an earlier test result from the seller or you may ask the seller for a new test to be conducted by a qualified radon tester. Before you accept the seller's test, the EPA says you should determine:

❑ The results of previous testing.

❑ Who conducted the previous test: the home owner, a radon professional, or some other person.

❑ Where in the home the previous test was taken, especially if you plan to live in a lower level of the home. (For example, the test may have been taken on the first floor. However, if you want to use the basement as living space, test there.)

❑ What, if any, structural changes, alterations, or changes in the HVAC system have been made to the house since the test was done. (Such changes may affect radon levels.)

If you decide that a new test is needed, discuss it with the seller as soon as possible. If you decide to use a qualified radon tester, contact your state radon office to obtain a copy of its approved list of radon-testing companies (see the EPA's Web site). If the home has never been tested for radon, have a test conducted as soon as possible. Include the following provisions in your purchase contract:

❑ Where the test will be located

❑ Who should conduct the test

❑ What type of test is to be done

❑ When the test is to be done

❑ How the seller and the buyer will share the test results and test costs (if necessary)

❑ When radon mitigation measures will be taken and who will pay for them

Tell me more

Make sure that the test is done in the lowest level of the home suitable for occupancy. This means the lowest level that you are going to use as living space which is finished or does not require renovations prior to use. A state or local radon official or qualified radon tester can help you make some of these decisions.

Since you cannot see or smell radon, special equipment is needed to detect it. When you're ready to test your home, you can order a radon test kit by mail from a qualified radon measurement services provider or laboratory. You can also hire a qualified radon tester, very often a home inspector, who will use a radon device(s) suitable to your situation. The most common types of radon-testing devices are:

❑ *Passive Devices:* These are radon-testing devices that do not need power to function. These include charcoal canisters, alpha-track detectors, charcoal liquid scintillation devices, and electric ion chamber detectors available in hardware, drug, and other stores. These devices are exposed to the air in the home for a specified period of time and then sent to a laboratory for analysis.

❑ *Active Devices:* These are radon-testing devices that require power to function. They include continuous radon monitors and continuous working-level monitors that continuously measure and record the amount of radon or its decay products in the air. Many of these devices provide a report of this information that can reveal any unusual or abnormal swings in the radon level during the test period. A qualified tester can explain this report to you. In addition, some of these devices are specifically designed to deter and detect test interference. Some technically advanced active devices offer anti-interference features. While these tests may cost more, they may ensure a more reliable result, according to the EPA.

105. What are lead-based paint hazards?

If the home you're buying was built before 1978, you have certain rights concerning lead-based paint and lead poisoning hazards. For starters, the home seller or her real estate agent must provide you with the EPA pamphlet entitled "Protect Your Family from Lead in Your Home," or other EPA-approved lead hazard information. The same party must also disclose what the seller knows about the home's lead-based paint or lead-based paint hazards and give you any relevant records or reports.

Like asbestos, lead paint was a compound commonly used in products found in and around homes until its adverse affects on health were discovered. Lead may cause a range of health effects, from behavioral problems and learning disabilities to seizures and death. According to the EPA, children six years old and under are at most risk because their bodies are growing quickly.

Tell me more

As a buyer, you have at least ten days to conduct an inspection or risk assessment for lead-based paint or lead-based paint hazards. However, to have the right to cancel the sale based on the results of an inspection or risk assessment, you will need to negotiate this condition with the seller (in other words, make sure you include it as a contingency in your purchase contract). The seller must attach a disclosure form to the agreement of sale which will include a lead warning statement. The buyer, seller, and real estate agent(s) will also sign an acknowledgment that these notification requirements have been satisfied.

Lead can be found both on the inside and outside of a home, though some of the most common sources include:

❏ *House Paints:* Most houses built before 1939 had lead-based paint applied to the interior or exterior surfaces, and some home paints produced up to 1977 contained small amounts of lead. Some of these paints still remain inside older homes and may be particularly hazardous if in poor condition (chipped or peeling) or if disturbed by sanding or abrasion (creating lead dust).

❏ *Lead in the Soil:* While lead is a naturally occurring element found in small amounts nearly everywhere, the soil near heavily used streets and roads may contain lead as a result of past use of lead in gasoline. Lead may also be present in the soil adjacent to houses with lead-based paint. Lead buildup in the soil may contribute to the high levels of lead in household dust.

❏ *Drinking Water:* Some water pipes in older homes were made of lead. In both old and new homes, lead solder was used in copper piping. Both can be a source of lead in drinking water.

Also at risk are homes located next to heavily traveled roads or highways that have lead-containing exterior paint or that are adjacent to bridges or steel structures which have been renovated and may have lead contamination in surrounding soils, says the EPA. These homes require additional testing for lead.

If the home you are buying falls into these risk categories, you will want to have lead testing done prior to closing. Testing methods range from small home test kits to actual laboratory analyses of paint samples. Ask your local health department for more information about having your home's paint, as well as household dust and soil from your yard and even the home's drinking water tested for lead. Correcting the problem of lead soil contamination is also a job for professionals who specialize in these intricate projects.

106. What disclosure requirements exist concerning lead-based paint hazards?

The EPA has established strict guidelines for home sellers under its Residential Lead-Based Paint Hazard Reduction Act. Federal law now imposes the requirements listed below on sellers of residential housing built prior to 1978:

❑ Sellers must disclose the presence of any lead-based paint hazards actually known to the seller. This disclosure must be made prior to the seller's acceptance of the purchaser's offer. An offer may not be accepted until after the disclosure requirements are satisfied and the purchasers have had an opportunity to review the disclosure language, and to amend their offer, if they wish.

❑ If the seller is aware of the presence of lead-based paint and/or lead-based paint hazards in the property being sold, the disclosure must include any information available concerning the known lead-based paint and/or lead-based paint hazard, including the following:
  • The seller's basis for determining that lead-based paint and/or lead-based paint hazards exist.
  • The location of the lead-based paint and/or lead-based paint hazards.
  • The condition of the painted surfaces.

❑ If a lead-based paint hazard is not known to the seller, the disclosure must include a statement disclaiming such knowledge.

❑ The seller must supply a list of any records and reports pertaining to lead-based paint and/or lead-based paint hazards, copies of which must be provided to the purchasers.

❑ The disclosure must also include the government-mandated lead warning statement, found on the front side of the form.

❑ Sellers must provide purchasers with a copy of the federal pamphlet entitled "Protect Your Family from Lead in Your Home" (available from real estate professionals).

❑ Sellers must permit a purchaser a ten-day period (unless the parties mutually agree, in writing, upon a different period of time) to have the property tested for lead-based paint before the purchasers become obligated under the buy-and-sell agreement.

❑ A civil fine of $10,000 may be levied against any seller or real estate agent who fails to live up to the obligations imposed by this law.

Tell me more

Obtain more detailed information about dealing with lead in a home from the following sources:

U.S. Department of Housing and Urban Development (HUD)
451 7th Street, SW (Room B-133)
Washington, DC 20410
Attn: Office of Lead-Based Paint Abatement & Poison Prevention

(202) 755-1805
www.hud.gov

U.S. Environmental Protection Agency (EPA)
401 M Street, SW (TS-799)
Washington, DC 20460
Attn: TSCA Hotline
(202) 554-1404
www.epa.gov

National Lead Information Center Hotline
1-800-LEAD-FYI

American Industrial Hygiene Association (AIHA)
2700 Prosperity Avenue, Suite 250
Fairfax, VA 22031
(703) 849-8888
www.aiha.org

107. What is clear title?

One of the key steps that will need to be taken between purchase contract
signing and closing involves your new home's title, which is the legal term
for one's ownership interest in land. Before anyone can transfer "title" to
another owner (in this case, you), a title search must be conducted by a
lawyer or title insurance firm to make sure the title is indeed theirs to "convey" to you. In order for this clean exchange of ownership to take place,
the property must have what is known as "clear title."

Clear title basically means that the property is free from liens, defects,
or other encumbrances (except those which you have agreed to accept—
such as a mortgage that you will assume). If these contingencies (or any
others listed in the purchase contract) are not met, the deal can be nullified
and the earnest money returned to the buyer.

Tell me more

The average real estate transaction will probably go through without any
substantial title issues, also known as "clouds." As long as property owners
operate within the legal limits of the law and pay their bills within a reasonable amount of time, it's not hard to maintain clear title throughout the
extent of their ownership.

There are always exceptions to the rule, and I myself ran into a major
title stumbling block when I tried to purchase a condominium about six
years ago. The place was perfect and the price was right, but the owner

had gotten himself into a legal entanglement that clouded the title on this particular property. Originally, he was in a "rent to own" situation with his seller, who owed money to a group of professionals who schlepped down to the courthouse one day and slapped a lien on the property. The current owner inherited that lien when an improper title search was conducted years earlier.

The estimated value on the property was about $60,000, but between the owner's mortgage and two liens placed on the property, the amount he owed on it was about $120,000. I waited patiently for two months as lawyers and lenders tried to hash it out but, in the end, wound up walking away from the deal because the title was more "completely overcast" than "cloudy." Hopefully, you'll never find yourself in that situation.

108. What does a title report include?

Once a title search is performed on your new home, the preliminary report will show any impediment that would prevent clear title from passing to you. The report will include the following information:

❑ Taxes on subject property, amount owed, amount paid, and assessor's parcel number

❑ Easements of record, if applicable

❑ Restrictions on subject property, if applicable

❑ Liens and/or judgments of record, if applicable

❑ Exact vesting of owner of record

The title search will also verify the extent of your ownership rights or interest. The most common form of interest is "fee simple" or "fee," which is the highest type of interest an owner can have in land. Liens, restrictions, and interests of others excluded from title coverage will be listed numerically as exceptions in the report, and you may also have to consider interests of any third parties, such as easements granted by prior owners that limit use of the property.

109. What kinds of things can "cloud" a title?

Title defects go beyond just liens. Other examples of situations that can cloud a property's title include:

❑ Lost or forged deeds

❑ A married signer who represents himself or herself as single

❑ Claims of undisclosed heirs

❑ Impersonation of another

❑ Clerical error at the courthouse when earlier documents were recorded

❏ Incorrect legal description
❏ Instruments signed by minors or mentally incompetent persons
❏ Title taken as a result of an improperly probated will
❏ Confusion of title resulting from similar names

110. What is title insurance?

Title insurance ensures that you have clear title to the property. If there are any problems or discrepancies found later, you can always go back to the title insurance company and have them clear them up if necessary. It's basically a form of insurance contract that guarantees to indemnify an owner or mortgagee of property for damages suffered as a result of undiscovered title defects that arise later.

Tell me more

When you buy a home, most lenders will require that you pay a fee to the title insurance company for the lender's title insurance policy. This fee is generally paid at closing and covers a onetime premium. The policy assures your lender that there are no liens or judgments against the property, and that the mortgage will be in "first position" (the first to be paid in the case of a foreclosure, a sale, or refinance). An additional title insurance policy will also protect you from liability for any defects in the title that may not arise in a standard title search.

Along with the lender's policy, you may also want to purchase an owner's title insurance policy, which is an agreement that the insurer will pay all losses involved in any claim covered by the policy terms. The policy provides two types of coverage:

1. If the insured title is contested, the insurer will defend the title at no expense to you.
2. If the title is defective and the problem cannot be resolved, title insurance protects you from financial loss. You'll be reimbursed up to the amount of the policy, which is typically the full amount of your loss.

An owner's policy typically costs $3.00 to $4.00 per $1,000 of the mortgage loan, or $600 to $800 for a $200,000 home. Whether you purchase this additional insurance is your choice, and you'll probably want to discuss the options with your lender, attorney, and/or real estate professional before deciding.

PART III

SEALING THE DEAL

CHAPTER SEVEN

SECURING YOUR MORTGAGE LOAN

111. What's the first step in securing a mortgage?

The first thing you'll want to do is review your finances, check your credit (particularly if you have a hunch that a past blemish might affect the lender's decision), and compare lending institutions (such as your local bank, credit union, online lender, and/or mortgage broker), then select the best match for your financial situation.

Just because a lender handed you a prequalification letter—or a more detailed preapproval—last month doesn't mean you have to go back to that lender for your loan. In the past, banks were the most logical starting point, but these institutions are usually the best choice for buyers with excellent credit. Another option is credit unions, which serve only their own membership with low-fee mortgages and loans. Online companies (see Question 38) like LendingTree.com offer a one-stop-shopping environment in which consumers can obtain rate quotes from a dozen lenders at a time, while independent mortgage brokers (see Question 116) specialize in matching consumers to the right loan program—even if that consumer has poor credit or a past bankruptcy.

Tell me more

To make sure you get the best rate and service offerings, you'll want to shop around and check out your options before making a decision. But first, order a copy of your credit report from all three reporting agencies (see Question 30) and check it for any errors. Mortgage lenders are sticklers about having even the smallest of unpaid bills paid off prior to closing, and the sooner you take care of any discrepancies or overlooked bills, the better. (If you do catch an error, don't be too surprised: It's estimated that half of all credit reports contain errors significant enough for an individual to be denied a loan.)

While you're sorting out your own financial picture, start tracking the movement of interest rates in the market. Your local paper should include a daily picture of current mortgage rates and an indication of whether they're going up or down. Use this information to help make decisions regarding the loan, lender, and type of loan product that will best suit you.

112. How do I choose my loan type?

As mentioned in Chapter 2: Nailing Down the Finances, today's lenders are offering home buyers a wide range of home loan choices, from 100 percent financing to loans with home equity lines of credit built into them, and everything in between. To help whittle down your choices, ask yourself the following questions:

❑ *How long do I plan to stay in my home?* If you're looking at five years or less, it may behoove you to opt for a fifteen-year loan, which allows you to start paying off your principal balance faster.

❑ *How large a monthly payment can I comfortably afford?* If your monthly resources are limited, you'll want a thirty-year loan that's more expensive in the long run, but that offers a lower monthly payment. If your financial situation changes, you can always make an extra payment or two a year and reduce the loan time considerably, provided the loan has no prepayment penalties (fees charged for paying off your loan early).

❑ *How much money do I have for a down payment?* Some of your down payment can come from "gift" funds from, say, a friend or relative, but lenders also like to see the buyer take an interest in the property by forking over at least some of their own hard-earned cash up front. There are also 100 percent financing programs, however, so check around if the down payment is a sticking point for you (and check back to Chapter 2 for information on gift down-payment programs).

❑ *Do I expect my income to remain stable, increase, or decrease?* Be honest with yourself on this answer, or risk getting in over your head on your mortgage loan. Unless you're absolutely positive that a corner office and bigger paycheck are waiting around the next corner, it's best to base your purchase on what you can afford right now.

Tell me more

Countrywide Home Loans, one of the nation's largest mortgage lenders, gives borrowers the following tips for selecting the right type of mortgage to meet their individual situations:

If you: Plan to live in your home for many years.

You'll want a: Low-interest rate over a long period of time. Since you're going to be making payments for years to come, your best strategy may be to take a fixed-rate loan and pay points to get your rate as low as possible.

If you: Plan to sell or refinance your home in just a few years.

You'll want to: Avoid points and closing costs since the difference in interest payments won't typically make up for your out-of-pocket costs at closing. Also try for a smaller down payment. A fixed-period adjustable-rate mortgage (ARM) is a good choice for holding rates down for a set number of years.

If you: Want to pay off your home loan by the time your children are in college.

You'll want a: Shorter-term loan such as a fifteen-year fixed-rate home loan, which is a smart way to ensure you can use income for other goals later in life. Plus you build equity faster.

If you: Want to budget for a fixed payment each month.

You'll want to: Look for a fixed-rate loan that has a principal and interest payment that stays the same for the entire term of the loan.

If you are: Comfortable with periodic changes to the interest rate if it means you can get more home now.

You'll want to: Look at ARMs, a great solution for people who have incomes that are going to grow and who will quickly refinance or be able to afford a larger payment in a few years should interest rates rise.

113. How can I best compare loans?

After assessing your own mortgage needs, the next step is to look for the best deal possible by comparing the products offered by several lenders, including banks, credit unions, online lenders, and mortgage brokers. The Internet is one of the best ways to do this, although it will require that you hand over some personal and financial data via the Web in order for the company to "shop" your information around and find one or more lenders willing to lend on your terms. Don't get too caught up in looking only at the interest rate, since points and other fees can add up to thousands of dollars and minimize any benefit you would gain from saving a half percentage point on the interest rate.

When shopping for a loan, review its terms, particularly these areas:

❑ The presence of prepayment penalties
❑ The expected down payment

❏ The mortgage insurance requirements
❏ The interest rate lock-in period (see Question 125)
❏ The monthly payment schedule

Tell me more

Select the loan with the rate and terms that suit your situation best. If you're planning to sell your home in the next two to four years, for example, you'll definitely want a loan with no prepayment penalties. If one lender stands out as meeting all of your criteria, ask which documents you'll need to provide for the approval process (see Question 115).

Also available during this process are a number of community and government programs that are particularly useful for first-time home buyers. If you need homebuyer counseling or assistance, flip back to Chapter Two: Nailing Down the Finances for more information on how to find such resources in your area.

114. How do I apply for a home loan?

Applying for a home loan can be simple, exhaustive, or anywhere in between, depending on the lender's requirements and your own financial situation. If your credit is good to excellent, you have an adequate down payment, and have a solid job history, the process will probably be pretty simple. If you don't fit into one or more of these categories, the application and approval process could require more documentation and backup.

If you didn't obtain a prequalification letter and/or preapproval prior to shopping for your home (see Question 25), you'll be starting at square one right now in your hunt for a home loan.

115. What documentation will I need to apply for a loan?

Most lenders use a straightforward application process that requires a ratified sales contract, an earnest money deposit, and a uniform residential loan application. You will need to bring proof of the first two along with you to the meeting (or deliver it via fax or mail to a lender not located nearby), and you will be asked to either fill out the loan application or have your loan officer conduct an interview and fill it out for you.

Tell me more

Here are the basic documents that your lender will expect:

❏ *Your Ratified Sales Contract*: This is the purchase contract that both you and the seller have signed off on. It's the starting point for the loan application interview, since this is the document that specifies the amount of your down payment, the price you will pay for your house, the type of mortgage financing you're seeking, and your planned closing and occupancy dates.

❑ *Earnest Money Deposit:* This "good-faith" payment will be deposited in an escrow account and applied to your closing costs when the deal closes. Your lender may request a receipt showing the deposit amount and when it was deposited in the escrow account.

❑ *Uniform Residential Loan Application (see appendix for a sample residential loan application):* Using a four-page standard residential mortgage loan application you will answer questions about your income, assets, liabilities, and credit, as well as information regarding the property you're buying. You may be asked to fill this out prior to meeting with the lender, or a loan officer will interview you by phone and fill out the application. In order to fill out the application accurately, you'll want to have the following documents handy, plus the following documents and information for yourself, your spouse, and any coborrowers who will be on the loan:

- Social security number
- Documentation of your current residence status (if you are not a U.S. citizen)
- Street addresses for your dwellings over the last two years
- W-2 forms for the last two years of employment and current pay stubs for the last month (or federal and/or business income tax returns for the last two years if you're self-employed)
- Documentation of other income sources such as alimony and child support that you wish to be included in your monthly income tally
- Contact information, account numbers, and balances for all checking and savings accounts, as well as three months of statements for any certificates of deposit or brokerage accounts
- Information regarding life insurance policies, automobiles, or other significant assets that you want to have considered when figuring your net worth
- Documentation of liabilities, such as child support or alimony, as well as information on debts like credit cards (the lender can usually pull the balances and required information on the former from your credit report)
- Your current monthly housing expenses
- A copy of any decrees or agreements relating to divorces or marital separations

- If you're using a "gift" as a source of closing funds, a copy of the gift letter and documentation that shows fund availability
- If you're applying for a Veterans Administration loan, an original VA certificate of eligibility, or a statement of service letter (for active-duty personnel)
- A check for the application fee, which will cover a credit report fee and, in some cases, the home appraisal fee (the latter varies by lender)

Expect several follow-up calls from your lender or mortgage broker as she goes through your documentation and finds "gaps" that need further explanation (such as a letter of explanation for a negative mark on your credit report by a certain debtor). The approval process may be as short as a few days or as long as a week or two, depending on your situation. Try not to get too frustrated every time your loan officer calls for "one more piece of documentation." Lenders set their own standards and requirements for approving loans, and all of the information you provide will ultimately help you in securing your new home.

116. What is a mortgage broker?

A mortgage broker is an individual or company that brings borrowers and lenders together to originate a mortgage loan. Intermediaries, these professionals require a fee or commission to get the job done, and they can act in the interest of both the borrower and lender. They negotiate, originate, and process residential real estate loans on behalf of the consumer. Because they operate independently of any lender, good mortgage brokers tend to be sharp, knowledgeable individuals who have access to an extensive selection of mortgage products and experience in comparing loans, rate, and terms.

Tell me more

According to the National Association of Mortgage Brokers, over 50 percent of Americans use mortgage brokers for financing. The group says brokers provide consumers with "choice, convenience, and experience." And although they will cost a little more than going directly to the lender, I myself have found them to be extremely flexible (One lender's requirements are too strict on the credit check? A mortgage broker can quickly point you to another who isn't so stringent.)

117. Should I use a mortgage broker?

Making mortgage brokers particularly attractive is their experience working in the "subprime" credit market, and the way they use flexible loan products that allow buyers with less-than-perfect credit scores or low- to moderate-income levels to become home owners.

It works like this: The broker allows wholesale lenders to cut origination costs by providing such services as preparing the borrower's loan package, preparing the loan application, helping with the funding process, and counseling the borrower. The National Association of Mortgage Brokers says that brokers help keep loan rates low because of their minimal overhead and setup costs, and that the broker will seek the loan that best suits the borrower's financial circumstances, needs, and goals. From the consumer's perspective, with rare exceptions, the broker does not get paid unless and until the loan closes. Thus, the broker has the ultimate incentive to provide the best possible customer service to the consumer.

One mortgage broker says she spends most of her time shopping for the best, most customized programs available on the market for her individual home buyers. "We pull credit reports at the beginning, then shop it around from that point for the best deal," she says, adding that the consumer who goes to each lender or online source individually risks blemishing their own credit history. "When a consumer shops on their own, they may get their credit pulled several times as they go from lender to lender, thus jeopardizing their credit score and the chance for the best possible approval."

Tell me more

Unlike individual lenders, credit unions, and banks, mortgage brokers tend to "think outside the box" when it comes to financing. Much like an independent real estate agent, they don't get paid until you get to the closing table, so it's in their best interest to toss out the cookie-cutter approach and instead focus on individualized options for each borrower. In exchange, you will pay "points," or up-front charges expressed as a percentage of the loan. One point, for example, is one percent of the loan price. If the lender quotes a one-point fee on a $100,000 loan, for example, and the broker adds one point, the borrower pays a total of $2,000, of which $1,000 goes to the broker.

There are a number of ways to find a mortgage broker in your area; a referral from a friend, family member, or colleague is among the best ways to track down a reputable professional. You can also check your local yellow pages, or consult a Web site like The National Association of Mortgage

Brokers (www.namb.org), which includes a "Find a Broker" section for consumers.

118. Besides funding, what does my lender have to provide?

By law, your lender will have to provide you with several documents and pieces of information, the most important of which is required by RESPA (the Real Estate Settlement Procedures Act, covered in more detail in Chapter 8), a federal statute that requires lenders to disclose certain costs in the sale of residential property.

Lenders are also required by law to provide you with several informational bulletins, depending on what type of loan you take out. For the most part, these requirements force banks and lenders to educate you—up front—on exactly how much it's going to cost to buy your home, including all fees and closing costs. That way, you don't get smacked with "hidden" fees at the closing table.

Tell me more

Legally, your lender is required to furnish you with several types of documents and information after you've applied for a mortgage loan. The information includes, but is not limited to, the following:

❑ *The Annual Percentage Rate:* Also known as the APR, this percentage figure includes interest plus certain closing costs and any points and other finance charges. It factors these up-front costs over the term of the loan. The APR must be disclosed to you according to federal truth-in-lending laws within three business days of when you apply for a loan, or prior to or at closing for a refinance.

❑ *A Good-Faith Estimate:* Within three days of submitting your loan application, your lender is required by federal law to hand over an itemized estimate of the costs to close your mortgage loan. The numbers will not be precise, but rather an "estimate" of how much money you'll need to bring to the closing table. It also includes the seller's closing costs.

❑ *A Guide to Settlement Costs:* Within three days of accepting your written application, your lender must hand over a copy of the government publication "Settlement Costs: A HUD Guide" (which is also available online at www.hud.gov/offices/hsg/sfh/res/sfhrestc .cfm). The guide walks you through the settlement process, your financial responsibilities, your rights, and an item-by-item explanation of the closing services and costs.

❑ *ARM Disclosures and Explanation:* Federal law requires your lender to give you information either when you receive an application form for an ARM or when you pay a nonrefundable fee, whichever comes first. You should also be given a written summary of the key terms and costs of the loan, the past performance of the index to which the interest rate will be tied, and a copy of the booklet "Consumer Handbook on Adjustable-Rate Mortgages," which is available online in PDF format at www.federalreserve.gov/pubs/brochures/arms/arms.pdf.

According to the Department of Housing and Urban Development (HUD), one of the purposes of RESPA is to help consumers become better shoppers for settlement services. RESPA requires that borrowers receive disclosures at various times. Some disclosures spell out the costs associated with the settlement, outline lender servicing and escrow account practices, and describe business relationships between settlement service providers. Here are three others that your lender will be required to hand over, if applicable:

1. *Servicing Disclosure Statement:* RESPA requires the lender or mortgage broker to tell you in writing, when you apply for a loan or within the next three business days, whether it expects that someone else will be servicing your loan (collecting your payments).

2. *Affiliated Business Arrangements:* Sometimes, several businesses that offer settlement services are owned or controlled by a common corporate parent. These businesses are known as "affiliates." According to HUD, when a lender, real estate broker, or other participant in your settlement refers you to an affiliate for a settlement service (such as when a real estate broker refers you to a mortgage broker affiliate), RESPA requires the referring party to give you an affiliated business arrangement disclosure. This form will remind you that you are generally not required, with certain exceptions, to use the affiliate and are free to shop for other providers.

3. *HUD-1 Settlement Statement (see sample form in appendix):* One business day before the settlement, you have the right to inspect the HUD-1 settlement statement. This statement itemizes the services provided to you and the fees charged to you. This form is filled out by the settlement agent who will conduct the settlement. Be sure you have the name, address, and telephone number of the settlement agent if you wish to inspect this form. The fully completed

HUD-1 settlement statement generally must be delivered or mailed to you at or before the settlement. In cases where there is no settlement meeting, HUD says the escrow agent will mail you the HUD-1 after settlement. In such cases, you have no right to inspect it one day before settlement.

119. What authorizations and approvals will my lender request?

Expect your lender to ask for several authorizations and approvals during the loan application process, including the following forms to confirm information you provided on the application:

- ❏ Employment verification
- ❏ Past mortgage or home rental payment history
- ❏ Bank deposits
- ❏ Authorization to check your credit

Tell me more

When checking your credit, your lender must also abide by what is known as the Fair Credit Reporting Act (FCRA), which limits that company to using the information on the report only for the purpose of qualifying you for the loan. During this process, the lender is not allowed to ask any of your personal references, family, or colleagues about your character or your ability to pay debts unless the lender asks your permission to do so. Lenders are also strictly forbidden, under the Equal Credit Opportunity Act (ECOA), to discriminate based on race, color, national origin, sex, marital status, or religion.

120. Should I sign IRS Form 4506?

During the loan application process you may be asked to sign an IRS Form 4506, also known as a "Request for Copy or Transcript of Tax Form." This form allows the lender to receive copies of your tax return directly from the IRS; it applies mostly to self-employed professionals who don't have W-2 statements from an employer.

Since the mortgage process itself is a very exploratory event, most borrowers don't mind signing another form and opening up yet another aspect of their financial lives to the lender. However, in this age of increased privacy and security concerns, you may want to think carefully before signing this form, particularly if you're shopping your loan around to multiple lenders.

Tell me more

It's a good idea to retain previous years' tax returns, but sometimes keeping paper documents is easier said than done. For that reason, lenders have access to Form 4506, which allows them to delve into your tax return archives and retrieve those necessary to complete your loan application.

You can use Form 4506 either to request a copy of your tax return or to designate a third party to receive the tax return. Such requests typically take up to sixty calendar days to process, and the form must be signed and dated by the taxpayer. There is a $39 fee for each return requested.

Sounds simple enough, but as mentioned previously, the thought of one or more lenders gaining access to tax returns, which contain everything from social security numbers to wages to personal deductions, doesn't sit well with every borrower. If you're concerned about issues like privacy and identity theft—or if you're concerned that numerous requests will somehow raise red flags with the IRS—then you'll want to work with a lender and/or loan product that doesn't require you to sign on the dotted line of an IRS Form 4506.

As a consumer in today's mortgage market, you're in the driver's seat. Simply ask the lender to waive the signing of the form, point you in the direction of a program that doesn't require the form, or move on to another lender. If you're working with a mortgage broker or real estate agent, be sure to make this request clear early in the process so that he can help you find the right program.

121. What factors affect my interest rate?

Nothing will dictate your interest rate more than your own credit history and debt-to-income ratio. It's pretty simple: Those borrowers with good credit ratings get good rates; those with poor credit histories usually have to settle for higher rates, based on perceived risk. Unfortunately, that means home buyers are often penalized on their past financial histories (no matter how much they've "cleaned up their act" in the last year or two), while those with cleaner records are offered the best possible rates.

If you have good credit and if your monthly income far surpasses your monthly debt obligations, your chances of getting approved at a lower interest rate are very good. However, if your monthly income barely takes care of your minimum debt obligations, even the best credit report won't help you receive the lowest available interest rate.

Tell me more

For obvious reasons, you'll want to consult your own credit history (if you haven't done so already) to clean up any errors on your report and find out just where you stand. By doing this, you'll be better prepared to discuss mortgage interest rates with your lender of choice or to move on to another source if necessary.

In addition to your credit history, the actual amount of your loan can affect your interest rate, particularly if the amount being financed exceeds loan limits set forth by government groups like Fannie Mae, the nation's largest source of financing for home mortgages. The good news is that Fannie Mae recently announced that it will apply new federal data on mean (average) home prices to increase its single-family mortgage loan limit to $333,700 for 2004, from $322,700 in 2003.

Fannie Mae adjusts its conforming loan limits annually. The conforming loan limits are based on the October-to-October changes in the mean (average) home price, as published by the Federal Housing Finance Board (FHFB). According to Fannie Mae, the group's average loan is well below the conforming limit, or $150,000 for a single-family property.

The length of your loan also affects your interest rate, with shorter-term loans of fifteen to twenty years fetching lower rates than those that extend over thirty years. If you don't mind the higher monthly payment—and if you're intent on paying down your principal balance sooner than you would with a thirty-year loan—then a shorter-term loan might be a good option.

Interest rates also vary by type of loan, with ARMs allowing you to get started at a rate lower than what's being offered on fixed-rate loans. However, your payments could get higher when the interest rate changes, so you'll want to weigh out the positives and negatives on that option.

If you have a down payment worth more than 20 percent of the home selling price (say $30,000 or more on a $150,000 home), you should be able to get the best possible rate. If you're putting down 5 percent or less ($7,500 or less on a $150,000 home), expect to pay a slightly higher rate since you're starting the homeownership experience with less collateral.

One last note about interest rates: When you're looking at the rates offered by various lenders, you'll see the acronym "APR" used frequently. While the definition doesn't warrant an entire section, you should know that the APR is a number that includes most of the fees that you'll pay to obtain a loan, such as the application fee, credit report fee, mortgage insurance premiums, and documentation fees, and is stated as an interest rate.

The federal truth-in-lending law requires mortgage companies to disclose the APR when they advertise a rate in an effort to present the "true" costs of the loan to you, the borrower.

122. When is an ARM the best choice?

Here are two examples of situations where ARMs could work out in your favor:

1. If you're not planning on owning your home for more than two to five years, and if you're currently in a low-interest-rate environment. By opting for an ARM, you'll be able to take advantage of the very low rate without worrying about how many percentage points it will increase over the next thirty years.
2. If your credit isn't good enough to qualify for a conventional mortgage at a decent rate, and if the lender offers a program that locks in an ARM rate for two years, then switches to a thirty-year loan after you've "proved" yourself as a creditworthy customer (Read: You've paid your mortgage and the rest of your bills on time for the two-year period.) Talk to your lender about these options, particularly if the credit issue is stalling your homebuying process.

123. What should I know about points?

There are two types of points that lenders charge at closing: origination points and discount points. The two point types differ in where they are actually applied in the loan process:

1. Origination points are charged to recoup some costs related to the loan origination process, such as your loan officer's compensation.
2. Discount points are used to "buy" your interest rate lower. This is known as a rate "buy-down." Generally, a full discount point will lower your fixed interest rate .25 percent or your adjustable rate .375 percent for the entire term of the loan.

Tell me more

Origination points are used at the discretion of the lender. They're not usually tax deductible and are considered a "necessary evil" of the mortgage loan process, with the majority of lenders using them. Different lending institutions handle this process differently, and in some cases the origination points may be negotiable. Be sure to ask your lender how such chargeable items are handled.

Discount points are different. They are fees that you pay up front to lower your mortgage interest rate on a fixed-rate mortgage and are yet another way to obtain a lower interest rate on your loan. The process is fairly simple: You prepay the interest on your loan in a lump sum up front in order to reduce the amount that you pay each month. One point equals 1 percent of your loan balance, so if your loan balance is $150,000 then one point will equal $1,500.

The more points you're willing to pay up front, the lower your mortgage interest rate. Whether or not you decide to pay points up front depends on two factors: 1) whether you can afford to make those up-front payments and 2) how long you expect to have the mortgage. The first is self-explanatory, while the second is important because the longer you plan to keep your mortgage, the more sense it will make to pay for points now and pay less interest over the life of the loan.

124. Are there tax advantages to paying points?

According to the IRS, paying discount points can present tax advantages to buyers, since they may be deductible as home mortgage interest (only if you itemize deductions on Form 1040, Schedule A). If you can deduct all of the interest on your mortgage, you may be able to deduct all of the points paid on the mortgage.

Tell me more

The IRS says you can deduct the points in full in the year they are paid, if all the following requirements are met:

- ❏ You are legally liable for the debt, and the loan is secured by your main home (your main home is the one you live in most of the time).
- ❏ Paying points is an established business practice in your area.
- ❏ The points paid were not more than the amount generally charged in that area.
- ❏ You use the cash method of accounting. This means you report income in the year you receive it and deduct expenses in the year you pay the points.
- ❏ The points were not paid for items that usually are separately stated on the settlement sheet such as appraisal fees, inspection fees, title fees, attorney fees, and property taxes.

❑ You provided funds at or before closing that were at least as much as the points charged, not counting points paid by the seller. (You cannot have borrowed the funds from your lender or mortgage broker.)

❑ You use your loan to buy or build your main home.

❑ The points were computed as a percentage of the principal amount of the mortgage.

❑ The amount is clearly shown on your settlement statement.

Points that do not meet these requirements may be deductible over the life of the loan, according to the IRS. Check with your accountant or tax preparer for the most updated information on this topic. You can also check with IRS Publication 936, "Home Mortgage Interest Deduction," which is available online in a PDF format at www.irs.gov/pub/irs-pdf/p936.pdf.

125. What does it mean to "lock in a rate?"

After shopping around for a mortgage and selecting a lender, your next step will be to lock in a rate on your loan. Also called a "rate lock" or "rate commitment," this is basically a lender's promise to hold a specific rate and a certain number of points for you for a certain period of time. Some lenders offer this "lock-in" when you file your loan application, while others will not offer it until the loan is approved.

Unlike a loan commitment or "approval," a rate lock-in is simply a promise to keep charges and interest rates at a predetermined level, even if the market fluctuates while the loan is being processed.

Tell me more

Because interest rates fluctuate along with the overall economy and the stock market—and because it takes several weeks (or more) to prepare, assess, and document a loan application—the sooner you can lock in a rate, the better. Realize, however, that by locking in a rate you will also be unable to take advantage of any "decreases" in the cost of the mortgage, such as a lower market interest rate, unless the lender is willing to then lock in the lower rate when it becomes available. If the market is characterized by falling interest rates, you'll want to ask the lender about this option up front.

How your lock-in is presented depends on the individual lender. Some use preprinted forms that explain the exact terms of the lock-in agreement, while others may simply offer an oral commitment in person or by phone.

If possible, try to get the commitment in writing since oral agreements are hard to prove should a dispute crop up down the road.

Something else to be aware of: Lenders may charge a fee to lock in the interest rate and points for your loan. The fee may be charged up front and may not be refunded if the loan doesn't ultimately close. Inquire about the lender's policies before accepting the lock-in, or ask that the fee be levied at the closing table to ensure that you don't pay for it if your loan application is not approved.

126. Should I lock in a rate?

Here are a few key questions to ask your lender before asking for or accepting a lock-in rate:

- ❑ Do you offer a lock-in of interest rate and points?
- ❑ When can I lock in these items? (When I apply for the loan? When the loan is approved?)
- ❑ Do you charge a fee to lock in an interest rate?
- ❑ Does the length of the lock-in determine that fee?
- ❑ Will the lock-in be in writing?
- ❑ If rates drop during the lock-in period, can I lock in at the lower rate?
- ❑ If the answer is yes to the above question, do you charge an additional fee for this service?
- ❑ Can I float my interest rate and points now and lock them in at a later date?
- ❑ What rate will be charged if the lock-in expires prior to my closing date?

Tell me more

Besides the "true" lock-in, in which the interest rate and points are locked in by the lender, there are two other options that you might want to consider, depending on the lender, your situation, and the current mortgage market. They are:

1. *Locked-In Interest Rate with Floating Points:* The lender will let you lock in the interest rate but allow the points to rise or fall to coincide with changes in market conditions. Should interest rates drop during this time, the points may also fall, and vice versa.
2. *Floating Interest Rate with Floating Points:* The lender will lock in your interest rate and points between the time you file your applica-

tion and closing. This is a good option if you're in an environment where interest rates are steady or falling. If rates increase, however, expect to pay a higher rate.

Lock-ins are valid for a set number of days, typically 30 to 60, although lock-ins as short as 7 days or as long as 120 are also used in the industry. The period needs to be long enough to allow for settlement and any other contingencies set forth by the lender. Ask your real estate agent or attorney how long home closings generally take to complete in your area (thirty to sixty days is considered the industry norm, although I've closed homes in ten working days), and keep in mind that the longer the lock-in rate, the higher the fee you will pay for that commitment.

127. Do I need private mortgage insurance (PMI)?

Private mortgage insurance (PMI) is insurance against a loss by a lender in the event of a default by the borrower. Issued by a private insurance company, a portion of the premium is generally paid for at closing, with the rest paid as part of the monthly mortgage payment. The size of your down payment will dictate whether you need this insurance or not: Put down 20 percent or more, and your lender will not take out PMI on your new loan. Fork over less up front, however, and expect to pay for this coverage, which protects the mortgage lender in case you default on your loan.

Tell me more

PMI can be a mixed blessing for home buyers. Low down-payment mortgages have gained in popularity in recent years, making it possible for more people to become home owners. For those loans, mortgage insurance serves as a cushion for lenders who take the risk, thus allowing borrowers to purchase a more expensive home than they might otherwise be able to afford. On the flip side, the coverage is an added expense for the borrower who can't afford a 20 percent down payment.

If you're going to need PMI, you should know that most monthly plans require that a portion of your mortgage insurance premium be paid up front at closing, with the rest paid as part of your monthly mortgage payment. Under an annual plan, you'll pay the entire first-year premium at closing. There are also single-premium plans that require a onetime single PMI premium.

So you're probably asking yourself, just how much does it cost? Well, the PMI premium is based on your loan-to-value ratio, the type of loan and the amount of coverage required by the lender. Your good-faith estimate of closing costs (see Question 36) will include the estimated premium and monthly cost for PMI. On a $150,000 loan with 10 percent down ($15,000), expect to pay about $60 a month for PMI.

If PMI is in the cards for your loan, you can take solace in the fact that you will be able to cancel it when you've paid 20 percent or more of your principal loan balance. The Homeowners Protection Act of 1998 went into effect in 1999 and established clear rules for automatic termination and borrower cancellation of PMI on home mortgages. These protections apply to certain home mortgages signed on or after July 29, 1999, for the purchase, initial construction, or refinance of a single-family home.

128. What is a good-faith estimate?

When you were shopping around for your mortgage loan, the lenders or mortgage brokers you worked with probably gave you a rough idea of your closing costs. Once you apply for your loan, lenders are required to put those costs in writing via a good-faith estimate, in accordance with RESPA, within three business days of your application. Under the Truth in Lending Act (TILA), the lender must also provide a disclosure estimating the costs of the loan you applied for, including your total finance charge and the APR, within the same three days.

Tell me more

RESPA governs the home loan application and closing process and ensures that buyers receive timely notification of closing and related costs. This document lists the estimated costs you will have to pay at or before loan closing. It also identifies some of the companies that are expected to provide services in connection with your loan, like credit bureaus, appraisers, and closing agents.

Your good-faith estimate will include some or all of the following charges. Most of the charges have been covered in this book (see especially Chapter 2 on financing), with further explanation below on the additional charges not yet addressed in other chapters:

❑ *Application Fee and Credit Report:* Imposed by your lender, the application fee covers the initial costs of processing your loan request and usually includes a credit report check. The application fee with a credit report can range from $400 to $525. Appraisal Fee: This fee covers an independent appraisal of the home you want to purchase.

❑ *Attorney Fees:* Attorney fees are typically based upon the purchase price of the home and the complexity of the sale and can range anywhere from $500 to $1,200 and up.

❑ *Documentation Fees:* Some lenders charge fees for underwriting, processing, and documentation preparation. Expect to pay less than 1 percent of the loan amount for these additional charges.

❑ *Home and Pest Inspections:* The costs for these services vary depending upon the location and size of the property, and the professionals you choose.

❑ *Homeowners and Hazard Insurance:* Prices for homeowners insurance (see Question 129) vary depending upon the value of the home, the location, and the insurance agency.

❑ *Interim Interest or Daily Rate of Interest:* This is based on your closing date and covers loan interest from the day of closing through the end of the month. The fee will range from zero to thirty days' interest and is payable to the lender.

❑ *Loan Origination Fees and Discount Points:* One point equals one percent of the loan amount (see Question 123).

❑ *Mortgage Insurance (PMI):* See Question 127.

❑ *Survey:* Depending on the size of the property and the state you live in, surveys can cost between $250 and $450.

❑ *Title Fees Typically Including the Following:*
  • *Document Preparation Fee:* A flat fee paid to the title company that ranges from $50 to $200.
  • *Title Search:* The cost for a title search is based upon the purchase price and may cost approximately $250 to $500.
  • *Title Insurance:* Lenders' title insurance is approximately .2 percent to .5 percent of the loan amount, paid by you, while your title insurance ranges between .3 percent and .6 percent of the purchase price of the home.

❑ *Government Fees:* These fees include city, county, and state transfer taxes; prepaid property taxes; and recording fees.

❑ *Property Taxes:* Expect to pay four to eight months' worth of taxes at closing. The money will be held in an escrow account to ensure that sufficient funds are available to cover these expenses once you've bought your home.

As you carefully review your good-faith estimate, keep in mind that the fees listed on the form are estimates and are not set in stone. The actual charges you will pay in connection with your loan may be higher or lower, but this document will give you a good general idea of how much your loan will cost.

129. What is homeowners insurance?

Homeowners insurance protects your property against loss from liability, theft, and most common disasters, including acts of terrorism (unless previously excluded from the policy). A standard homeowners insurance policy insures both the home itself and its contents. Such policies come "packaged," which means they cover both damage to the property and your liability or legal responsibility for any injuries and property damage that you, your family members, or your pets may inflict on others while they are on your property.

Rates on homeowners insurance policies vary widely, depending on location, your own financial and insurance history, and the insurance history of the home itself. The policies cover most disasters, although there are exceptions to the rule. Flood insurance, for example, must be purchased separately (your real estate agent or attorney will know if your home is in a "flood zone"). Earthquake coverage must also be bought separately, if required. Maintenance-related issues (such as a leaking roof) are your own responsibility and are not covered by homeowners insurance.

Tell me more

A standard homeowners insurance policy includes four basic types of coverage:

1. *Coverage for the Structure of Your Home:* This pays for the repair or rebuilding of your home should it be damaged or destroyed by fire, hurricane, or other disaster. When examining this portion of the policy, be sure that it covers the cost of rebuilding your home. The policy also covers "detached" structures, such as sheds, for roughly 10 percent of the amount of insurance you have on the structure of the home.
2. *Coverage for Your Personal Belongings, or the Home's "Contents":* Along with the physical structure, your own belongings are also covered by the homeowners insurance policy. Most companies provide coverage for 50 to 70 percent of the amount of insurance you have on the home itself. So if you have $175,000 worth of insurance on the home, you would have $87,000 to $123,000 worth of coverage for your contents.

3. *Liability Protection:* This protects you against lawsuits for property damage or bodily injury inflicted on others by you, your family members, and/or pets. For example, if your son accidentally destroys your neighbor's garage door, you are covered. If he backs into your door, however, you're not covered. This portion of your policy covers the costs of defending yourself in court plus any court awards, up to the policy limit, which generally starts at $100,000.

4. *The Cost of Living Elsewhere Because of a Fire or Other Disaster:* This part of the policy pays for the hotel bills, restaurant meals, and other living expenses incurred while your home is being rebuilt. Most policies provide coverage for about 20 percent of the insurance on your house, but this number can be increased at your request.

130. How much homeowners insurance do I need?

When purchasing homeowners insurance, use the following rule of thumb: The coverage should be at least the replacement cost of your new home. This ensures that your home will be completely rebuilt in case of a total loss. In other words, you can't base the homeowners insurance coverage on what it cost to build the home in the first place, since appreciation and inflation both influence the rising cost of new homes.

Because it's in a lender's best interest to make sure its investment is insured against potential losses, most will want the first year's premium paid at or before closing. As mentioned in Chapter 2, you can also have this premium added to your monthly housing payment, along with your property taxes. In such cases, the lender then pays your insurance bill out of escrow when it receives premium notices from your insurance company.

There are no hard-and-fast rules on just how much you should pay for homeowners insurance, since certain areas of the country are more prone to natural disasters like flooding, earthquakes, hurricanes, and tornadoes. The price you pay for homeowners insurance can vary by hundreds of dollars, depending on a number of factors, including which company you're buying insurance from. There are several Web sites where you can shop around for insurance rates, including www.homeownerswiz.com, www.homeowners-insurance-quotes-inc.com, and www.2020insurance.com.

Tell me more

When you're shopping around, the Federal Consumer Information Center suggests keeping these "12 Ways to Save Money on Your Homeowners Insurance" in mind:

Before You Buy Your Home

1. *Consider the cost before you buy your home:* You may pay less for insurance if you buy a house close to a fire hydrant or in a community that has a professional rather than a volunteer fire department. It may also be cheaper if your home's electrical, heating, and plumbing systems are less than ten years old. If you live in the eastern United States, for example, consider a brick home that's more wind resistant. If you live in an earthquake-prone area, look for a wooden-frame house because it is more likely to withstand this type of disaster. Choosing wisely could cut your premiums by 5 to 15 percent.

2. *Shop around:* It will take some time, but it could save you a good sum of money. Ask your friends, check the yellow pages, or call your state insurance department. You can also access insurance information for your state on the Internet at www.naic.org/consumer/state/usamap.htm. States often make information available on typical rates charged by major insurers, and many states provide the frequency of consumer complaints by company.

3. *Raise your deductible:* Deductibles are the amount of money you have to pay toward a loss before your insurance company starts to pay a claim, according to the terms of your policy. The higher the deductible, the more money you can save on your premiums. Nowadays, most insurance companies recommend a deductible of at least $500. If you can afford to raise your deductible to $1,000, you may save as much as 25 percent. Remember, if you live in a disaster-prone area, your insurance policy may have a separate deductible for certain kinds of damage. If you live near the coast in the eastern part of the United States, for example, you may have a separate windstorm deductible. If you live in a state vulnerable to hailstorms, you may have a separate deductible for hail; if you live in an earthquake-prone area, your earthquake policy has a deductible; and if you're out west, where wildfires run rampant in the summer, expect to see wildfire deductibles.

4. *Purchase your home and auto policies from the same insurer:* Some companies that sell homeowners, auto, and liability coverage will take 5 to 15 percent off your premium if you buy two or more policies from them. But make certain this combined price is lower than buying the different coverages from different companies.

5. *Don't confuse what you paid for your home with rebuilding costs:* The land under your house isn't at risk from theft, windstorm, fire,

and the other perils covered in your homeowners policy. So don't include its value in deciding how much homeowners insurance to buy. If you do, you will pay a higher premium than you should.

6. *See if you can buy group coverage:* If your employer administers a group insurance program, check to see if a homeowners policy is available and is a better deal than you can find elsewhere. In addition, professional, alumni, and business groups often work out a package with an insurance company, which includes a discount for association members. Ask your association's director if an insurer is offering a discount on homeowners insurance to you and your fellow graduates or colleagues.

7. *Seek out other discounts:* Companies offer several types of discounts, but they don't all offer the same discount or the same amount of discount in all states. That's why you should ask your agent or company representative about any discounts available to you. For example, since retired people stay at home more than working people, they are less likely to be burglarized and may spot fires sooner. Retired people also have more time for maintaining their homes. If you're at least fifty-five years old and retired, for example, you may qualify for a discount of up to 10 percent at some companies.

Once You Have Purchased Your Home

8. *Make your home more disaster resistant:* Find out from your insurance agent or company representative what steps you can take to make your home more resistant to windstorms and other natural disasters. You may be able to save on your premiums by adding storm shutters, reinforcing your roof, or buying stronger roofing materials. Older homes can be retrofitted to make them better able to withstand earthquakes. In addition, consider modernizing your heating, plumbing, and electrical systems to reduce the risk of fire and water damage.

9. *Improve your home security:* You can usually get discounts of at least 5 percent for a smoke detector, burglar alarm, or dead bolts. Some companies offer to cut your premium by as much as 15 or 20 percent if you install a sophisticated sprinkler system and a fire and burglar alarm that ring at the police, fire, or other monitoring stations. These systems aren't cheap, and not every system qualifies for a discount. Before you buy such a system, find out what kind your insurer recommends, how much the device would cost, and how much you'd save on premiums.

10. *Stick with the same insurer:* If you've kept your coverage with a company for several years, you may receive a special discount for being a long-term policyholder. Some insurers will reduce their premiums by 5 percent if you stay with them for three to five years and by 10 percent if you remain a policyholder for six years or more. But make certain to periodically compare this price with that of other policies.

11. *Review the limits in your policy and the value of your possessions at least once a year:* You want your policy to cover any major purchases or additions to your home. But you don't want to spend money for coverage you don't need. If your five-year-old fur coat is no longer worth the $5,000 you paid for it, you'll want to reduce or cancel your floater (extra insurance for items whose full value is not covered by standard homeowners policies) and pocket the difference.

12. *If you're on a government plan, seek out private insurance*: If you live in a high-risk area—say, one that is especially vulnerable to coastal storms, fires, or crime—and have been buying your homeowners insurance through a government plan, you should check with an insurance agent or company representative or contact your state department of insurance for the names of companies that might be interested in your business. You may find that there are steps you can take that would allow you to buy insurance at a lower price in the private market.

CHAPTER EIGHT

THE HOME BUYER'S LEGAL RIGHTS

131. What is the Fair Housing Act?

Created in 1988, the Fair Housing Act protects home buyers and renters from illegal discrimination. As a buyer, you have the right to buy any home you can afford in any neighborhood, and the act makes it illegal to discriminate because of such factors as race, color, national origin, religion, sex, disability, or familial status (meaning whether you have children or are pregnant).

Real estate professionals, lenders, or others involved with the home-buying process who unfairly deny someone the right to own (or rent) a home are said to be "discriminating" and thus violating the Fair Housing Act.

132. What should I do if I suspect that I am a victim of discrimination?

Fair Housing violations are more common than most people would think in this day and age. They can range from the single mother denied the right to purchase a condo in a neighborhood perceived to be, but not legally registered as, an over-55 community to the minority home buyer who is "steered" to neighborhoods by a real estate agent who "thinks" they belong in a certain area, and everything in between.

You may or may not experience issues like these during your own home purchase, but it's still important to be aware of these types of discrimination and of your legal rights, should they occur. Often, the problems crop up during the lending process, where again no one can refuse to give you a loan based on race, color, national origin, religion, sex, familial status, or handicap. (A lender is allowed to offer a loan on less favorable terms, or even turn down your application, based on valid issues like insufficient income, unacceptable credit history, or poor past track record with mortgage loans.)

Tell me more

According to the U.S. Department of Housing and Urban Development (HUD), it is also illegal to threaten, coerce, intimidate, or interfere with anyone exercising a fair housing right or assisting others who exercise that right; and to advertise or make any statements that indicate a limitation or preference based on race, color, national origin, religion, sex, familial status, or handicap. For example, it is illegal to advertise that a house is for sale to "whites only," says HUD.

If you think that any of your fair housing rights have been violated, discuss your concerns with the person or people involved. If you're not satisfied after discussing your complaints, access HUD's Office of Fair Housing and Equal Opportunity (FHEO) at 1-800-669-9777 or online at www.hud.gov/complaints/housediscrim.cfm. From the Web site you can print out a form and mail it to HUD at:

Office of Fair Housing and Equal Opportunity
Department of Housing and Urban Development
Room 5204
451 Seventh Street SW
Washington, DC 20410-2000

133. What is RESPA?

References to RESPA (Real Estate Settlement Procedures Act) have appeared throughout this book, but it's also helpful to know exactly what this law is and what it means for you as a buyer. In the past, much of what went on between the signing of the purchase agreement and the actual settlement was "behind closed doors," with the buyer unaware of some of the relationships between the various service providers (such as appraisers, title companies, and lenders) and uninformed about important aspects of the deal, like closing cost estimates.

That changed when RESPA came along in 1974 and laid down the law on certain requirements and timelines that the folks who are helping to close your transaction must follow. Primarily concerned with closing costs and settlement procedures, RESPA is designed to help home buyers be better shoppers in the homebuying process and, as such, requires that consumers receive disclosures at various times in the transaction and outlaws kickbacks that increase the cost of settlement services.

Tell me more

RESPA is a federal law regulating a lender's closing or settlement practices. HUD says the purposes of RESPA are:

❑ To help consumers become better shoppers for settlement services
❑ To eliminate kickbacks and referral fees that unnecessarily increase the costs of certain settlement services

RESPA requires that lenders make disclosures and treat you fairly by:

❑ Giving you a copy of HUD's booklet "Settlement Procedures and You" within three days after you apply for a loan.
❑ Giving you a good-faith estimate of the closing (or "settlement") costs within three days after you apply for a loan.
❑ Itemizing all loan closing charges on a uniform settlement statement (USS), also known as the HUD-1 form. This law also gives you the right to inspect the HUD-1 form at least twenty-four hours before the closing on your home. To exercise this important but often over-looked right, HUD advises asking your closing agent or lender for a copy of the HUD-1 form sooner.
❑ Prohibiting lenders and agents from receiving hidden kickbacks or referral fees for referring customers to anyone for any transaction involving a federally insured loan (see Question 134).
❑ Restricting the amount of money a lender can ask you to put in escrow.

Let's look at loan transfers, for example. Your new home loan has a value, which means the lender you just signed up with can sell it to another company. In fact, that same loan may change hands several times in the next few years. Under RESPA, your original lender is required to disclose this information—when you make your loan application—as well as the percentage of loans that lender has assigned, sold, or transferred over the past two years. Your lender also must disclose his or her capacity to service loans, and you will be asked to sign a statement saying that you have read and understood the disclosure.

According to HUD, if your lender transfers the servicing of your loan to another lender, he must give you no less than a fifteen-day notice before the transfer. This notice must include the date of the transfer; the name, address, and toll-free or collect call telephone number of the new servicer; as well as the name of an employee of the new servicer whom you can call. If you send timely payments to the lender who transferred your loan, rather than to the new lender servicing your loan, you may not be charged a late fee during a sixty-day period after the date of the transfer.

Also covered under RESPA are affiliated business arrangement (AfBA) disclosures, which are required whenever a settlement service provider involved in a RESPA-covered transaction refers the consumer to a provider with whom the referring party has an ownership or other beneficial interest. According to HUD, the referring party must give the AfBA disclosure to the consumer at or prior to the time of referral. The disclosure must describe the business arrangement that exists between the two providers and must give the borrower an estimate of the second provider's charges.

RESPA covers loans secured with a mortgage placed on a one to four-family residential property, including purchase loans, assumptions, refinances, property improvement loans, and equity lines of credit. If during your homebuying process you feel that one or more service providers have violated RESPA, you will want to file a complaint outlining the violation and identifying the violators by name, address, and phone number. Complainants should also provide their own name and phone number for follow-up questions from HUD. Requests for confidentiality will be honored. Complaints should be sent to:

Director, Office of RESPA and Interstate Land Sales
U.S. Department of Housing and Urban Development
Room 9146
451 7th Street, SW
Washington, DC 20410

134. What are illegal kickbacks and referral fees?

RESPA was enacted because Congress felt that consumers needed protection from unnecessarily high settlement charges caused by certain abusive practices that have developed in some areas of the country. Those include fees, kickbacks, or "anything of value" in exchange for referrals.

As a home buyer working with what you assume are competent professionals, it can be difficult to detect (or even suspect) someone who is taking such kickbacks in exchange for business.

Tell me more

According to HUD, it is illegal under RESPA for anyone to pay or receive a fee, kickback, or anything of value as the result of agreeing to refer settlement service business to a particular person or organization. For example, your mortgage lender may not pay your real estate broker $250 for referring you to the lender. It is also illegal for anyone to accept a fee or part of a fee for services if that person has not actually performed settlement services for the fee. For example, a lender may not add to a third party's fee, such as an appraisal fee, and keep the difference.

As a buyer, you should also be aware of which payments are legal and permitted. According to HUD, RESPA does not prevent title companies, mortgage brokers, appraisers, attorneys, settlement/closing agents, and others who actually perform a service in connection with the mortgage loan or the settlement from being paid for the reasonable value of their work.

135. What should I do if I suspect a fee is illegal?

If a participant in your settlement appears to be taking a fee without having done any work, you should advise that person or company of the RESPA referral fee prohibitions. Also realize that it is a crime for someone to pay or receive an illegal referral fee. The penalty can be a fine, imprisonment, or both. You may be entitled to recover three times the amount of the charge for any settlement service by bringing a private lawsuit. If you are successful, the court may also award you court costs and your attorney's fees, according to HUD.

If you suspect a problem in any of these areas, HUD says the best place to have it fixed is at its source (the lender, settlement agent, broker, etc.). If that approach fails and you think you have suffered because of a violation of RESPA, Equal Credit Opportunity Act (see Question 137), or any other law, you may be entitled to sue in a federal or state court.

Tell me more

According to HUD, most settlement service providers are supervised by a governmental agency at the local, state, and/or federal level. Your state's attorney general may have a consumer affairs division, for example, and if you feel that a provider of settlement services has violated RESPA or any other law, you can complain to that agency or association.

Lastly, if you have a question any time during the life of your loan, RESPA requires the company collecting your loan payments (your "servicer") to respond to you. Write to your servicer and call it a "qualified written request under Section 6 of RESPA." A "qualified written request" should be a separate letter and not mailed with the payment coupon, HUD advises. Describe the problem and include your name and account number. The servicer must investigate and make appropriate corrections within sixty business days.

136. What is the Truth in Lending Act?

In 1968, Congress laid down the law when it passed the Consumer Credit Protection Act, which required creditors (for the first time) to state the cost of borrowing in a common language so that you, as a consumer, can figure out exactly what the charges are, compare costs, and shop around for the best deal. The act was particularly important in that it spawned a number of other consumer protection or "truth in lending" laws, requiring that consumers be informed as to why their credit was denied and be allowed to access their credit records and handle billing disputes.

Each of the new laws was designed to reduce the problems and confusion about consumer credit, which over the years has become increasingly more complex to understand and work with. Because your credit rating plays a key role in the home loan process, this bill is particularly important for you as a new home buyer.

Tell me more

The Consumer Credit Protection Act is aptly named in that it protects you, the consumer, from being discriminated against by lenders for reasons pertaining to your credit history and rating. The law says, for example, that you:

❑ Cannot be denied a credit card just because you're a single woman
❑ Can fix errors on your monthly bill without damaging your credit rating
❑ Cannot have credit denied or shut down just because you've reached the age of 62
❑ Can limit your risk if a credit card is lost or stolen

You may hear the Consumer Credit Protection Act referred to as the Truth in Lending Act (TILA) during the mortgage process. Essentially, the establishment of the former led to a number of TILAs, which mandate that lenders disclose certain costs and terms that relate to your loan. You typically obtain these TILA disclosures when you receive an application for a loan, although you may also get additional disclosures before the loan closes.

The Truth in Lending Act requires lenders to disclose the terms and costs of all loan plans, including:

❑ The annual percentage rate (APR), points, and fees
❑ The total of the principal amount being financed
❑ The payment due date and terms (including any balloon payment [if applicable] and late payment fees)
❑ The application fee
❑ Any annual or onetime service fees

- ❏ Prepayment penalties
- ❏ The address of the property for which the loan is being secured (if applicable)
- ❏ Key features of variable-rate loans, including the highest rate the lender would charge, how it is calculated, and the resulting monthly payment
- ❏ Total finance charges
- ❏ Whether the loan is assumable

As a borrower, you should know that federal law mandates that neither the lender nor anyone else involved in the transaction may charge a fee until you have received this information. Also key is the fact that lenders who advertise their services to the public must adhere to TILA disclosure requirements with respect to the loan rate and terms. That means those "no money down" ads that appear in the newspaper must follow these four guidelines:

1. Specific credit terms (such as "no money down" and "5 percent APR") that are used in the advertisements must be made available to applicants.
2. If an advertisement includes a rate, it must state the rate as an APR. Recall that this rate takes into account additional costs, such as fees and points, incurred in the first year of the loan.
3. If the APR may be increased after that one-year period, the advertisement must reflect that information.
4. The ad can also include a simple annual rate or periodic rate, applied to an unpaid balance. It may be stated in conjunction with, but not more conspicuously than, the APR.

TILA applies to each individual or business that offers or provides credit to consumers, credit that is subject to a financial charge or payable by a written agreement in more than four installments; credit that is used for personal, family, or household purposes; and loan balances that equal or exceed $25,000 and are secured by a real property or dwelling. The act also provides consumers with rights in connection with certain types of credit transactions, including the right to cancel certain real estate lending transactions within three days (also known as a "right of rescission"), regulation of certain credit card practices, and a means for fair and timely resolution.

As you can see, TILA and related consumer protection acts are designed to help you navigate the homebuying process without getting railroaded by unexpected fees, unresolved credit issues, and other hazards. It's all about disclosure and basically opening up to the public a process that for years was handled behind closed doors and only revealed to the consumer at the closing table, if then.

The fact that the laws exist does not necessarily mean all lenders abide by them, as evidenced by a 2003 court case involving a Boston bank and a home buyer. The alleged TILA violation involved a prepayment clause in the mortgage note provided to the buyers in connection with their "high-cost" mortgage loan. The buyers claimed that the lender failed to disclose that no penalty would be due if the borrowers refinanced with the original lender.

The federal Truth in Lending Act may permit a consumer to file a lawsuit if a creditor fails to correctly provide the required disclosures. The court may order actual damages suffered as a result of a violation, statutory damages, court costs, and attorney's fees. Under certain circumstances, consequential damages such as emotional distress may be ordered. If during your homebuying process you feel that a lender or other service provider has violated your consumer rights, consult with a real estate attorney to discuss your next course of action.

137. What is the Equal Credit Opportunity Act?

Knowing that credit is used by millions of consumers to finance homes (and obtain other types of loans) every year, the Federal Trade Commission (FTC) established the Equal Credit Opportunity Act (ECOA) to ensure that those consumers are given an equal chance to obtain credit. This doesn't mean all consumers who apply for credit get it, according to the FTC, which cites factors such as income, expenses, debt, and credit history as other considerations for creditworthiness.

Tell me more

The ECOA protects you when you deal with any creditor who regularly extends credit, including banks, small loan and finance companies, retail and department stores, credit card companies and credit unions. Anyone involved in granting credit, such as real estate brokers who arrange financing, is covered by the law. Businesses applying for credit also are protected by the law.

According to the FTC, when you apply for credit, a creditor may not:

❑ Discourage you from applying because of your sex, marital status, age, race, national origin, or because you receive public assistance income.

❏ Ask you to reveal your sex, race, national origin, or religion. A creditor may ask you to voluntarily disclose this information (except for religion) if you're applying for a real estate loan. This information helps federal agencies enforce antidiscrimination laws. You may be asked about your residence or immigration status.

❏ Ask if you are widowed or divorced. When permitted to ask marital status, a creditor may only use the terms "married," "unmarried," or "separated."

❏ Ask about your marital status if you are applying for a separate, unsecured account. A creditor may ask you to provide this information if you live in "community property" states: Arizona, California, Idaho, Louisiana, Nevada, New Mexico, Texas, and Washington. A creditor in any state may ask for this information if you apply for a joint account or one secured by property.

❏ Request information about your spouse, except when your spouse is applying with you, your spouse will be allowed to use the account, you are relying on your spouse's income or on alimony or child support income from a former spouse, or you reside in a community property state.

❏ Inquire about your plans for having or raising children.

❏ Ask if you receive alimony, child support, or separate maintenance payments, unless you are first told that you do not have to provide this information if you won't rely on these payments to get credit. A creditor may ask if you have to pay alimony, child support, or separate maintenance payments.

❏ Consider whether you have a telephone listing in your name. A creditor may consider whether you have a phone.

❏ Consider the race of people in the neighborhood where you want to buy, refinance, or improve a house with borrowed money.

❏ Consider your age, unless:
  • You are too young to sign contracts, generally younger than eighteen years of age.
  • You are sixty-two or older, and the creditor will favor you because of your age.
  • It is used to determine the meaning of other factors important to creditworthiness. For example, a creditor could use your age to determine if your income might drop because you are about to retire.
  • It is used in a valid scoring system that favors applicants sixty-two and older. A credit-scoring system assigns points to answers you

provide to credit application questions. For example, your length of employment might be scored differently depending on your age.

As a consumer, the ECOA also states that you have the right to:

❏ Have credit in your birth name (Mary Smith), your first and your spouse's last name (Mary Jones), or your first name and a combined last name (Mary Smith-Jones).
❏ Get credit without a cosigner, if you meet the creditor's standards.
❏ Have a cosigner other than your husband or wife, if one is necessary.
❏ Keep your own accounts after you change your name or marital status, reach a certain age, or retire, unless the creditor has evidence that you are not willing or able to pay.
❏ Know whether your application was accepted or rejected within thirty days of filing a complete application.
❏ Know why your application was rejected. The creditor must give you a notice that tells you either the specific reasons for your rejection or your right to learn the reasons if you ask within sixty days. Acceptable reasons include: "Your income was low," or "You haven't been employed long enough." Unacceptable reasons are: "You didn't meet our minimum standards," or "You didn't receive enough points on our credit-scoring system." Indefinite and vague reasons are illegal, so ask the creditor to be specific.
❏ Find out why you were offered less favorable terms than you applied for—unless you accept the terms. Ask for details. Examples of less favorable terms include higher finance charges or less money than you requested.
❏ Find out why your account was closed or why the terms of the account were made less favorable unless the account was inactive or delinquent.

For women home buyers, the FTC says keep in mind that a good credit history (basically, a record of how you paid past bills) often is necessary to get credit. Unfortunately, this hurts many married, separated, divorced, and widowed women. There are two common reasons women don't have credit histories in their own names: They lost their credit histories when they married and changed their names, or creditors reported accounts shared by married couples in only the husband's name. If you're married, divorced, separated, or widowed, the FTC advises you to contact the local credit bureau(s) to make sure all relevant information is in a file under your own name.

138. What should I do if I suspect a lender has discriminated against me?

If you suspect that a lender is in violation of the ECOA, the FTC suggests the following steps:

❑ Complain to the creditor. Make it known that you're aware of the law. The creditor may find an error or reverse the decision.

❑ Check with your state's attorney general to find out if the creditor violated state equal credit opportunity laws. Your state may decide to prosecute the creditor.

❑ Bring a case in federal district court. If you win, you can recover damages, including punitive damages. You also can obtain compensation for attorney's fees and court costs. An attorney can advise you on how to proceed.

❑ Join with others and file a class action suit. You may recover punitive damages for the group of up to $500,000 or 1 percent of the creditor's net worth, whichever is less.

❑ Report violations to the appropriate government agency. If you are denied credit, the creditor must give you the name and address of the agency to contact. While some of these agencies don't resolve individual complaints, the information you provide helps them decide which companies to investigate.

Tell me more

If you feel a lender may have discriminated against you in violation of this federal law, the FTC says you should contact the appropriate federal agency, depending on the type of lender involved. Here's a list of contacts for the most popular home lending institutions:

❑ For nationally chartered banks: Comptroller of the Currency Compliance Management Mail Stop 7-5, Washington, DC 20219.

❑ For state-chartered banks insured by the Federal Deposit Insurance Corporation, but not members of the Federal Reserve System: Federal Deposit Insurance Corporation Consumer Affairs Division, Washington, DC 20429.

❑ For federally chartered or federally insured savings and loans: Office of Thrift Supervision Consumer Affairs Program, Washington, DC 20552.

❑ For federally chartered credit unions: National Credit Union Administration Consumer Affairs Division, Washington, DC 20456.
❑ For state member banks of the Federal Reserve System: Consumer and Community Affairs Board of Governors of the Federal Reserve System, 20th & C Streets, NW Washington, DC 20551.
❑ For discrimination complaints against all kinds of creditors: Department of Justice Civil Rights Division, Washington, DC 20530.

139. What rights do I have concerning my mortgage application?

While it may seem as if you're sitting on the outside looking in as lenders pore over your financial history and ultimately decide whether to cut that five-, six-, or even seven-figure check to cover the cost of your home, you are protected under a number of other laws and acts designed to give home buyers a hand during this very complex process.

You have already learned about the key laws in place to protect buyers, but there are a few others that HUD highlights as being particularly helpful for home buyers.

Tell me more

According to HUD, there are several federal laws that provide you with protection during the processing of your loan. You already know that the ECOA and Fair Credit Reporting Act prohibit discrimination and provide you with the right to certain credit information, but you should also know that frequently there are differences in the types and amounts of settlement costs charged to the borrower.

For example, some borrowers are charged greater fees for mortgages depending on their creditworthiness. These differences may be justified, or they may be unlawfully discriminatory. It is important that you examine your settlement documents closely, especially lines 808–811 on the HUD-1 settlement statement. Do not hesitate to compare your settlement costs with those of your friends and neighbors.

If you feel you have been discriminated against by a lender or anyone else in the homebuying process, you may file a private legal action against that person or complain to a state, local, or federal administrative agency. You may want to talk to an attorney, or you may want to ask the federal agency that enforces the ECOA (the Board of Governors of the Federal Reserve System) or the Fair Housing Act (HUD) about your rights under these laws.

According to HUD, your lender or mortgage broker is required to act on your application and inform you of the action taken no later than thirty days after it receives your completed application. Your application will not be considered complete, and the thirty-day period will not begin, until you provide to your lender or mortgage broker all of the material and information requested.

If, by chance, your application is denied, your lender or mortgage broker must give you a statement of the specific reasons why he denied your application or tell you how you can obtain such a statement. The notice will also tell you which federal agency to contact if you think the lender or mortgage broker has illegally discriminated against you.

140. What is predatory lending?

Just what it sounds like, predatory lending is the practice of making unaffordable loans based on the assets of the borrower rather than on the borrower's ability to repay. Unlike the subprime lending market, which makes legal, legitimate loans available at higher interest rates to those with past credit or payment issues, predatory lenders engage in fraud or deception to conceal the true nature of the loan obligation.

Predatory lenders "prey" on unsuspecting or unsophisticated borrowers who are often so desperate to get into homes of their own that they essentially "sign their lives away" to make it happen. These lenders have come under increasing scrutiny over the last few years, thanks to the media attention given to several high-profile lawsuits in this arena.

Tell me more

Predatory lending is a practice by which unscrupulous lenders take advantage of consumers (especially those with previous credit problems) by providing loans that have exorbitantly high fees and interest rates. As a home buyer, you should be aware of the fact that a loan from a predatory lender may end up costing you more—and even your home—in the long run.

In addition to roping borrowers into higher fee and interest rate loans, these lenders:

❏ Make loans without confirming the borrower's ability to repay the debt. When this happens, foreclosure rates increase as borrowers struggle to keep up with the housing payments.
❏ Encourage borrowers to repeatedly refinance their home loans in a short period of time. In doing so, the lenders charge high fees and points—a process that's also known as "loan flipping."

❑ Act in a fraudulent or deceptive manner to hide the true nature of the loan obligations. Such tactics are meant to snag unsuspecting home buyers who are not well versed on their legal rights and who are eager to become property owners.

141. How can I tell if my lender is using predatory-lending tactics?

If your own financial situation causes you to seek out nontraditional lenders, be especially aware of any lender whose strategies seem to fit any or all of these practices. Here are a few more characteristics of predatory lending:

❑ High closing costs
❑ Balloon payments that are due at the end of the loan
❑ Fees that you don't understand
❑ Any type of "mandatory" credit, life, or disability insurance
❑ Loans with high interest rates and penalties for prepayment
❑ Loan fees that exceed 5 percent of the total loan amount
❑ A loan offer that comes by way of an unsolicited telemarketer or door-to-door salesperson

Tell me more

In pinpointing tactics that predatory lenders commonly use, HUD says to watch out for the following situations:

❑ A lender or investor tells you that they are your only chance of getting a loan or owning a home. You should be able to take your time to shop around and compare prices and houses.
❑ The house you are buying costs a lot more than other homes in the neighborhood but isn't any bigger or better.
❑ You are asked to sign a sales contract or loan documents that are blank or that contain information that is not true.
❑ You are told that Federal Housing Administration insurance protects you against property defects or loan fraud—it does not.
❑ The cost or loan terms at closing are not what you agreed to.
❑ You are told that refinancing can solve your credit or money problems.
❑ You are told that you can only get a good deal on a home improvement if you finance it with a particular lender.

If you think you might be the victim of a dishonest lender, you can get free help and advice. For more information on your options, contact the U.S. Department of Housing and Urban Development at 1-800-669-9777, or visit the department's predatory-lending Web site at www.hud.gov/offices/hsg/sfh/pred/predlend.cfm.

142. What if there are termites in the home?

Most lenders will require a recent termite inspection and certification as a condition for home loan approval. The inspection must be done within thirty days of settlement. In most states, if the inspector finds evidence of prior infestation that has been treated but damage that has not been repaired, the lender will require that damage be repaired by the seller prior to settlement.

See Question 102 for more information on the termite inspection process and lenders' requirements. Traditionally, the responsibility has been on the seller to cover the cost of ridding the home of termites and repairing the damage, as required by the lender.

143. What if there is radon in the home?

Radon is a little trickier, since many buyers don't test for the toxic gas when they buy a home. If you happen to be buying in an area where radon is prevalent, however, you will want to have one of the various radon tests mentioned in Chapter 6 completed prior to purchase.

The remediation of radon is doable, but who actually foots the bill for the repairs will be negotiated between yourself and the seller. According to the Environmental Protection Agency (EPA), radon levels can be brought down to well below what it calls the "action level" in most houses. Radon mitigation systems that continuously remove radon from the area below a foundation are the most effective, according to the EPA. If the home has been tested for radon in the past, the EPA says you should ask the following questions before accepting the seller's existing test:

❏ What were the results of previous testing?
❏ Who conducted the previous test (the home owner, a radon professional, or some other person)?
❏ Where in the home was the previous test taken? Consider this particularly if you plan to live in a lower level of the home. For example, the test may have been taken on the first floor. However, if you want to use the basement as living space, test there as well.
❏ What, if any, structural changes, alterations, or changes in the heating, ventilation, and air-conditioning (HVAC) system have been

made to the house since the test was done? The EPA says such changes may affect radon levels.

Tell me more

If you are going to pay for the radon remediation, the EPA's publication "Consumer's Guide to Radon Reduction" recommends asking the contractor to prepare a contract before any work starts. Carefully read the contract before you sign it, and make sure everything in the contract matches the original proposal. The contract should describe exactly what work will be done prior to and during the installation of the system, what the system consists of, and how the system will operate.

Carefully consider optional additions to your contract that may add to the initial cost of the system but may be worth the extra expense. Typical options might include a guarantee that the contractor will adjust or modify the system to reach the promised radon level or an extended warranty and/ or a service plan. The contract should also include the following:

❑ The total cost of the job, including all taxes and permit fees; how much, if any, is required for a deposit; and when payment is due in full

❑ The time needed to complete the work

❑ An agreement by the contractor to obtain necessary licenses and follow required building codes

❑ A statement that the contractor carries liability insurance and is bonded and insured to protect you in case of injury to persons, or damage to property, while the work is being done

❑ A guarantee that the contractor will be responsible for damage and cleanup after the job

❑ Details of warranties, guarantees, or other optional features, including the acceptable resulting radon level

❑ A declaration stating whether any warranties or guarantees are transferable if you sell your home

❑ A description of what the contractor expects you to do (for example, make the work area accessible) before work begins

144. What if there is mold in the home?

Another hot button for home buyers these days is toxic mold—a fairly newfound point of litigation and contention among home buyers, home sellers, insurance companies, and just about anyone else who is involved in the real estate transaction. An increasing number of attorneys are handling cases relating to mold exposure, and a large number of homeowners insurance providers have "dropped" such coverage from their policies, essentially removing themselves from the risk of large lawsuits over mold.

Tell me more

The fact is, mold exists everywhere, all of the time, and generally doesn't cause anyone health concerns. It can, however, be an issue for those who are unusually sensitive to mold (by causing respiratory problems). Black or "toxic" mold in particular can be especially problematic and has received increased attention thanks to a 2001 case in which a Texas family won $32.1 million (later cut to $4 million) in a case involving extensive mold damage to their home.

So what's a home buyer to do? For starters, a good home inspector has probably already boned up on the various issues surrounding mold and is already trained to recognize the "bad" forms of mold in a home's structure. The Southern Pine Council advises home buyers to consider the following tips when walking through prospective new homes:

❑ Consider the architecture. Is it appropriate for the region? Have the design and style weathered the rigors of the native climate over the years, or are there signs that moisture or other exposures have taken their toll on certain areas of the home?

❑ Consider hiring an independent home inspector. Find a certified inspector in your area at the National Association of Home Inspectors Web site, www.NAHI.org.

❑ Find out if the home is in a floodplain. Has it ever flooded? Is the height of the foundation above the Federal Emergency Management Agency (FEMA)–designated base flood elevation (BFE)? If so, how high is the foundation above the BFE? If flooded, was the home thoroughly cleaned and disinfected to remove moisture and prevent mold? Flood maps are available from FEMA.

❑ Trust your eyes and nose. Look for signs of moisture problems or water damage. Check for mold on surfaces; water spots on the ceiling; or other telltale water damage around doors, window casements, or under cabinets. Any home will smell a little musty if left unoccupied for a while, but areas with strong musty odors may mean trouble.

If you or an inspector do find "bad" mold in the home (not to be confused with a strip of mildew or nontoxic mold found behind an air-conditioning unit), you and/or your real estate agent or attorney will need to sit down with the seller to figure out who will take responsibility for its removal and remediation. Simply sponging up the mold probably will not solve the problem, as it is necessary to clean up mold contamination, not just kill the mold.

Because toxic mold is a fairly new issue for home buyers, there are few precedents set and even fewer historical examples to refer to when attempting to remediate the problem in order to close your mortgage loan. Your best bet will be to educate yourself on the problem through publications like the National Association of Home Builders Household Mold Resource Center, online at www.moldtips.com, and discuss it with your agent, inspector, attorney, and seller to come up with a plan of action that works in your favor.

145. What if a home inspector finds other defects in the home?

Here's another important area where you have some well-defined rights as a home buyer. As long as you're not purchasing your home "as is" (meaning, just as it is right now, with no guarantee of repairs on the owner's part), you have the right to negotiate for the repair of any problems that the inspectors discover during the inspection process.

If you were on site for the actual inspection, then any major issues listed on the report probably won't come as a surprise. If you weren't there and if you're just now getting an eyeful of the furnace, pool, and roof problems that exist in the home, don't panic. These issues don't necessarily mean that you should walk away from the home, but they do bode well for any further negotiating that will need to take place in order to get the most pertinent issues solved prior to closing.

Tell me more

Unlike an appraisal or termite inspection, says the American Society of Home Inspectors (ASHI), a professional home inspection is an examination of the current condition of your prospective home. A home inspector, therefore, will not pass or fail a house but rather describe its physical condition and indicate what may need repair or replacement. From there, it's up to you whether you want to exert your rights as a home buyer and demand that any or all of the problems be fixed prior to closing.

Remember that the seller also has rights and that he or she can refuse to make any such repairs, thus making your purchase contract null and void. This is why it's good to have the home inspection done as early as possible in the process, just in case. Working in your favor is the fact that findings in the inspection report may have a bearing on the value of the property and may be useful in negotiating for repairs to substandard components.

As you go over your home inspection report, remember that no house is perfect. If the inspector finds problems, it doesn't necessarily mean you shouldn't buy the house, only that you will know in advance what to expect. A seller may be flexible with the purchase price or contract terms if major problems are found. If your budget is very tight, or if you don't wish to become involved in future repair work, this information will be extremely important to you.

Ed Frank, president of InspectAmerica Engineering, P.C., in White Plains, New York, also says, "There's hardly a perfect home," and reminds buyers that a good inspector will always find some defects. Buyers should weigh the positives against the negatives, remember that every deal is different and negotiable, and that there are many factors to consider. For example, a lot depends upon whether the real estate market is currently a buyer's or seller's market (see Questions 4 and 5 for more information on market dynamics).

While a home inspection is not a guarantee that problems won't develop after you move in, ASHI says that if you believe a problem was already visible at the time of the inspection and should have been mentioned in the report, your first step should be to call and meet with the inspector to clarify the situation. Misunderstandings are often resolved in this manner, according to ASHI's informational guide "The Home Inspection and You," which also advises buyers to consult with a local mediation service to help settle any such disagreements.

146. Do I need a home warranty?

In Chapter 5 we covered the issue of home warranties—who pays for them, and what they cover. Here, we'll look a little more closely at the value of having such coverage when purchasing an existing home.

Home warranties cover repair and replacement costs for appliances and other systems associated with a home. They can be purchased by either the home buyer or seller, and they are often paid for at closing. These warranties cover any home, no matter the age of the structure, and serve to replace items that fail on their own (versus homeowners insurance, which covers items damaged by fires or natural disasters).

Tell me more

Home warranties have become very popular in the last few years and serve as a key selling point on existing homes, where a refrigerator, an air-conditioning condenser, or a bathroom pipe can break without notice and without a manufacturer's warranty. Independent companies sell these policies, which are frequently paid for by the home seller. If your seller isn't offering such a warranty, you may want to negotiate for one, or simply buy one on your own.

Keep an eye out for warranty coverage that only kicks in once the home is actually in your possession. If you're working with a real estate agent, ask for literature from warranty providers. Here are three companies that currently offer the coverage:

First American Home Buyers Protection
P.O. Box 10180
Van Nuys, CA 91410-0180
800-698-0422
www.firstam.com/warranty

Old Republic Home Protection
P.O. Box 5017
San Ramon, CA 94583-0917
800-445-6999
www.orhp.com

American Home Shield
P.O. Box 849
Carroll, IA 51401-9901
800-827-4636
www.americanhomeshield.com

The typical home warranty policy is effective for one year with an option to renew coverage upon expiration. The renewal cost might be higher than the fee paid for the initial policy, which usually ranges from $350 to $450, depending on the company and the coverage. After keying my zip code into one home warranty provider's Web page, the site produced the following "Basic Contract Coverage" list for home buyers:

❑ Telephone wiring
❑ Central air conditioning
❑ Microwave (built-in) only
❑ Plumbing stoppages
❑ Oven/range/cooktop
❑ Kitchen refrigerator
❑ Garbage disposal

- ❏ Electrical system
- ❏ Plumbing system
- ❏ Heating system
- ❏ Instant hot water dispenser
- ❏ Trash compactor
- ❏ Ceiling and exhaust fans
- ❏ Dishwasher
- ❏ Water heater
- ❏ Central vacuum system
- ❏ Ductwork
- ❏ Toilets

If your home seller isn't willing to cough up the funds for a home warranty, you'll have to decide whether or not the extra coverage is warranted, then purchase one yourself if so desired. Remember that the home warranty contract covers failures due to normal wear and tear of systems and appliances located within the foundation of the home during the contract term. Go over your contract carefully, for most cover only those systems and appliances specifically mentioned and exclude all others.

CHAPTER NINE

THE CLOSING PROCESS

147. What happens at the closing table?

The words "closing table" sound ominous if you've never been there before, but really all you'll be doing is sitting around a conference table at a title firm or other location to read and sign a bundle of papers that will finalize your home purchase. At closing, you'll be asked to sign legal documents that record your commitment to repay your mortgage loan and that give the lender the right to the home if you're unable to pay.

If no major hiccups took place between contract signing and closing, then the date that this occurs will probably be the same date you chose during the initial negotiations. If not, then the date may be sooner or later, depending on the situation.

Tell me more

A real estate closing is typically a formal meeting attended by the buyer, the seller, the listing agent and selling agent, and the settlement agent. Your mortgage broker may also attend, and depending on where you live, the closing could also be attended by your attorney, an escrow agent, the lender, and/or the title insurance company. In addition to making sure that the documents are read and signed, most of the parties are there for their "cut" of the transaction, as everyone from the mortgage broker to the real estate agent gets paid at closing.

The closing of a real estate transaction takes the title to the home out of the seller's name and puts it in your name. You will also receive the keys to your new home. Depending on the complexity of the deal (and how much talking goes on at the table!), your closing will probably take an hour or two at the most. Closings are usually scheduled at a time of day convenient to all parties involved.

The actual closing procedures depend on where in the country you're located and what the protocol is for a closing in that area. Regardless of your location, however, you can assume that the meeting will take place at the office of an attorney, an escrow company, or a title company. More likely than not, the closing will be attended by the buyer(s), any involved real estate agents, and the seller.

When you arrive at the closing, be ready to sign your name a good number of times—so many that you may walk away from the table with a cramp in the hand that's holding the keys to your new home! The primary items that will be signed, sealed, and delivered at the closing table include (but are not limited to):

- ❏ The settlement statement
- ❏ The contract
- ❏ The loan papers (for you)
- ❏ Title insurance (for you)
- ❏ The title or deed (which will be transferred into your name)
- ❏ The down payment and closing costs (via your cashier's check)
- ❏ Payoffs of any existing mortgages
- ❏ Funds available to the sellers upon recording of the new deed

148. What should I bring to closing?

Before you pile into the car for the trek to the closing table, look at the following checklist:

The Preclosing Checklist

- ❏ Schedule the closing within your lender's commitment period (otherwise, you're not meeting the terms of your loan agreement).
- ❏ If you're currently renting, give your landlord sufficient notice. Make sure you know how to get back your security deposit.
- ❏ Order your homeowners insurance policy for your new home.
- ❏ Inspect the home again. If there is damage to the property, make sure the seller fixes it prior to closing.
- ❏ If the home is new, make a list with the contractor of any minor items that need to be completed after the closing. It's a good idea to hold back money in an escrow account until the work is completed. If major work remains unfinished, it may be in your best interest to postpone the closing.
- ❏ Verify that the seller will vacate the house before your closing date.
- ❏ Make your own arrangements for moving into your new home on or after the closing date.

❑ Ask your lender for a final printout of your closing costs.

❑ Review the closing costs list and raise questions over any fees that were not previously discussed, or that don't look right to you.

❑ Get a certified check or money order for the closing costs and down payment. (This is very important as the settlement service provider will not accept a personal check to pay for closing costs.)

❑ Check with your agent to make sure you have everything in order.

❑ Make sure you know:
  • The date of the closing
  • The time (specify A.M. or P.M.)
  • The place
  • The complete name of your closing agent or company

❑ On the day of the closing, bring along any receipts for closing-related expenses you've already paid, such as:
  • Deposit
  • Mortgage application fees
  • Inspection fees (including any termite, home inspection, or other services that you may have already paid for, but that could still show up on the settlement statement as closing costs)

❑ Be sure to bring the homeowners insurance policy or binder.

149. How does the closing typically unfold?

When you arrive at the closing, you will be escorted to a conference table, where all parties will converge to watch you sign a number of important papers and documents. Closings are conducted differently, depending on the closing agent and your location, but here's a general overview of how the meeting will proceed:

❑ The closing agent will review the settlement sheet with you and the seller and answer any questions. Both you and the seller will sign the settlement sheet.

❑ The closing agent will ask you to sign the other loan documents, such as the mortgage note and truth in lending statement. You will also provide evidence of required insurance and inspections (if not already provided).

❑ If everyone agrees that the papers are in order, you and the seller will submit a certified or cashier's check to cover the closing costs and the balance of funds due (if applicable). The check from the lender covering the mortgage amount will then be submitted to the closing agent.

- ❑ If the lender will be paying your annual property taxes and home-owner's insurance for you, an escrow account (or reserve) will be established.
- ❑ You will receive the keys to your new home.

Tell me more

Once the closing is complete, the closing agent will officially record your mortgage and deed at the local government clerk's office or registry of deeds. This legal transfer of the property could take a few days to complete, depending on what it is and how busy that office is at the time. Once the deed is recorded, you are officially the owner of the home.

150. What is a closing statement?

You should have already received a good-faith estimate, and you may have even asked for a preview of your HUD-1 settlement twenty-four hours prior to closing. Now comes the real thing: the closing statement. It's still a HUD-1 statement, but this time the numbers are solid and truly represent the financial aspects of the transaction. You'll find a sample HUD-1 form in the appendix of this book.

The HUD-1 statement sets out the financial agreement between the parties, the costs each much pay, and any other related information regarding the real estate transaction. The closing agent should walk you through the statement line by line (after handing a copy to all involved parties) and allow for any questions that you might have on the charges.

Tell me more

The HUD-1 statement that you receive at the closing table represents your precise cost of home ownership. Unlike the earlier "estimates" that you should have received, the closing statement is an accurate reflection of exactly how much the loan and related services are going to cost you. The HUD-1 is a standardized form from the U.S. Department of Housing and Urban Development (HUD) that itemizes all of the expenses and credits related to the settlement. There is a sample HUD-1 form in the appendix of this book, but here are a few of the key areas that you'll want to look at carefully before signing:

- ❑ The appraisal fee and the cost of doing a credit check. If you paid a loan origination fee, which covers the appraisal and credit check, you should be credited for these two items on the closing statement.

❑ The underwriting fee. This may be broken down into administration
  fee and document preparation fee.
❑ Fees listed under "title charges." You'll see a settlement or closing
  fee that's used to pay the closing agent's salary. You'll also see a title
  insurance fee.
❑ Government recording and transfer charges. These vary by location,
  so check with your closing agent on the particulars for this section.
❑ Tax service fee of $50 to $75. This protects the mortgage lender
  and/or owner if you fail to pay property taxes.
❑ The interest charge. This is the amount of interest that you owe the
  lender for the remainder of the current month. If you close on January 20, for example, you'll owe interest from January 20 to January
  31.
❑ Below the interest charge you'll see a number representing how
  much you'll need to put into escrow accounts for mortgage insurance (that's the PMI, which you can read more about in Chapter 7),
  homeowners insurance, taxes and—if required—flood insurance.
❑ Attorney's fees.

Other fees on your closing statement could include:

❑ Courier fees
❑ Notary fees
❑ Documentation fee
❑ Overnight delivery fee
❑ Points
❑ Processing fees

Be sure to bring along your good-faith estimate to the closing so that
you can compare it to the HUD-1 document and make sure that no hidden
or additional charges have been added unexpectedly since the first document was developed. Realize that actual costs can vary, but that they
shouldn't vary by more than $500 either way. If they do—or if you feel that
the lender has tacked on "hidden" fees—be sure to bring it up at the closing table and/or discuss the issue with your attorney before signing any
documents.

151. What are prorated fees?

On your closing statement you'll see reference to prorations or prorated
fees, which are the same thing. At the closing, certain costs are often pro-

rated (or distributed) between the buyer and the seller, with property taxes being the most commonly prorated fees. That's because property taxes (unlike, say, a telephone bill) are billed every month of every year on the property and paid at the end of the year for which they are assessed.

That means if you purchased your home on May 30, 2005, the seller possessed and/or lived in the home for the first five months of the year. As such she owes you five months' worth of property taxes for the year 2005, which you won't pay until early 2006. To make such situations more equitable, the tax bill is prorated, with the seller crediting you, the buyer, for five months' worth of property taxes at the closing table.

Tell me more

Prorations are simply a fair way to split recurring costs between buyer and seller. In addition to property taxes, similar adjustments are made for the following fees:

❑ Homeowners association dues
❑ Special assessments
❑ Fuel costs
❑ Utility costs (if billed on an annual or a semiannual basis)

Any prorations should be clearly spelled out on your HUD-1 closing statement. Go over them carefully, and better yet, talk to your real estate agent and/or seller about them prior to closing so that there are no surprises on closing day. If you're purchasing a town house in May for which homeowners association dues are $1,200 and billed on January 1 for the upcoming year, expect to see a prorated fee of $700 on your closing statement, with the same amount recorded as a "credit" on the seller side.

You may also want to notify utility companies of the upcoming ownership change and even request a reading on the day of settlement, with the bill for presettlement charges to be mailed to the seller at his or her new address or to the settlement agent. This will eliminate the odds of receiving a bill for power, telephone, and other utilities used when the seller still possessed the property.

152. What fees am I responsible for?

As you pore over your closing statement, keep in mind that every deal is different, but that the buyer and seller are generally going to be responsible for the following fees (some prorated, some not):

The Buyer Pays For

- ❑ Title insurance premiums
- ❑ Escrow fees
- ❑ Notary fees
- ❑ Document preparation fees
- ❑ Document recording fees
- ❑ Prorated share of the property taxes
- ❑ Buyer-ordered inspections (such as a home inspection, roof inspection)
- ❑ Special delivery/courier fees
- ❑ All new loan charges (except those that the seller is required to pay)
- ❑ New loan interest (from the closing day to thirty days prior to first payment date)
- ❑ Fire insurance premium for the first year
- ❑ Preliminary change of ownership fee
- ❑ Assumption/change of record fees for takeover of an existing loan

The Seller Pays For

- ❑ Real Estate Commission documentation preparation
- ❑ Deed document recording fee
- ❑ County transfer tax
- ❑ Loan fees required by the buyer's lender
- ❑ Notary fees
- ❑ Homeowners association transfer fee
- ❑ Prorated share of homeowners association dues
- ❑ Bonds or assessments (according to the sales contract)
- ❑ Termite inspection and subsequent repairs
- ❑ Natural hazards disclosure report
- ❑ City transfer/conveyance tax (if applicable)
- ❑ Special courier/delivery fees
- ❑ Payoff of all loans in the seller's name
- ❑ Interest accrued to the previous lender
- ❑ Lender payoff fees
- ❑ Home warranty
- ❑ Any delinquent taxes
- ❑ Any judgment, tax liens, etc. against the seller
- ❑ Prorated share of the property taxes
- ❑ Recording charges to clear all documents of record against the seller

Tell me more

If any of the charges look unfamiliar or incorrect to you, bring it up at the closing table and ask for an explanation or resolution. Expect the seller to do the same. I've attended closings where the seller's closing costs actually exceeded mine due to unpaid utility bills and a property tax obligation that was supposed to have been taken care of through a PITI (see Question 47) arrangement with his lender. It pays to pore over your statement and make sure everything is in order before signing on the dotted line.

153. What is a walk-through?

A walk-through is a physical examination of a property that typically occurs immediately prior to closing to ensure that no changes have taken place and no new damage has been done to the property. This is the time to scour around the home (which should now be vacant, if it wasn't already) and make sure that the owner didn't replace the refrigerator with an old, rusty unit, for example. It's also the time to confirm that fixtures (curtains, blinds, etc.) and chattels (another term for personal property) that are supposed to be included in the sale are indeed on the premises.

154. What should I look for during the walk-through?

Before you make your way to the closing table, you'll definitely want to schedule a final walk-through of the home. This should take place immediately prior to closing on the home, although it may take place a few days or even weeks prior to closing. Preferably, you'll want to conduct both, since the earlier walk-through will help you confirm that the seller did indeed make the repairs as required (and give the seller time to correct the problems before closing if they haven't been done). You may want to ask your home inspector along on that walk-through, particularly if the repairs involved were hidden to the naked eye, such as a repair to an air-conditioning unit or roof.

The closing day walk-through will be different and will be focused mainly on ensuring that the home is in the same condition as it was when you made your offer and signed on the dotted line of the purchase contract. Here are a few key questions to keep in mind as you navigate through the now-vacant home:

❑ Did the seller's move result in any new damage in the home? Inspect the floors for mars or rips, and check out the wall corners, door frames, and other areas prone to such damage.

❑ Are all major systems in the home working properly? Do a quick test of appliances, furnaces, and air-conditioning units to make sure everything is still in good working order.

❑ Are all the items that the seller agreed to leave still in the home, and are they the same items you saw two months ago when you made the offer?

❑ Are all the items that the seller agreed to remove indeed gone? If that old rusty shed is still out in the backyard, speak up about it.

Tell me more

Chances are good that your walk-through will go smoothly, thus paving a clear path to the closing table. However, if the condition of the home has changed since the last time you were in it, now is the time to speak up. You'll have a better shot at getting the problems fixed now, before the property deed officially changes hands. It may seem like an eleventh-hour repair is out of reach, but you'd be surprised at how many last-minute problems crop up at the closing table anyway, so don't be shy about having your demands met.

One way to do this is by negotiating a repair or replacement fund, then having the seller deposit those funds into an escrow account or attorney's trust fund. You would then tap those funds to bring the home back to the state it was in when you agreed to buy it. Either your attorney or real estate agent can help you set this fund up and negotiate an amount that exceeds the repair estimate, just in case.

Depending on the scope and severity of the problem, you might also consider negotiating a flat rate to be paid from the seller to you at closing. If you're going to do this, make sure you have a good handle on exactly how much the repair will cost, lest you find yourself coming up short financially when it's time to get the work done. If the situation cannot be resolved prior to closing, then you may also consider delaying the closing until a resolution is reached.

155. What can I do to ensure a smooth closing?

For the closing process to go smoothly, all parties must bring the necessary documentation and be prepared to pay their closing costs. Your closing agent or mortgage broker will inform you of the exact amount of your cashier's check, so that you can go to the bank and have that check prepared ahead of time, and in the right amount.

The seller and her attorney or real estate agent are responsible for preparing and bringing the deed and the most recent property tax bill. They also will bring other documents required by the contract, including the property insurance policy, termite inspection, documents showing the removal of liens, and a bill of sale for personal property.

By the closing date, you should have most, if not all, of the required items taken care of. Here's a look at the basic items that you and/or your agent or broker should have spent the last month or two wrapping up for closing. If you've missed any of these important necessities, be sure to have them taken care of before your settlement date:

- ❑ Purchase homeowners insurance (see Questions 129 and 130).
- ❑ Find out what company should be named as the beneficiary under the homeowners insurance commitment clause. It may be the lender, or another firm, if the lender assigned the loan to another company. Be sure to bring the correct binder (which is the one-page copy of the insurance policy that names the beneficiary) to closing.
- ❑ Purchase title insurance.
- ❑ Obtain a cashier's check in the amount of your total closing costs.
- ❑ Iron out any problems regarding what chattel, appliances, fixtures, and other items are to be left in—or removed from—the home.

One of the best ways to make sure your closing day goes smoothly and results in your walking away with a set of keys jingling sweetly in your hand is to simply ask a lot of questions, no matter how silly or mundane they may seem. First-time home buyers in particular tend to hold back on the questioning, but there's really no reason to do so. Everyone involved in the transaction is aware of the fact that the homebuying process is one of the most complex financial transactions, so treat it as such, and ask away without fear. You'll be glad you did.

156. What if I can't be at the closing?

As crucial as it may seem to be present at the closing table, most lenders are willing to accommodate what is known as a "mail-away" closing. It's in your best interest to try to be there, but if you absolutely cannot be at the closing at the designated time, let your real estate agent, closing agent, lender, or all of the above know as early as possible so that they can make provisions to get the transaction closed without your physical presence.

In such a situation, you may also appoint someone to act on your behalf via a power of attorney. Discuss this with your lawyer, who is a likely candidate to handle the closing should you not be able to attend.

Tell me more

The Internet, fax machines, and overnight mail services have virtually elimi-
nated the need for proximity to process and close a loan. That means that
even if you can't physically be at the closing, there are two different ways
to get the home closed. They are:

1. Conduct a mail-away closing.
2. Assign your power of attorney to someone you trust, who can sign
   the documents on your behalf.

Every state has its own specific requirements, so check with your closing agent for guidelines on the latter. If you select the mail-away process,
your lender will coordinate overnight delivery of the documents to ensure
a timely closing. The same works for the seller, who can also opt for a mail-
away closing if he's not in town on the specified date. Once all the documents are prepared, the loan package is overnighted to the seller with very
specific instructions on how and where to sign each document.

Realize that if either or both parties are out of town or inaccessible on
the closing date, your actual settlement will take longer than the one to two
hours that a typical meeting will take. Also realize that receiving information via overnight mail—or having someone else sign on your behalf—
precludes you from being able to ask last-minute questions about your loan
documentation and other paperwork.

157. Can the transaction get held up at the closing table?

Like any financial transaction, there's always something that can come up
and sideline the process, either by delaying it temporarily or by stopping it
completely. Real estate is no different. In fact, closing or settlement is considered one of the top ten most problematic areas of the real estate transaction. Because of the nature of the process, the closing itself can get hung
up on the financing side, on the legal aspects of title, and on other factors
involving the final transfer of property from the seller to you, the buyer.

That doesn't mean that you're destined to run into issues while gathered around the conference table, eye to eye with the seller, real estate
agent(s), and other real estate service providers. In fact, I've never run into
any major problems with closing, other than the "clouded title" property
that was discussed in Chapter 6. As a buyer, however, you must be aware
of what *could* go wrong and be prepared for unexpected situations, just in
case.

Tell me more

There are several preclosing steps that you can take to make sure your
end of the closing goes smoothly. This includes reviewing your closing

documents (which you can request from your closing agent); going over your loan documents; and reading through your abstract of title and survey, as well as any other documents related to the transaction.

If you (or your attorney or real estate agent) notice anything strange or out of order, don't wait until you're at the closing table to point it out. Instead, call it to the attention of the lender and/or closing agent immediately.

Because keeping your own end of the transaction in order is enough work for you as the buyer, you probably won't have the impetus or time to keep track of what the other parties are doing. However, you should know that there are a few common issues that can come up at the last minute.

Here's a laundry list of possible issues that can delay or halt the closing process:

On the Part of the Lender

❑ The lender didn't properly prequalify the borrower.
❑ The lender, for whatever reason, decides that it doesn't want to lend money to the borrower.
❑ The lender tries to raise the loan's rates, points, or fees.
❑ The borrower doesn't qualify for the loan because of late submittal of information.
❑ The lender asks for a last-minute reappraisal of the property.
❑ The lender, for whatever reason, decides not to lend money on the particular property.
❑ The lender misplaces an important file.

On the Part of the Buyer

❑ The buyer gave misleading information on the loan application.
❑ The buyer submitted incorrect tax information to the lender.
❑ The buyer gave misleading information to the real estate agent.
❑ The buyer finds herself lacking the adequate down-payment funds.
❑ The buyer demands too many repairs or fixes during the final walkthrough.
❑ The buyer decides that another property is a better deal than the home in question.
❑ The buyer did not sign and return paperwork in a timely fashion.

On the Part of the Escrow Company

❑ The company didn't notify the closing agents about unsigned documents.

❑ The company didn't obtain information from lien holders, benefi-
ciaries or lenders in a timely fashion.

❑ The company misplaced important paperwork or prepared paperwork incorrectly.

❑ The company failed to share valuable, pertinent information with
the involved parties in a timely fashion.

On the Part of the Seller

❑ The seller experiences an illness or divorce or otherwise loses the
motivation to sell.

❑ The seller has a property with hidden defects that are discovered
prior to selling.

❑ The seller takes items from the property that the buyer thought were
included in the deal.

❑ The seller cannot clear up liens against the property or other issues.

❑ The seller was not the 100 percent, rightful owner of the property.

❑ The seller can't make it to the closing table and has not assigned
power of attorney to a third party.

As you can see, most of the problems involve a lack of communication
between parties and could be minimized by a competent facilitator who is
in charge of making sure that the deal is seen through to the closing table.
This person can be a real estate agent, the title company, the mortgage
broker (who, unlike the lender, is very interested in seeing the sale through
to close in order to get paid), and/or an attorney working in your best
interest.

158. How can a lawyer help ensure a smooth closing?

In Chapter 5 we discussed the issue of attorneys, with the focus on why
you might be required (by law) to have one at the closing table working in
your favor. What we didn't discuss yet are the primary reasons why an
attorney's fees could well be worth their weight in gold. While not all transactions involve complex legal issues, many of them comprise a number of
topics and concerns that you may not be knowledgeable about.

An attorney working for a home buyer, for example, generally handles
issues such as how to take title, information on type of property to be
purchased (that is, single family, multifamily), and financing issues. According to the Massachusetts Bar Association, an attorney will also:

- ❑ Review the offer to purchase.
- ❑ Review or prepare the purchase and sale agreement (P&S) and negotiate about its terms, including who should hold the deposit.
- ❑ Advise concerning financing and tailoring of purchase and sales terms to the lender's requirements.
- ❑ Review the various inspections.
- ❑ Review the title examination with the bank's attorney.
- ❑ Attend the closing and review the papers that the buyer is required to sign.
- ❑ Set up escrows and special arrangements to correct the title, complete construction, or ensure possession.
- ❑ Arrange title insurance protection for the buyer against losses due to title defects, if desired.
- ❑ Arrange transfer of security deposits and notices to tenants.

Some of these tasks will be completed long before closing, but since everything during the transaction process revolves around that date, the attorney's role in the overall purchase is fairly clear. Well versed in the transaction process, a real estate attorney (which you can find in your local yellow pages, by asking your real estate agent, or through an online resource like www.realestateattorneys.com) is well equipped to handle any problems as they arise and to avert such issues before they become real problems.

159. Should I hire an attorney?

As an attorney, Joan Yudkin has seen more than her fair share of real estate closings. Based in Sudbury, Massachusetts, Yudkin says, "Buying a new home or condominium is exciting, but it can also be stressful if you do it without the proper professionals." Family and friends may tell you that you do not need to bother hiring a lawyer, but as someone who has been representing clients in the purchase and sale of real estate for over twenty years, Yudkin says she's seen the pitfalls that may occur if you do not have an attorney.

Tell me more

"Keep in mind, buying real estate will be your largest investment, and it's important to protect that asset," says Yudkin, who gives buyers these six reasons why they should consider hiring an attorney to represent them in the real estate transaction:

1. After your offer is accepted, you will have to sign a P&S, which is a legal document. The P&S sets forth the obligations of both buyer and seller and the consequences of not going through with the deal. Before you sign the P&S, it should be reviewed by a lawyer.

2. An addendum should be attached to the P&S that specifically protects you as a buyer. A lawyer can draft this addendum, which includes paragraphs to ensure that the property is transferred to you in good condition and to ensure the return of your deposit if the seller cannot meet his or her obligations.

3. If the seller has an attorney, it will make any further negotiations easier if you also have a lawyer. Remember too that it is also very hard to negotiate and represent yourself in emotional situations such as buying a home.

4. Unless you have a buyer-broker, all brokers are working for the seller, and there is no one looking out for you. A lawyer will represent you and work to protect your interests. If you do have a buyer-broker, a lawyer will work with the broker to ensure that you have the proper legal protections.

5. Your lender will assign the drafting of your mortgage documents to a "bank" attorney. Remember that the bank attorney is representing the bank's interest, which may be different from yours. The bank attorney is under no obligation to provide legal advice to you in the event that problems arise with the seller. By having your own attorney, you will have someone protecting your interests throughout the process.

6. At the closing, problems may arise concerning issues discovered at the final walk-through inspection. Bank attorneys do not get involved in these disputes. By having your own attorney, those issues can be immediately resolved, and you will get the home that was promised to you.

Whether you have an attorney by your side at closing is entirely up to you. Just keep these tips and information in mind as you make an informed decision regarding the use of an attorney.

160. What should I take away from the closing table?

After your loan and other documents are signed, sealed, and delivered (hopefully in a timely, positive, and nonstressful manner), you'll be free to leave the closing agent's office and start moving into your new home. Before you walk out the door, make sure you have your copies of all of the related paperwork, which should be kept in a safe place for future reference.

The property survey, for example, will come in handy should you wish to make any changes to the physical structure, while your loan papers will most likely include a first payment invoice to use just in case the lender doesn't mail one out to you in time for that first payment.

Tell me more

Expect to walk out of the closing meeting with a thick folder of paperwork that includes a mix of original and copied documents that you should hang on to. Here are a few of the key closing documents that you will receive at the closing meeting:

- ❑ HUD-1 settlement statement (see Question 150).
- ❑ Truth in lending (TIL) statement: This outlines the costs of your loan, the annual percentage rate, and the cost of your mortgage as a yearly rate. The TIL statement also discloses the other terms of the loan, including the finance charge, the amount financed, the payment amount, and the total payments required.
- ❑ The note: The mortgage (or promissory) note represents your promise to pay the lender according to the agreed terms of the loan, including the dates on which your mortgage payments must be made and the location to which they must be sent. This document also explains the penalties that will be assessed if you fail to make your monthly mortgage payments.
- ❑ The mortgage: This is the legal document that secures the note and gives the lender a legal claim against your home should you default on the note's terms. While you have possession of the property, the lender has an ownership interest (also known as an "encumbrance") until the loan has been fully repaid. Some states use a "deed of trust" in lieu of a mortgage. By signing a deed of trust, you receive title to the property but convey title to a neutral third party (a "trustee") until the loan balance is paid.
- ❑ Affidavits: Depending on how the real estate transaction process is handled in your area, you may be asked to sign an affidavit of occupancy, which states that you will use the property as a principal residence. There could be other affidavits to sign, depending on your lender. If you have concerns about such documents, ask up front about which you will be required to sign.
- ❑ The deed: The seller will sign the deed at closing, thus transferring ownership to you. Your name and the names of any other buyers

appear on the deed, which you will receive a copy of at closing. As mentioned earlier in this chapter, the closing agent then records the deed, which will be sent to you after it is recorded.

In your closing packet, you should also have a copy of your appraisal, your survey, any documents pertaining to real estate agents' roles in the transaction (such as a disclosure stating a real estate licensee's fiduciary duties to buyer and seller), a copy of the purchase contract, and the seller's property disclosure statement. If any of the documents are missing, ask the closing agent for copies before you leave the office.

CHAPTER TEN

Post-Sale Concerns

161. When is my first house payment due?

Depending on your lender's policies, you will most likely have a short re-prieve between the time you paid your last rent payment and the time the first payment is due on your new home. I've closed on homes in November and not had to make that first payment until early January, which freed up some of my cash for holiday spending, since my last rent payment was made on November 1.

Shortly after closing, your lender will mail you a bill for the first payment. You may also receive a first bill in your closing packet, to use just in case the lender doesn't mail you a bill in time to pay the first payment. Keep in mind that you're responsible for that initial payment even if the lender doesn't contact you between the closing date and the due date of your mortgage payment.

Tell me more

Since mortgage payments are a great way to boost (and, unfortunately, ruin) your credit rating, it's imperative that you attempt to always make your mortgage payment on time. Most companies will give you a ten- to fifteen-day grace period to give you time to mail the check and to give them time to process the payment.

In addition to sending out your monthly statements and collecting payments, your lender is also responsible for issuing an annual IRS Form 1098, which you and/or your accountant will use to record your total mortgage interest payment for the prior year. The statements are typically mailed out after January 31 of each year.

162. What will my monthly mortgage loan statements look like?

At a minimum, the monthly statement that you receive from your lender will include:

❑ Your account number
❑ The total amount due (principal and interest plus taxes and insurance, if applicable)
❑ A total amount due should the payment arrive after the grace period
❑ The due date
❑ A customer service phone number

The statement will also include some or all of the following information:

❑ The current statement date
❑ The loan's maturity date
❑ The interest rate
❑ The current principal balance
❑ The current escrow balance (how much tax and insurance reserves have been paid in)
❑ The interest paid year to date
❑ The taxes paid year to date
❑ Any past-due amounts
❑ Outstanding late charges

163. What payment alternatives do lenders offer?

If writing out monthly checks isn't your favorite pastime, most mortgage lenders are more than happy to automatically deduct the total payment from your bank account each month. This is known as an "automatic deduction," and you will most likely be given the option to enroll in the program after closing. To sign up, you'll have to provide an authorization form and a voided check (or savings account slip) to set up the draft process. Your lender will then debit your account on a fixed day every month, thus ensuring a timely, accurate payment process.

164. Do I need to retain my closing and home-related expenses?

Absolutely. Now that you're a home owner, or very close to becoming one, you will definitely want to create an organized filing system to handle the myriad mortgage loan, insurance, tax, and improvement- and repair-related paperwork that you'll be collecting. You can do this using a simple accordion file, with tabs indicating the various expenses, or using a filing system organized by month, with bills filed according to the date paid.

Computer software packages like Microsoft Money (www.microsoft .com/money) and Quicken (www.quicken.com) can also help you keep track of household expenses, although you will also want a physical filing system in which to retain hard copies of your paperwork (such as your homeowners insurance policy), statements (like your utility bill stub), and receipts (the money you shelled out to repair your driveway).

Tell me more

Moving into a new home—especially if it's your first—is very exciting, but it also brings with it fiscal responsibility that you didn't previously have as renter or as someone who lived in another person's home. One of the most important responsibilities will be setting up files to keep track of everything that has to do with your new home.

Like any new system, the initial setup will involve some time on your part, but the work you do now will pay off in the future when, for example, you need to call for warranty service on your six-month-old refrigerator or show your accountant how much mortgage interest you paid during the previous year. Ultimately, you'll want to have easy access to information pertaining to the home purchase (this will hopefully be neatly contained in the folder you received at the closing table), as well as maintenance and improvement expenses that accumulate over time.

One valid reason to track expenses—no matter how insignificant they may seem—is that when you sell your home, you may be able to deduct some of them when reporting a capital gain from the sale of the home. If you need more impetus to start a filing system, consider how impressed your buyer will be if you can hand over copies of maintenance and improvement receipts, along with any extended warranties and owner's manuals, to go with the home.

165. How do my mortgage payments affect my taxes?

Your filing system will come in handy particularly when tax time rolls around, especially during the year after you purchased the home, during which time you will be eligible for a number of deductions. Columbia, Maryland–based Fiducial, the ninth largest accounting firm in the nation, offers these five tips to help new home owners avoid common financial mistakes:[1]

1. Check closing statements for all deductible items: Many new home owners miss deductible items buried in their closing documents. It's

[1]Reprinted courtesy of small business services provider Fiducial. For more information, see www .Fiducial.com. Copyright 2004 Fiducial, Inc. All Rights Reserved.

important to read these documents carefully and review them with a tax professional at the time of sale.

2. Establish the basis of the home: The amount paid for a home is the starting point in determining the home's basis. The basis includes most settlement or closing costs and any debt assumed—all of which are on a home buyer's HUD-1 settlement statement. The basis of the home is important in determining all available tax deductions that can be taken. Home owners should be sure to adjust the basis if they make home improvements that increase its value to take advantage of future tax-saving opportunities.

3. Don't forget that seller-paid points are deductible: Many home owners forget to include these fees when they are preparing their taxes for the year. Even professional tax preparers often overlook this deduction.

4. Deduct nonamortized points from a prior refinance: If home owners pay points to obtain a refinance loan, the points are deductible, but they must be amortized over the life of the loan. If the home owner sells or refinances the home again and the original loan is paid off early, the balance of nonamortized points can be taken as an itemized deduction that year.

5. Keep records of moving expenses: There are a number of deductions that can be taken related to moving expenses. New home owners should keep all receipts and proper records to take advantage of tax savings. Expenses that can be deducted include any expense in moving household goods, travel, or lodging incurred en route to the new home and storage of home furnishings.

Tell me more

Since housing costs typically make up the bulk of a home owner's monthly budget, having all of the paperwork at your fingertips can also help you set up a household budget. For 2001, for example, housing accounted for one-third of spending by U.S. households, twice the amount spent in 1972, reports the Urban Land Institute. Using a software program or even a manual system, you can create a financially responsible plan for the future.

166. What is a homestead exemption?

In an effort to boost home ownership, a number of states have instituted tax breaks for home owners within their boundaries. Known as "homestead exemptions," these incentives can provide significant financial rewards for primary dwellings (not for properties that you rent out to others, or for second homes).

Most of the exemptions either minimize the amount of a home's assessed value that can be levied with property taxes, or limit the amount of appreciation that a home's assessed value can rack up in a year's time. Some states offer a combination of the two benefits.

Tell me more

Homestead exemptions are allowed in some states to owners of principal, full-time residences, and they allow for a predetermined deduction of a dollar amount from the assessed value to determine property taxes. In fourteen states a fixed amount of the homestead value is exempt from the property tax, ranging from $1,000 in Oklahoma to $52,500 in some areas of South Carolina. In other states, the exempt value is determined as a percentage of market value. Ohio, for example, exempts 12.5 percent of an owner's property, South Dakota provides a 100 percent exemption from state taxes, while Michigan offers a full exemption for homestead property.

One state provides a $25,000 deduction in the assessed value of a home for property tax liability. The tax break was created in 1992 by an amendment to the state constitution governing how properties with homestead exemptions can be assessed. Known as the Save Our Homes (SOH) amendment, the law sets a 3 percent maximum limit on annual valuation increases of homestead property for ad valorem tax purposes. The amendment does not limit the tax rate itself, but the "increase in assessed value" of the property.

For home owners, this homestead exemption deduction translates to a savings of between $700 and $800 a year, depending on the area's tax assessment rates. Such homestead exemptions also offer protection from losing a primary residence due to bankruptcy or debt (although they do not apply to nonpayment of tax or mortgage payments).

The total dollar amount that a home can be homesteaded depends on where you live. In California, for example, all privately owned homes are eligible for a $7,000 homestead exemption from property taxes, while elderly taxpayers who meet income guidelines, as well as veterans, are eligible for an additional exemption. Also in California, property tax assessments are capped at 2 percent annually, then uncapped when a property is sold, at which point the property is taxed at fair market value.

Other states with homestead exemptions include Louisiana, Nevada, New York, and Texas. You'll want to check with your local tax collector's office for more details on what breaks you might be entitled to as a new home owner. Do this as soon as possible after closing, as there are typically strict deadlines on when you can file for a homestead exemption.

167. How do I apply for a homestead exemption?

Using Florida as an example, the initial application for property tax exemption must be made between January 1 and March 1 of the year for which the exemption is sought. Initial application should be made in person at the property appraiser's office. Every person who has legal or equitable title to real property in the state, and who resides on the property on January 1 and in good faith makes it his or her permanent home, is eligible for a homestead exemption.

Tell me more

For more information about property taxes, contact your county property appraiser or tax collector. There you can obtain an application for any applicable exemptions, find out what the deadlines are, and apply for all the tax breaks you're entitled to as a home owner.

For state-specific information, visit these online government resources. If the page doesn't take you directly to a property tax–related page, browse through the site for "homestead exemption," "property tax," or "tax law" for more detailed information:

Alabama
www.ador.state.al.us/advalorem/index.html

Alaska
www.dced.state.ak.us

Arizona
www.revenue.state.az.us

Arkansas
www.accessarkansas.org/

California
www.boe.ca.gov/

Colorado
www.dola.state.co.us/propertytax/index.htm

Connecticut
www.opm.state.ct.us

Delaware
http://delaware.gov/yahoo/Government

District of Columbia
http://cfo.dc.gov/

Florida
www.myflorida.com/dor/property/

Georgia
www.state.ga.us

Hawaii
www.ehawaiigov.org/

Idaho
www.state.id.us

Illinois
www.revenue.state.il.us/LocalGovernment/PropertyTax/

Indiana
www.in.gov/

Iowa
www.state.ia.us/tax/educate/78573.html

Kansas
www.ksrevenue.org/pilrd.htm

Kentucky
www.lrc.state.ky.us

Louisiana
www.legis.state.la.us/tsrs/search.htm

Maine
http://janus.state.me.us/legis/statutes/36/title36ch0sec0.html

Maryland
www.dat.state.md.us/

Massachusetts
www.dor.state.ma.us

Michigan
www.michigan.gov/treasury

Minnesota
www.house.leg.state.mn.us

Mississippi
www.mstc.state.ms.us/taxareas/property/main.htm

Missouri
www.moga.state.mo.us/

Montana
http://leg.state.mt.us/css/mtcode_const/const.asp

Nebraska
http://pat.nol.org

Nevada
www.leg.state.nv.us/

New Hampshire
www.gencourt.state.nh.us

New Jersey
www.state.nj.us/treasury/taxation/index.html?lpt/
localtax.htm~mainFrame

New Mexico
www.state.nm.us/tax/ptd/ptd_info.htm

New York
www.orps.state.ny.us/index.cfm

North Carolina
www.ncga.state.nc.us/

North Dakota
www.state.nd.us/lr/cencode/t57.html

Ohio
www.legislature.state.oh.us/

Oklahoma
www.lsb.state.ok.us/

Oregon
www.leg.state.or.us/

Pennsylvania
www.dgs.state.pa.us

Rhode Island
www.rilin.state.ri.us/

South Carolina
www.sctax.org/Tax + Information/property/property.htm

South Dakota
http://legis.state.sd.us/

Tennessee
www.comptroller.state.tn.us

Texas
www.cpa.state.tx.us/taxinfo/proptax/tc02/index.html

Utah
http://tax.utah.gov

Vermont
www.leg.state.vt.us

Virginia
http://policylibrary.tax.state.va.us/OTP/Policy.nsf

Washington
www.dor.wa.gov/content/taxes/property/prop.rnls

West Virginia
www.state.wv.us

Wisconsin
www.dor.state.wi.us/

Wyoming
http://revenue.state.wy.us/

168. How do property taxes work?

If you didn't opt for the PITI (see Question 47) system of collecting property taxes (and homeowners insurance) through your monthly mortgage
payment, expect to receive an annual property tax bill and a monthly, a
biannual, or an annual insurance bill, depending on how your insurer handles the process.

Each municipality handles property taxes in a different way. Some bill
the county taxes at one time during the year, with school taxes billed separately on a different statement. Others aggregate all of the taxes on one bill
that's sent at the end of the year (to pay for the current year's taxes), with

a small discount for those home owners who pay their bill on or before March 31 of the following year.

Tell me more

Your local tax collector will most likely combine onto one bill the charges levied against your property by a number of different taxing authorities, including the county itself, the school system, the city where you reside, and even groups like the local transit authority.

To figure your property taxes, the tax collector works from what is known as an "assessed value," which can be higher or lower than the price you paid for the home. My $300,000 Florida home is assessed at $236,200, for example, while my $125,000 Pennsylvania country home is assessed at $75,800. After taking into consideration any exemptions (see Question 166), the tax collector will then divide the final value by 1,000 and multiply it by what is known as a millage rate. So for my less expensive home, a total millage rate of 7.345 multiplied by 75.8 finds me paying $556.75 annually for county and township taxes (school fees are higher and are billed separately).

You will receive real estate tax bills directly from your local tax collector, usually in plenty of time to plan for their payment. Most offer diminishing discounts to those who pay three, two, or one month ahead of the deadline, with penalties being imposed (generally 10 percent per month) for payments that aren't postmarked by the deadline date.

Your property tax bill will include a few other key facts about your property, including some or all of the following information:

❑ Parcel number (your home's legal description)
❑ Site address
❑ Class (most likely residential)
❑ Date of purchase
❑ Date home was built
❑ Home description (one story, two story)
❑ Acreage/lot size

One last note about property taxes. As a home buyer, you should know that the various "caps" that states place on home appreciation rates mean you can't look at last year's tax obligations to determine your future payments, especially if the seller has owned the dwelling for multiple years. The issue has become particularly germane in today's real estate environment, which is characterized by double-digit appreciation rates.

Let's say you purchase a home from someone who has owned it for forty years and is currently paying about $3,054 in taxes on a property assessed at $144,797 (taking into account a $25,000 homestead exemption). If sold in 2003, the transaction would have triggered a reassessment to fair market value and bring the home's value to $262,201. That means a property tax bill of about $6,086.

169. How do homeowners insurance payments work?

Your insurer will mail you either a monthly, a biannual, or an annual statement from which you will pay your homeowners insurance. Most insurers will also automatically withdraw those amounts from your checking or savings account on the predetermined dates, so if you're interested in that service, be sure to ask about it.

Tell me more

As a new home buyer with a mortgage loan on your property, you should know that nonpayment (and the subsequent cancellation) of a homeowners insurance policy will trigger a chain of unfavorable events, starting with a notice from your mortgage company telling you that it's going to secure its own insurance on its investment at your expense. The lender will buy the policy with little regard to price, and as such your "new" policy will probably be much more expensive than the one you let lapse.

Because of this—and because hazard and liability insurance are vital when you own a large investment such as a home—it's in your best interest to keep your homeowners policy paid and up-to-date.

170. How can I lower my property taxes?

Many of us receive those annual property tax bills and pay the "amount due" without question. Others take their gripes right to their county appraiser's office to demand reassessments and possible tax rate reductions.

Which group you fall into is your choice, but you should be aware that the "squeaky wheels" in this case often do indeed get the grease. Meaning: They walk away with lower property tax bills after bringing to their tax collectors' attention the fact that their properties' assessed values are incorrect.

Tell me more

A tax assessment is an estimate of what your property is worth. The value placed on the property determines what portion of the local property tax levy will be billed to your property. Once determined, the value is multiplied by the tax rates to determine how much you, as a property owner, pay. Some states base their assessment on full market value (or some fraction thereof). The responsibility for the assessment function generally falls to a local official, either appointed or elected.

Luckily, the local official's word is not the final one in most cases. To deal with the fact that home owners are able to dispute their tax assessments, most municipalities have property tax dispute processes in place. If assessors have overvalued your property, for example, getting an independent appraiser to conduct an appraisal can help prove that the property's assessed value should indeed be lower than what's reflected on your bill. This is important because a high assessment can cost you money that would be better spent on other expenses.

Each state, county, and city has its own way of handling property tax disputes. Here's how a "small claims" tax appeal works in one U.S. county:

❑ A taxpayer may choose to use simplified small claims procedures if the dispute concerns the valuation or classification of property in which the property is real property (your home), or in which the full cash value of all real and personal property, as assessed, does not exceed $1 million. You may also use the small claims procedure for disputes concerning all other taxes where the total amount of the taxes, the interest at the time of assessment, and the penalties in dispute are less than $5,000.

❑ The filing fee is $90 for a small claims tax court appeal, and $190 for any other tax court appeal.

❑ The state's property tax assessment appeals are decided by either a judge or commissioner/judge pro tem of the tax court. There are no juries in the small claims division of the tax court.

❑ Lawyers are permitted in small claims tax court, but they are not required. In small claims tax court, you may be represented by a person who is not a lawyer if the judge allows such representation. Typically, this includes a son or daughter representing an elderly parent or relative. You must request, in writing, the judge's permission before relying on anyone other than a lawyer to represent you.

❑ Your case is against the county and its assessor, who are called the defendants. The county attorney or a representative of the assessor's office may represent the assessor.

❑ After you file the property tax appeal, you will receive notice of a hearing date for your case. The notice will be sent to the address shown on the petition. If you move, it is your responsibility to inform the tax court of your new address.

❑ In the time between the setting of the trial date and the trial, you may still negotiate with the county attorney or assessor to reach a settlement.

If you do decide to dispute your property tax assessment, be assured that you are in good company. There have been a number of high-profile cases publicized over the last few years. In 2004, for example, a group of famous folks in Greenwich, Connecticut, brought their property tax gripes to the town's Board of Assessment Appeals. Among them was Diana Ross, who claimed that the $168,000 annual tax bill on her five-acre estate was too high. She pinpointed the problem to a $13.4 million appraisal that "exaggerated" the value of the improvements she'd made to the property, which she's owned since 1988.

At press time, the dispute had yet to be resolved, but this is just one example of a home owner's right to protest a property tax bill and/or assessment that seems out of whack.

171. What should I do before moving into my new home?

Ah, there's nothing quite like moving day. Depending on your current living situation, you'll either be elated at the thought of getting your manageable amount of "stuff" into your new dwelling, or completely dread the idea of having to move your mountains of possessions and furniture into your new home. Either way, it has to be done, so take a deep breath and realize that with a little preparation, a lot of "throwing away," and some extra muscles from your friends and family, you'll be in your new place in no time flat.

Tell me more

As someone who has moved a lot in her lifetime, I feel compelled to give you this advice as a future home owner: Toss out (or sell) as much as you can before you move, because once it gets into your new home, it'll probably just sit there accumulating dust anyway. Using what I call the "six-month rule" (some go with shorter time frames, but I like to hang on to things until the bitter end), I ask myself: Have I used this in the last six months, or am I going to use it in the next six months? If the answer is no to both questions, it either goes to my local charity, is sold at a garage sale, or is put out on the curb for the garbage service to haul away.

Another good step to take involves advance planning. When you start your house hunt, you should already be thinking about how you and any-one else who is moving with you can simplify the process. That means checking out moving van rental rates (or, moving company rates for longer hauls) ahead of time and making reservations once your closing date is determined; enlisting friends and family to help you load and unload; and coordinating the start-up of your power, cable, water, and phone service.

To make the process manageable, create a folder or use a tablet (with pocket, for scribbled notes and related clippings) solely for your move and refer to it often. Use this prepurchase checklist to make sure you cover the key moving bases:

❑ Make agreements with the seller (at the time of the contract, or at least a few weeks prior to closing) about your possession of the home and moving date. To avoid unnecessary hassles, you may want to get these commitments in writing.

❑ About the actual move itself, ask yourself:
  • Am I going to want to do the entire move myself?
  • If so, do I have adequate manpower and vehicles to get it done?
  • Will I want a professional mover to handle the entire process?
  • What are movers' rates, and can I afford to outsource this task to such a company?
  • Is the mover insured, and does the company come with good references?

❑ Make a list of everyone who will need to be contacted at your new home (utilities, post office, schools, work) and make a list of any important items you'll need to purchase for your new home (shower curtain, toaster, etc.)

❑ Begin packing as early as possible, particularly items that you don't use every day. The sooner you box them up, the less you'll have to worry about as moving day approaches.

❑ Allocate an area of your existing home or apartment as a staging area where you can store those boxes for the actual move. Mark every box and carton to make unpacking easier.

As moving day nears, continue the packing and planning process, and make the necessary calls to utilities and other service providers (such as an alarm company) to alert them to your move. You'll also want to check out the postal service's Web site (https://moversguide.usps.com), where you can not only make address changes online but also get helpful moving tips and community information.

172. How should I pack up my existing possessions for the move?

On its Web site, the U.S. Post Office® offers the following packing tips to movers:

- ❏ Get more boxes than you think you will need.
- ❏ Get smaller boxes for books, and use bigger boxes for lighter items.
- ❏ Pack room by room, keeping similar items together.
- ❏ Reinforce the bottoms of boxes with at least one strip of packing tape.
- ❏ Pack boxes firmly to prevent the contents from shifting during your move.
- ❏ Use crumpled paper for padding. Seal boxes tightly with wide packing tape.
- ❏ Pack records and CDs vertically in boxes; don't stack them flat.
- ❏ Place heavier items in the bottom of the box and lighter items on top.
- ❏ Separate items with paper to prevent scratches caused by rubbing.
- ❏ Remove lids from jars and ceramics. Wrap each separately.
- ❏ Seal any opened boxes and bottles before packing them to avoid spills and leakage.
- ❏ Use towels, linens, curtains, etc. to pad boxes of fragile items. Clearly mark these boxes "FRAGILE."
- ❏ Use a jumbo box for lamp shades and cushion them well.
- ❏ When disassembling furniture, beds, lamps, etc., put the hardware into a plastic bag along with any assembly tips and tape it onto the item itself.
- ❏ If possible, ask your mover if you can leave clothes in dresser drawers. Find out from your movers how they want hanging clothes packed.
- ❏ Make a master list of all household items and your belongings.
- ❏ Pack rugs last so they can be the first items unloaded and placed at your new location.
- ❏ Number boxes when they are packed and sealed. Clearly indicate on the box its room destination. Write on the master list the contents of the numbered boxes.

Before you move, you should also fill a box of essentials and label it "Open Me First." Put this box to the side to be loaded last (so it's unloaded first) or move it yourself. Include in the box items like basic tools such as flashlights, a pocket knife, a hammer, screwdrivers, nails, masking tape, a tape measure, and lightbulbs; bathroom essentials such as hand towels, soap, toilet paper, shampoo, and shower curtains; and kitchen items such as paper towels, a coffeemaker and filters, paper plates and cups, plastic utensils, dish detergent, a sponge, pet foods, dishes, and trash bags.

173. What if I discover a defect that wasn't disclosed to me?

Depending on the condition of your home and how well (or how poorly) its past owners took care of the property, expect to find at least a few hidden problems that you didn't notice during your previous visits. Some homes may be in "move-in" condition, complete with instructions on how to use the landscape lighting and sprinkler system, while others will take a bit more elbow grease.

Serious defects are another matter entirely, and one that has attracted a lot of attention from lawyers, the media, and real estate professionals in the last few years. Because sellers are required by law to disclose any defects in the home (plus any repairs made or knowledge of damage to the home) on their seller disclosure form (see a sample form in the appendix of this book), you as a buyer have legal recourse, should you discover later that a defect was not disclosed.

Tell me more

Ask any real estate attorney at which point in the home sale the most lawsuits are filed, and he'll probably tell you "after the sale." That's because a seller can be liable for defects in the house she sells, even defects of which she was unaware. Depending on the severity of the defect, she may even have to return a portion of the home's selling price—or even the whole kit and caboodle (in exchange for taking the home back). If the defects were intentionally kept from the buyer, she's in even more trouble and may have to pay your attorney's fees and damages.

Through a safety net enforced with your own walk-throughs, a qualified home inspection, and the seller's disclosure form, you should be able to ward off or alleviate any long-term defects in your home that go above and beyond the typical repairs and maintenance that a home owner has to make on a home anyway. You should also realize that homes are complex structures made up of various systems, any of which can break down or fail at any given time.

Let's look at foundations, as an example. In a recent Louisiana case, a buyer purchased a home and then realized that a room described on a floor plan diagram as being 13 × 24 feet was in reality only 13 × 20 feet. He consulted with the sellers about rescinding the sale, but they refused. The buyer took the seller to court, which found that the buyer was entitled to rescind the sale, based on the fact that he was given incorrect measurements of the home—and despite the fact that he had visually inspected the home prior to purchase. The suit took three years to resolve.

Another Louisiana case found the buyer getting a reduced price, but not entitled to a rescission of the purchase. After purchasing the home, he found that the backyard flooded during heavy rain. In that case, the court found that the defect wasn't serious enough for a rescission but did order the purchase price reduced by $20,000, to make up for the inconvenience.

Each state handles the nondisclosure issue differently. In Arizona, for example, the state REALTOR organization's residential resale contract stipulates that a buyer and seller agree to mediate most disputes arising out of the purchase and sale of the home, including a claim that the seller failed to disclose known defects. Taking the case to small claims court is another option if the cost to repair the undisclosed defect is $2,500 or less. If the buyer is unable to resolve the nondisclosure dispute through mediation, and if the cost to repair the defect exceeds $2,500, filing a lawsuit in superior court may be the buyer's only option.

174. What steps should I take if I discover a major defect postsale?

If after closing the transaction and taking possession of the property you come upon a major defect that was not disclosed by the seller, your first call should be to the seller, who may cough up the money required for the repair in lieu of being taken to court over it. This scenario is somewhat unrealistic, since human nature will probably prompt the seller to say something like, "We never disclosed it because we didn't know anything about it." And because the seller disclosure form only asks for "known" defects, the seller could very well be in the clear.

Tell me more

If you have a firm sense that the seller acted in a fraudulent manner by falsifying a disclosure report, your next call should be to a lawyer, who will file a lawsuit against the seller. Find out how such cases have been handled in the past, and try to review any precedents to see who prevailed in those cases. Should you decide to file the suit and if you win, the seller will most likely be required to repair the defect plus pay court and even attorney's fees. To win the case, you'll need to prove that the seller was indeed aware of the defect and that she failed to disclose it. This means bringing repair estimates, inspection reports, appraisals, and/or statements from contractors or neighbors who knew about the problem prior to the sale.

As a buyer you should also know that purchasing a home as is (see Question 91) doesn't exempt the home seller from disclosing any known defects in the residence. While an as-is sale does mean that she doesn't have to pay for repairs, it doesn't mean she can avoid the issue of informing you about home defects that she is aware of. Also, if you do run into post-sale problems with your home, be sure to consult with an experienced real estate attorney who can help guide you through the legal process.

Appendix

There are myriad forms involved in the real estate transaction. Here you'll find four that you will certainly encounter during your own homebuying process: an offer to purchase and contract, a residential property condition disclosure statement, a residential loan application, and a HUD-1 form. Depending on the lender, mortgage broker, or real estate agent, your own forms may be slightly different from what you see here, but these samples will give you a general idea of what to expect.

I. Purchase Agreement

OFFER TO PURCHASE AND CONTRACT

_____, as Buyer, hereby offers to purchase and _____, as Seller, upon acceptance of said offer, agrees to sell and convey, all of that plot, piece or parcel of land described below, together with all improvements located thereon and such fixtures and personal property as are listed below (collectively referred to as the "Property"), upon the following terms and conditions:

1. REAL PROPERTY: Located in the City of _____ , County of _____, State of _____, being known as and more particularly described as:

Street Address_____Zip_____
Legal Description:_____

A portion of the property in Deed Reference: Book_____, Page No._____, _____ County.)

NOTE: Prior to signing this Offer to Purchase and Contract, Buyer is advised to review Restrictive Covenants, if any, which may limit the use of the Property, and to read the Declaration of Restrictive Covenants, By-Laws, Articles of Incorporation, Rules and Regulations, and other governing documents of the owners' association and/or the subdivision, if applicable.

2. FIXTURES: The following items, if any, are included in the purchase price free of liens: any built-in appliances, light fixtures, ceiling fans, attached floor coverings, blinds, shades, drapery rods and curtain rods, brackets and all related hardware, window and door screens, storm windows, combination doors, awnings, antennas, satellite dishes and receivers, burglar/fire/smoke alarms, pool and spa equipment, solar energy systems, attached fireplace screens, gas logs, fireplace inserts, electric garage door openers with controls, outdoor plants and trees (other than in movable containers), basketball goals, storage sheds, mailboxes, wall and/or door mirrors, and any other items attached or affixed to the Property, EXCEPT the following items:

_____
_____
_____.

3. PERSONAL PROPERTY: The following personal property is included in the purchase price:_____
_____
_____.

4. PURCHASE PRICE: The purchase price is $_____ and shall be paid as follows:
(a) $_____, EARNEST MONEY DEPOSIT with this offer
by____Cash____Personal check____bank check____certified check____other:
_____ to be deposited and held in escrow by _____ ("Escrow Agent") until the sale is closed, at which time it will be credited to Buyer, or until this contract is otherwise terminated. In the event: (1) this offer is not accepted; or (2) any of the conditions hereto are not satisfied, then all earnest monies shall be returned to Buyer. In the event of breach of this contract by Seller, upon Buyer's request, all earnest monies shall be returned to Buyer, but such return shall not affect any other remedies available to Buyer for such breach. In the event this offer is accepted and Buyer breaches this contract, then all earnest monies shall be forfeited upon Seller's request, but receipt of such forfeited earnest monies shall not affect any other remedies available to Seller for such breach.

NOTE: In the event of a dispute between Seller and Buyer over the return or forfeiture of earnest money held in escrow by a broker, the broker is required by state law to retain said earnest money in the broker's trust or escrow account until a written release from the parties consenting to its disposition has been obtained or until disbursement is ordered by a court of competent jurisdiction.

(b) $_____, ADDITIONAL EARNEST MONEY DEPOSIT to be paid to Escrow Agent no later than _____, TIME BEING OF THE ESSENCE WITH REGARD TO SAID DATE

(c) $_____, BY ASSUMPTION of the unpaid principal balance and all obligations of Seller on the existing loan(s) secured by a deed of trust on the Property in accordance with the attached Loan Assumption Addendum.

(d) $_____, BY SELLER FINANCING in accordance with the attached Seller Financing Addendum.

(e) $_____, BALANCE of the purchase price in cash at Closing.

5. CONDITIONS: (State N/A in each blank that is not a condition to this contract.)

(a) Buyer must be able to obtain a_____FHA_____VA (attach FHA/VA Financing Addendum) ____Conventional, Other: _____ loan at a_____Fixed Rate ____Adjustable Rate in the principal amount of _____ (plus any financed VA Funding Fee or FHA MIP) for a term of _____ year(s), at an initial interest rate not to exceed _____ % per annum, with mortgage loan discount points not to exceed _____ % of the loan amount. Buyer shall apply for said loan within _____ days of the Effective Date of this contract. Buyer shall use Buyer's best efforts to secure the lender's customary loan commitment letter on or before _____ and to satisfy all terms and conditions of the loan commitment letter by Closing. After the above letter date, Seller may request in writing from Buyer a copy of the loan commitment letter. If Buyer fails to provide Seller a copy of the loan commitment letter or a written waiver of this loan condition within five days of receipt of Seller's request, Seller may terminate this contract by written notice to Buyer at any time thereafter, provided Seller has not then received a copy of the letter or the waiver.

(b) There must be no restriction, easement, zoning or other governmental regulation that would prevent the reasonable use of the Property for:

_____ purposes.

(c) The Property must be in substantially the same or better condition at Closing as on the date of this offer, reasonable wear and tear excepted.

(d) All deeds of trust, liens and other charges against the Property, not assumed by Buyer, must be paid and satisfied by Seller prior to or at Closing such that cancellation may be promptly obtained following Closing. Seller shall remain obligated to obtain any such cancellations following Closing.

(e) Title must be delivered at Closing by GENERAL WARRANTY DEED unless otherwise stated herein, and must be fee simple marketable and insurable title, free of all encumbrances except: ad valorem taxes for the current year (prorated through the date of Closing); utility easements and unviolated restrictive covenants that do not materially affect the value of the Property; and such other encumbrances as may be assumed or specifically approved by Buyer. The Property must have legal access to a public right of way.

6. SPECIAL ASSESSMENTS: Seller warrants that there are no pending or confirmed governmental special assessments for sidewalk, paving, water, sewer, or other improvements on or adjoining the Property, and no pending or confirmed owners' association special assessments, except as follows:

_____
_____
_____.

(Insert "None" or the identification of such assessments, if any.) Seller shall pay all owners' association assessments and all governmental assessments confirmed through the time of Closing, if any, and Buyer shall take title subject to all pending assessments, if any, unless otherwise agreed as follows:

_____
_____.

7. PRORATIONS AND ADJUSTMENTS: Unless otherwise provided, the following items shall be prorated and either adjusted between the parties or paid at Closing: (a) Ad valorem taxes on real property shall be prorated on a calendar year basis through the date of Closing; (b) Ad valorem taxes on personal property for the entire year shall be paid by the Seller unless the personal property is conveyed to the Buyer, in which case, the personal property taxes shall be prorated on a calendar year basis through the date of Closing; (c) All late listing penalties, if any, shall be paid by Seller; (d) Rents, if any, for the Property shall be prorated through the date of Closing; (e) Owners' association dues and other like charges shall be prorated through the date of Closing. Seller represents that the regular owners' association dues, if any, are $_____ per _____.

8. CLOSING EXPENSES: Buyer shall be responsible for all costs with respect to any loan obtained by Buyer. Buyer shall pay for recording the deed and for preparation and recording of all instruments required to secure the balance of the purchase price unpaid at Closing. Seller shall pay for preparation of a deed and all other documents necessary to perform Seller's obligations under this agreement, and for excise tax (revenue stamps) required by law. If Seller is to pay any of Buyer's expenses associated with the purchase of the Property, the amount thereof shall be $_____, including any FHA/VA lender and inspection costs that Buyer is not permitted to pay, but excluding any portion disapproved by Buyer's lender.

9. FUEL: Buyer agrees to purchase from Seller the fuel, if any, situated in any tank on the Property at the prevailing rate with the cost of measurement thereof, if any, being paid by Seller.

10. EVIDENCE OF TITLE: Seller agrees to use his best efforts to deliver to Buyer as soon as reasonably possible after the Effective Date of this contract, copies of all title information in possession of or available to Seller, including but not limited to: title insurance policies, attorney's opinions on title, surveys, covenants, deeds, notes and deeds of trust and easements relating to the Property. Seller authorizes (1) any attorney presently or previously representing Seller to release and disclose any title insurance policy in such attorney's file to Buyer and both Buyer's and Seller's agents and attorneys; and (2) the Property's title insurer or its agent to release and disclose all materials in the Property's title insurer's (or title insurer's agent's) file to Buyer and both Buyer's and Seller's agents and attorneys.

11. LABOR AND MATERIAL: Seller shall furnish at Closing an affidavit and indemnification agreement in form satisfactory to Buyer showing that all labor and materials, if any, furnished to the Property within 120 days prior to the date of Closing have been paid for and agreeing to indemnify Buyer against all loss from any cause or claim arising therefrom.

12. PROPERTY DISCLOSURE AND INSPECTIONS:
(a) Property Disclosure:
_____Buyer has received a signed copy of the [Your State]Residential Property Disclosure Statement prior to the signing of this Offer to Purchase and Contract.
_____Buyer has NOT received a signed copy of the [Your State] Residential Property Disclosure Statement prior to the signing of this Offer to Purchase and Contract and shall have the right to terminate or withdraw this contract without penalty prior to WHICHEVER OF THE FOLLOWING EVENTS OCCURS FIRST: (1) the end of the third calendar day following receipt of the Disclosure Statement; (2) the end of the third calendar day following the date the contract was made; or (3) Closing or occupancy by the Buyer in the case of a sale or exchange.
_____Exempt from [Your State] Residential Property Disclosure Statement because

_____

_____.
_____The Property is residential and was built prior to 1978 (Attach Lead-Based Paint or Lead-Based Paint Hazards Disclosure Addendum.)

(b) Property Inspection: Unless otherwise stated herein, Buyer shall have the option of inspecting, or obtaining at Buyer's expense inspections, to determine the condition of the Property. Unless otherwise stated herein, it is a condition of this contract that: (i) the built-in appliances, electrical system, plumbing system, heating and cooling systems, roof coverings (including flashing and gutters), doors and windows, exterior surfaces, structural components (including foundations, columns, chimneys, floors, walls, ceilings and roofs), porches and decks, fireplaces and flues, crawl space and attic ventilation systems (if any), water and sewer systems (public and private), shall be performing the function for which intended and shall not be in need of immediate repair; (ii) there shall be no unusual drainage conditions or evidence of excessive moisture adversely affecting the structure(s); and (iii) there shall be no friable asbestos or existing environmental contamination. Any inspections shall be completed and written notice of necessary repairs shall be given to Seller on or before _____. Seller shall provide written notice to Buyer of Seller's response within _____ days of Buyer's notice. Buyer is advised to have any inspections made prior to incurring expenses for Closing and in sufficient time to permit any required repairs to be completed by Closing.

(c) **Wood-Destroying Insects:** Unless otherwise stated herein, Buyer shall have the option of obtaining, at Buyer's expense, a report from a licensed pest control operator on a standard form in accordance with the regulations of the [Your State] Pest Control Committee, stating that as to all structures, except _____, there was no visible evidence of wood-destroying insects and containing no indication of visible damage therefrom. The report must be obtained in sufficient time so as to permit treatment, if any, and repairs, if any, to be completed prior to Closing. All treatment required shall be paid for by Seller and completed prior to Closing, unless otherwise agreed upon in writing by the parties. The Buyer is advised that the inspection report described in this paragraph may not always reveal either structural damage or damage caused by agents or organisms other than wood-destroying insects. If new construction, Seller shall provide a standard warranty of termite soil treatment.

(d) **Repairs:** Pursuant to any inspections in (b) and/or (c) above, if any repairs are necessary, Seller shall have the option of completing them or refusing to complete them. If Seller elects not to complete the repairs, then Buyer shall have the option of accepting the Property in its present condition or terminating this contract, in which case all earnest monies shall be refunded. Unless otherwise stated herein, any items not covered by (b) (i), b (ii), b (iii) and (c) above are excluded from repair negotiations under this contract.

(e) **Acceptance: CLOSING SHALL CONSTITUTE ACCEPTANCE OF EACH OF THE SYSTEMS, ITEMS AND CONDITIONS LISTED ABOVE IN ITS THEN EXISTING CONDITION UNLESS PROVISION IS OTHERWISE MADE IN WRITING.**

13. **REASONABLE ACCESS:** Seller will provide reasonable access to the Property (including working, existing utilities) through the earlier of Closing or possession by Buyer, to Buyer or Buyer's representatives for the purposes of appraisal, inspection, and/or evaluation. Buyer may conduct a walk-through inspection of the Property prior to Closing.

14. **CLOSING:** Closing shall be defined as the date and time of recording of the deed. All parties agree to execute any and all documents and papers necessary in connection with Closing and transfer of title on or before _____, at a place designated by Buyer. The deed is to be made to _____.

15. **POSSESSION:** Unless otherwise provided herein, possession shall be delivered at Closing. In the event possession is NOT to be delivered at Closing: _____a Buyer Possession Before Closing Agreement is attached. OR, _____a Seller Possession After Closing Agreement is attached.

16. **OTHER PROVISIONS AND CONDITIONS:** (ITEMIZE ALL ADDENDA TO THIS CONTRACT AND ATTACH HERETO.)

17. **RISK OF LOSS:** The risk of loss or damage by fire or other casualty prior to Closing shall be upon Seller. If the improvements on the Property are destroyed or materially damaged prior to Closing, Buyer may terminate this contract by written notice delivered to Seller or Seller's agent and all deposits shall be returned to Buyer. In the event Buyer does NOT elect to terminate this contract, Buyer shall be entitled to receive, in addition to the Property, any of the Seller's insurance proceeds payable on account of the damage or destruction applicable to the Property being purchased.

18. ASSIGNMENTS: This contract may not be assigned without the written consent of all parties, but if assigned by agreement, then this contract shall be binding on the assignee and his heirs and successors.

19. PARTIES: This contract shall be binding upon and shall inure to the benefit of the parties, i.e., Buyer and Seller and their heirs, successors and assigns. As used herein, words in the singular include the plural and the masculine includes the feminine and neuter genders, as appropriate.

20. SURVIVAL: If any provision herein contained which by its nature and effect is required to be observed, kept or performed after the Closing, it shall survive the Closing and remain binding upon and for the benefit of the parties hereto until fully observed, kept or performed.

21. ENTIRE AGREEMENT: This contract contains the entire agreement of the parties and there are no representations, inducements or other provisions other than those expressed herein. All changes, additions or deletions hereto must be in writing and signed by all parties. Nothing contained herein shall alter any agreement between a REALTOR® or broker and Seller or Buyer as contained in any listing agreement, buyer agency agreement, or any other agency agreement between them.

22. NOTICE AND EXECUTION: Any notice or communication to be given to a party herein may be given to the party or to such party's agent. This offer shall become a binding contract (the "Effective Date") when signed by both Buyer and Seller and such signing is communicated to the offering party. This contract is executed under seal in signed multiple originals, all of which together constitute one and the same instrument, with a signed original being retained by each party and each REALTOR® or broker hereto, and the parties adopt the word "SEAL" beside their signatures below.

Buyer acknowledges having made an on-site personal examination of the Property prior to the making of this offer.

Date: _____ Date: _____
Buyer _____ _____ (SEAL) Seller
_____ (SEAL)
Date: _____ Date: _____
Buyer _____ _____ (SEAL) Seller
_____ (SEAL)

Escrow Agent acknowledges receipt of the earnest money and agrees to hold and disburse the same in accordance with the terms hereof.
Date_____
Firm: _____
By:_____
(Signature)
Selling Agent/Firm/Phone_____
Acting as ___Buyer's Agent ___Seller's (sub)Agent _____Dual Agent
Listing Agent/Firm/Phone_____
Acting as _____Seller's (sub)Agent____Dual Agent

II. Residential Property Condition Disclosure Statement

LOCATION OF SUBJECT PROPERTY:

SELLER IS __ IS NOT __ OCCUPYING THE SUBJECT PROPERTY.

Appliances/Systems/Services: (Circle whether the items are in working order)

Sprinkler system	N/A	Yes	No	Unknown
Swimming pool	N/A	Yes	No	Unknown
Hot tub/Spa	N/A	Yes	No	Unknown
Water heater	N/A	Yes	No	Unknown

___Electric ___Gas ___Solar

Water purifier	N/A	Yes	No	Unknown
Water softener	N/A	Yes	No	Unknown

___Leased ___Owned

Sump pump	N/A	Yes	No	Unknown
Plumbing	N/A	Yes	No	Unknown
Whirlpool tub	N/A	Yes	No	Unknown
Sewer system	N/A	Yes	No	Unknown

___Public ___Septic ___Lagoon

Air conditioning system	N/A	Yes	No	Unknown

___Electric ___Gas ___Heat pump

Window air conditioner(s)	N/A	Yes	No	Unknown
Attic fan	N/A	Yes	No	Unknown
Fireplaces	N/A	Yes	No	Unknown
Heating system	N/A	Yes	No	Unknown

___Electric ___Gas ___Heat pump

Buyer's initials_____

Humidifier	N/A	Yes	No	Unknown
Gas supply	N/A	Yes	No	Unknown

___Public ___Propane ___Butane

Propane tank	N/A	Yes	No	Unknown

___Leased ___Owned

Ceiling fans	N/A	Yes	No	Unknown
Electric air purifier	N/A	Yes	No	Unknown
Garage door opener/control	N/A	Yes	No	Unknown
Intercom	N/A	Yes	No	Unknown
Central vacuum	N/A	Yes	No	Unknown

Security system   N/A   Yes   No   Unknown
___Rent ___Own ___Monitored

Smoke detectors   N/A   Yes   No   Unknown
Dishwasher   N/A   Yes   No   Unknown
Electrical wiring   N/A   Yes   No   Unknown
Garbage disposal   N/A   Yes   No   Unknown
Gas grill   N/A   Yes   No   Unknown
Vent hood   N/A   Yes   No   Unknown
Microwave oven   N/A   Yes   No   Unknown
Built-in oven/Range   N/A   Yes   No   Unknown
Kitchen stove   N/A   Yes   No   Unknown
Trash compactor   N/A   Yes   No   Unknown

Seller's initials_____

Source of household water
___Public ___Private ___Well

Other items_____   Yes   No   Unknown
Other_____   Yes   No   Unknown
Other_____   Yes   No   Unknown

IF YOU HAVE ANSWERED UNKNOWN to any of the above, please explain. Attach
additional pages with your signature(s).

_____

_____

_____

Zoning, flood and water--Circle below:

1. Property is zoned: *(Check one)* ___residential ___ commercial ___ historical
___agricultural ___ industrial ___ office ___urban____ conservation ___ other
___unknown

2. Are you aware of any flood insurance requirements concerning the property?
Yes   No   Unknown

3. Do you have flood insurance on the property?   Yes   No   Unknown

4. Has the property been damaged or affected by flood, storm run-off, sewer backup,
drainage, or grading problems?   Yes   No   Unknown

5. Are you aware of any surface or ground water drainage systems which assist in
draining the property, e.g. french drains?   Yes   No   Unknown

6. Has there been any occurrence of water in the heating and air conditioning duct system?   Yes   No   Unknown

7. Are you aware of water seepage, leakage or other drainage problems in any of the improvements on the property?   Yes   No   Unknown

Additions/Alterations/Repairs:

8. Have any additions or alterations been made without required permits? Yes   No Unknown

9. Are you aware of previous foundation repairs? Yes   No   Unknown

10. Are you aware of any alterations or repairs having been made to correct defects or problems?   Yes   No   Unknown

11. Are you aware of any defect or condition affecting the interior or exterior walls, ceilings, slab/foundation, basement/storm cellar, floors, windows, doors, fences or garage?   Yes   No   Unknown

12. Has the roof ever been repaired or replaced during your ownership of the property? Yes   No   Unknown

13. Approximate age of roof, if known ____Number of layers, if known____ Unknown

14. Do you know of any current problems with the roof?   Yes   No   Unknown

15. Are you aware of treatment for termite or wood-destroying organism infestation? Yes   No   Unknown

16. Do you have a termite bait system installed on the property?   Yes No Unknown

17. If yes, is it monitored by a licensed exterminating company?
(Check one) ___ yes   no Annual cost $ _____

18. Are you aware of any damage caused by termites or wood-destroying organisms? Yes No   Unknown

19. Are you aware of major fire, tornado, or wind damage? Yes   No   Unknown

Environmental:
20. Are you aware of the presence of asbestos?   Yes   No   Unknown

21. Are you aware of the presence of radon gas?   Yes   No   Unknown

22. Have you tested for radon gas?   Yes   No   Unknown

23. Are you aware of the presence of lead-based paint? Yes No   Unknown

24. Have you tested for lead-based paint?   Yes   No   Unknown

25. Are you aware of any underground storage tanks on the property? Yes No Unknown

26. Are you aware of the presence of a landfill on the property?   Yes No Unknown

27. Are you aware of existence of hazardous or regulated materials and other conditions having an environmental impact?   Yes   No   Unknown

28. Are you aware of existence of prior manufacturing of methamphetamine? Yes No   Unknown

29. Have you had the property inspected for mold? Yes   No   Unknown

30. Have you had any remedial treatment for mold on the property? Yes No Unknown

31. Are you aware of any condition on the property that would impair the health or safety of the occupants?   Yes   No   Unknown

Property Shared in Common, Easements, Homeowners Association, Legal:

32. Are you aware of features of the property shared in common with adjoining landowners, such as fences, driveways, and roads, whose use or responsibility has an affect on the property?   Yes   No   Unknown

33. Other than utility easements serving the property, are you aware of easements or rights-of-way affecting the property?   Yes   No   Unknown

34. Are you aware of encroachments affecting the property? Yes   No   Unknown

35. Are you aware of a mandatory homeowners association? Yes   No   Unknown
Amount of dues $ _____ Special Assessment $ _____
Payable: *(Check one)* ___monthly ___ quarterly ___annually
Are there unpaid dues or assessments for the property? *(Check one)* ___ yes ___no
If yes, amount $____Manager's name:_____Phone no._____

36. Are you aware of any zoning, building code, or setback requirement violations?
Yes   No   Unknown

37. Are you aware of any notices from any government or government-sponsored agencies or any other entities affecting the property?   Yes   No   Unknown

38. Are you aware of any threatened or existing litigation or lawsuit(s), directly or indirectly affecting the property? Yes   No   Unknown

39. Is the property located in a fire district that requires payment? Yes No Unknown
Amount of fees $ _____ To whom paid _____
Payable *(Check one)* ___monthly ___quarterly ___annually

40. Is the property located in a private utility district?   Yes   No   Unknown
(Check applicable) water ___garbage ___sewer ___ other ____
If other, explain: _____
Initial membership fee $ _____ annual membership fee $ _____
If more than one (1) utility, attach additional pages.

Miscellaneous:

41. Are you aware of other defect(s), affecting the property, not disclosed above?
Yes   No   Unknown

42. Are you aware of any other fees or dues required on the property that you have not
disclosed?   Yes   No   Unknown
If you answered "YES" to any of the items 1–42 above, list the item number(s) and
explain. *(If needed, attach additional pages, with your signature(s), date(s) and location
of subject property.)*

On the date this form is signed, the seller states that based on seller's CURRENT
ACTUAL KNOWLEDGE of the property, the information contained above is true and
accurate.

Are there any additional pages attached to this disclosure *(circle one):*   Yes   No
If yes, how many?_____

Seller's signature_____ Date_____

A real estate licensee has no duty to the Seller or the Purchaser to conduct an independent
inspection of the property and has no duty to independently verify the accuracy or
completeness of any statement made by the seller in this disclosure statement.

The Purchaser is urged to carefully inspect the property and, if desired, to have the
property inspected by a licensed expert. For specific uses and restrictions for this
property, contact the City Planning Department. The Purchaser acknowledges that the
Purchaser has read and received a signed copy of this statement. This completed
acknowledgement should accompany an offer to purchase on the property identified.

Purchaser's Signature_____ Date_____

III. Uniform Residential Loan Application

This application is designed to be completed by the applicant(s) with the lender's assistance. Applicants should complete this form as "Borrower" or "Co-Borrower" as applicable.

Co-Borrower information must also be provided (and the appropriate box checked) when ☐ the income or assets of a person other than the "Borrower" (including the Borrower's spouse) will be used as a basis for loan qualification or ☐ the income or assets of the Borrower's spouse will not be used as a basis for loan qualification, but his or her liabilities must be considered because the Borrower resides in a community property state, the security property is located in a community property state, or the Borrower is relying on other property located in a community property state as a basis for repayment of the loan.

I. TYPE OF MORTGAGE AND TERMS OF LOAN

Mortgage Applied for: ☐ VA ☐ Conventional ☐ Other ☐ FHA ☐ FmHA	Agency Case Number	Lender Case No.

Amount $	Interest Rate %	No. of Months	Amortization Type: ☐ Fixed Rate ☐ GPM ☐ Other (explain): ☐ ARM (type):

II. PROPERTY INFORMATION AND PURPOSE OF LOAN

Subject Property Address (street, city, state, & zip code)	No. of Units

Legal Description of Subject Property (attach description of necessary)	Year Built

Purpose of Loan: ☐ Purchase ☐ Construction ☐ Refinance ☐ Construction-Permanent ☐ Other (explain):	Property will be: ☐ Primary Residence ☐ Secondary Residence ☐ Investment

Complete this line if construction or construction-permanent loan.

Year Lot Acquired	Original Cost $	Amount Existing Liens $	(a) Present Value of Lot $	(b) Cost of Improvements $	Total (a+b) $

Complete this line of this is a refinance loan.

Year Acquired	Original Cost $	Amount Existing Liens $	Purpose of Refinance	Describe improvements ☐ made ☐ to be made Cost: $

Title will be held in what Name(s)	Manner in which Title will be held	Estate will be held in: ☐ Fee Simple ☐ Leasehold (show expiration date):
Source of Down Payment, Settlement Charges and/or Subordinate Financing (explain)		

Borrower III. BORROWER INFORMATION Co-Borrower	
Borrower's Name (include Jr. or Sr. if applicable)	Co-Borrower's Name (include Jr. or Sr. if applicable)

Social Security Number	Home Phone (incl. area code)	Age	Yrs. School	Social Security Number	Home Phone (incl. area code)	Age	Yrs. School
☐ Married ☐ Separated	☐ Unmarried (include single, divorced, widowed)	Dependents (not listed Co-Borrower) no.: ages:		☐ Married ☐ Separated	☐ Unmarried (include single, divorced, widowed)	Dependents (not listed Borrower) no.: ages:	

Present Address (street, city, state, zip) ☐ Own ☐ Rent _____ No. Yrs.	Present Address (street, city, state, zip) ☐ Own ☐ Rent _____ No. Yrs.

If residing at present address for less than two years, complete the following:

Former Address (street, city, state, zip) ☐ Own ☐ Rent _____ No. Yrs.	Former Address (street, city, state, zip) ☐ Own ☐ Rent _____ No. Yrs.
Former Address (street, city, state, zip) ☐ Own ☐ Rent _____ No. Yrs.	Former Address (street, city, state, zip) ☐ Own ☐ Rent _____ No. Yrs.

Borrower IV. EMPLOYMENT INFORMATION Co-Borrower			
Name & Address of Employer ☐ Self-Employed	Yrs. on this job	Name & Address of Employer ☐ Self-Employed	Yrs. on this job
	Yrs. employed in this line of work/profession		Yrs. employed in this line of work/profession
Position/Title/type of Business	Business Phone (incl. area code)	Position/Title/type of Business	Business Phone (incl. area code)

If employed in current position for less than two years of if currently employed in more than one position, complete the following:

Name & Address of Employer ☐ Self-Employed	Dates (from - to)	Name & Address of Employer ☐ Self-Employed	Dates (from - to)
	Monthly Income $		Monthly Income $
Position/Title/type of Business	Business Phone (incl. area code)	Position/Title/type of Business	Business Phone (incl. area code)
Name & Address of Employer ☐ Self-Employed	Dates (from - to)	Name & Address of Employer ☐ Self-Employed	Dates (from - to)
	Monthly Income $		Monthly Income $
Position/Title/type of Business	Business Phone (incl. area code)	Position/Title/type of Business	Business Phone (incl. area code)

V. MONTHLY INCOME AND COMBINED HOUSING EXPENSE INFORMATION

Gross Monthly Income	Borrower	Co-Borrower	Total	Combined Monthly Housing Expense	Present	Proposed
Base Empl. Income*	$	$	$	Rent	$	▉
Overtime				First Mortgage (P&I)		$
Bonuses				Other Financing (P&I)		
Commissions				Hazard Insurance		
Dividends/Interest				Real Estate Taxes		
Net Rental Income				Mortgage Insurance		
Other: before completing see the notice in "describe other income," below				Homeowner Assn. Dues		
				Other:		
Total	$	$	$	Total	$	$

* Self Employed Borrower(s) may be required to provide additional documentation such as tax returns and financial statements.
Describe Other Income
Notice: Alimony, child support, or separate maintenance income need not be revealed if the Borrower (B) or Co-Borrower (C) does not choose to have it considered for repaying this loan.

B/C		Monthly Amount
		$

VI. ASSETS AND LIABILITIES

This statement and any applicable supporting schedules may be completed jointly by both married and unmarried Co-Borrowers if their assets and liabilities are sufficiently joined so that the Statement can be meaningfully and fairly presented on a combined basis; otherwise separate Statements and Schedules are required. If the Co-Borrower section was completed about a spouse, this Statement and supporting schedules must be completed about that spouse also.   Completed ☐ Jointly ☐ Not Jointly

ASSETS Description	Cash or Market Value	Liabilities and Pledged Assets. List the creditor's name, address and account number for all outstanding debts, including automobile loans, revolving charge accounts, real estate loans, alimony, child support, stock pledges, etc. Use continuation sheet, if necessary. Indicate by (*) those liabilities which will be satisfied upon sale of real estate owned or upon refinancing of the subject property.		
Cash deposit toward purchase held by:	$			
List checking and savings accounts below		LIABILITIES	Monthly Payt. & Mos. left to Pay	Unpaid Balance
Name and address of Bank, S&L, or Credit Union		Name and address of Company	$ Payt./Mos.	$
Account No.	$	Account no.		
Name and address of Bank, S&L, or Credit Union		Name and address of Company	$ Payt./Mos.	$
Account No.	$	Account no.		

Name and address of Bank, S&L, or Credit Union		Name and address of Company	$ Payt./Mos.	$
Account No.	$	Account no.		
Name and address of Bank, S&L, or Credit Union		Name and address of Company	$ Payt./Mos.	$
Account No.	$	Account no.		
Stock & Bonds (Company name/number & description)	$	Name and address of Company	$ Payt./Mos.	$
Life insurance net cash value Face Amount: $	$	Account no.		
Subtotal Liquid Assets	$	Name and address of Company	$ Payt./Mos.	$
Real estate owned (enter market value from schedule of real estate owned)	$			
Vested interest in retirement fund	$	Account no.		
Net worth of business(es) owned (attach financial statement)	$	Name and address of Company	$ Payt./Mos.	$
Automobiles owned (make and year)	$			
		Account no.		
Other assets (itemize)	$	Alimony/Child Support/ Separate Maintenance Payments Owed to:	$	
		Job Related Expenses (child care, union dues, etc.)	$	
Total Assets a.	$	Total Monthly Payments	$	
		Net Worth (a minus b) $	Total Liabilities b.	$

VI. ASSETS AND LIABILITIES (cont.)							
Schedule of Real Estate Owned (if additional properties are owned, use continuation sheet.)							
Property Address (enter S if sold, PS if pending sale or R if rental being held for income)	Type of Property	Present Market Value	Amount of Mortgage & Liens	Gross Rental Income	Mortgage Payments	Insurance, Maintenance, Taxes & Misc.	Net Rental Income
		$	$	$	$	$	$
	Totals	$	$	$	$	$	$

List any additional names under which credit has previously been received and indicate appropriate creditor name(s) and account number(s):

Alternate Name	Creditor	Account Number

VII. DETAILS OF TRANSACTION		VIII. DECLARATIONS				
			Borrower		Co-Borrower	
		If you answer "yes" to any questions a through i, please use continuation sheet for explanation	Yes	No	Yes	No
a. Purchase Price	$	a. Are there any outstanding judgments against you?	☐	☐	☐	☐
b. Alterations, improvements, repairs		b. Have you been declared bankrupt within the past 7 years	☐	☐	☐	☐
c. Land (if acquired separately)		c. Have you had property foreclosed upon or given title or deed in thereof in the last 7 years?	☐	☐	☐	☐
d. Refinance (incl. debts to be paid off)		d. Are you a party to a lawsuit?	☐	☐	☐	☐
e. Estimated prepaid items		e. Have you directly or indirectly been obligated on any loan which resulted in foreclosure, transfer of title in lieu of foreclosure, or judgment? (This would include such loans as home mortgage loans, SBA loans, home improvement loans, educational loans, manufactured (mobile) home loans, any mortgage, financial obligation, bond, or loan guarantee? If "Yes, " provide details including date, name and address of Lender, FHA or VA case number, if any, and reasons for the action.)	☐	☐	☐	☐
f. Estimated Closing Costs						
g. PMI, MIP, Funding Fee						
h. Discount (if Borrower will pay)						
i. Total Costs (add items a through h)						
j. Subordinate financing		f. Are you presently delinquent or in default on any Federal debt or any other loan, mortgage, financial obligation, bond, or loan guarantee? If "Yes," give details as described in the question.	☐	☐	☐	☐
k. Borrower's closing costs paid by Seller		g. Are you obligated to pay alimony, child support, or sep. maintenance?	☐	☐	☐	☐
l. Other Credits (explain)		h. Is any part of the down payment borrowed?	☐	☐	☐	☐
		i. Are you a co-maker or endorser on a note?	☐	☐	☐	☐
		j. Are you a U.S. Citizen?	☐	☐	☐	☐
		k. Are you a permanent resident alien?	☐	☐	☐	☐
m. Loan amount (exclude PMI, MIP, Funding Fee financed		l. Do you intend to occupy the property as your primary residence? If "Yes," complete question m below.	☐	☐	☐	☐
n. PMI, MIP, Funding Fee financed		m. Have you had an ownership interest in a property in the last 3 years?	☐	☐	☐	☐
o. Loan amount (add m & n)		(1) What type of property did you own -- principal resident (PR), second home (SH), or investment property (IP)?	—	—	—	—
p. Cash from/to Borrower (subtract j, k, l & o from i)		(2) How did you hold title to the home -- solely by yourself (S), jointly with your spouse (SP), or jointly with another person (O)?	—	—	—	—

IX. ACKNOWLEDGMENT AND AGREEMENT
The undersigned specifically acknowledge(s) and agree(s) that: (1) the loan requested by this application will be secured by a first mortgage or deed of trust on the property described herein; (2) the property will not be used for any illegal or prohibited purpose or use; (3) all statements made in this application are made for the purpose of obtaining the loan indicated here: (4) occupation of the property will be as indicated above; (5) verification or reverification of any information contained in the application may be made at any time by the Lender, it's agents, successors and assigns, either directly or through a credit reporting agency, from any source named in this application, and the original copy of this application will be retained by the Lender even if the loan is not approved; (6) the Lender, its agents, successors and assigns will rely on the information contained in the application and I/we have a continuing obligation to amend and/or supplement the information provided in this application if any of the material facts which I/we have represented herein should change prior to closing; (7) in the event my/our payments on the loan indicated in this application become delinquent, the Lender, its agents, successors and assigns, may, in addition to all their other rights and remedies, report my/our name(s)9s) and account information to a credit reporting agency; (8) ownership of the loan may be transferred to successor or assign of the Lender without notice to me and/or the administration of the loan account may be transferred to an agent, successor or assign of the Lender with prior notice to me; (9) the Lender, its agent, successors and assigns, make no representation or warranties, express or implied, to the Borrower(s) regarding the property, the condition of the property, or the value of the property.

Certification: I/we certify that the information provided in this application is true and correct as of the date set forth opposite my/our signature(s) on this application and acknowledge my/our understanding that any intentional or negligent misrepresentation(s) of the information contained in this application may result in civil liability and/or criminal penalties including, but not limited to, fine or imprisonment or both under the provisions of Title 18, United States Code, Section 1001, et seq. and liability for monetary damages to the Lender, its agents, successors and assigns, insurers and any other person who may suffer any loss due to reliance upon any misrepresentation which I/we have made on this application.

Borrower's Signature	Date	Co-Borrower's Signature	Date
X		X	

X. INFORMATION FOR GOVERNMENT MONITORING PURPOSES

The following information is requested by the Federal Government for certain types of loans related to a dwelling, in order to monitor the Lender's compliance with equal credit opportunity, fair housing and home mortgage disclosure laws. You are not required to furnish this information, but are encouraged to do so. The law provides that a Lender may neither discriminate on the basis of this information, nor on whether you choose to furnish it. However, if you choose not to furnish it, under Federal regulations this Lender is required to note race and sex on the basis of visual observation or surname. If you do not wish to furnish the above information, please check the box below. (Lender must review the above material to assure that the disclosures satisfy all requirements to which the Lender is subject under applicable state law for the particular type of loan applied for.)

BORROWER — ☐ I do not wish to furnish this information

CO-BORROWER — ☐ I do not wish to furnish this information

Race/National Origin:
- ☐ American Indian or Alaskan Native
- ☐ Asian or Pacific Islander
- ☐ Black, not of Hispanic Origin
- ☐ Hispanic
- ☐ White, not of Hispanic Origin
- ☐ Other, please specify

Sex: ☐ Female ☐ Male

To be completed by interviewer. This application was taken by:
- ☐ face-to-face interview
- ☐ by mail
- ☐ by telephone

Interviewer's Name (Print or Type)

Interviewer's Signature   Date

Interviewer's Phone Number (incl. area code)

Name and Address of Interviewer's Employer

IV. HUD-1 Form

A. U.S. DEPARTMENT OF HOUSING AND URBAN DEVELOPMENT SETTLEMENT STATEMENT				
B. TYPE OF LOAN			6. File Number	7. Loan Number
	1. o FHA	2. o FmHA		
3. o CONV. UNINS.	4. o VA	5. o CONV. INS.	8. Mortgage Insurance Case Number	
C. NOTE: This form is furnished to give you a statement of actual settlement costs. Amounts paid to and by the settlement agent are shown. Items marked "(p.o.c.)" were paid outside the closing; they are shown here for informational purposes and are not included in the totals.				
D. NAME AND ADDRESS OF BORROWER:	E. NAME AND ADDRESS OF SELLER:		F. NAME AND ADDRESS OF LENDER:	
G. PROPERTY LOCATION:	H. SETTLEMENT AGENT: NAME, AND ADDRESS			
	PLACE OF SETTLEMENT:		I. SETTLEMENT DATE:	

J. SUMMARY OF BORROWER'S TRANSACTION		K. SUMMARY OF SELLER'S TRANSACTION	
100. GROSS AMOUNT DUE FROM BORROWER:		**400. GROSS AMOUNT DUE TO SELLER:**	
101. Contract sales price		401. Contract sales price	
102. Personal property		402. Personal property	
103. Settlement charges to borrower(line 1400)		403.	
104.		404.	
105.		405.	
Adjustments for items paid by seller in advance		*Adjustments for items paid by seller in advance*	
106. City/town taxes to		406. City/town taxes to	
107. County taxes to		407. County taxes to	
108. Assessments to		408. Assessments to	
109.		409.	
110.		410.	
111.		411.	
112.		412.	
120. GROSS AMOUNT DUE FROM BORROWER		**420. GROSS AMOUNT DUE TO SELLER**	

200. AMOUNTS PAID BY OR IN BEHALF OF BORROWER:		500. REDUCTIONS IN AMOUNT DUE TO SELLER:	
201. Deposit of earnest money		501. Excess deposit (see instructions)	
202. Principal amount of new loan(s)		502. Settlement charges to seller (line 1400)	
203. Existing loan(s) taken subject to		503. Existing loan(s) taken subject to	
204.		504. Payoff of first mortgage loan	
205.		505. Payoff of second mortgage loan	
206.		506.	
207.		507.	
208.		508.	
209.		509.	
Adjustments for items unpaid by seller		*Adjustments for items unpaid by seller*	
210. City/town taxes to		510. City/town taxes to	
211. County taxes to		511. County taxes to	
212. Assessments to		512. Assessments to	
213.		513.	
214.		514.	
215.		515.	
216.		516.	
217.		517.	
218.		518.	
219.		519.	
220. TOTAL PAID BY/FOR BORROWER		520. TOTAL REDUCTION AMOUNT DUE SELLER	

300. CASH AT SETTLEMENT FROM/TO BORROWER		600. CASH AT SETTLEMENT TO/FROM SELLER	
301. Gross amount due from borrower(line 120)		601. Gross amount due to seller (line 420)	
302. Less amounts paid by/for borrower(line 220)		602. Less reductions in amount due seller (line 520)	
303. CASH (_ FROM) (_ TO) BORROWER		603. CASH (o TO) (o FROM) SELLER	

L. SETTLEMENT CHARGES		
700. TOTAL SALES/BROKER'S COMMISSION based on price $ @ %=	PAID FROM BORROWER'S FUNDS AT SETTLEMENT	PAID FROM SELLER'S FUNDS AT SETTLEMENT
Division of Commission (line 700) as follows:		
701. $ to		
702. $ to		
703. Commission paid at Settlement		
704.		
800. ITEMS PAYABLE IN CONNECTION WITH LOAN		
801. Loan Origination Fee %		
802. Loan Discount %		
803. Appraisal Fee to		
804. Credit Report to		
805. Lender's Inspection Fee		
806. Mortgage Insurance Application Fee to		
807. Assumption Fee		
808.		
809.		
810.		
811.		
900. ITEMS REQUIRED BY LENDER TO BE PAID IN ADVANCE		
901. Interest from to @$ /day		
902. Mortgage Insurance Premium for months to		
903. Hazard Insurance Premium for years to		
904. years to		
905.		
1000. RESERVES DEPOSITED WITH LENDER		
1001. Hazard Insurance months @ $ per month		
1002. Mortgage insurance months @ $ per month		
1003. City property taxes months @ $ per month		
1004. County property taxes months @ $ per month		
1005. Annual assessments months @ $ per month		
1006. months @ $ per month		
1007. months @ $ per month		
1008. Aggregate Adjustment months @ $ per month		

1100. **TITLE CHARGES**		
1101. Settlement or closing fee to		
1102. Abstract or title search to		
1103. Title examination to		
1104. Title insurance binder to		
1105. Document preparation to		
1106. Notary fees to		
1107. Attorney's fees to		
(includes above items numbers;)		
1108. Title Insurance to		
(includes above items numbers;)		
1109. Lender's coverage $		
1110. Owner's coverage $		
1111.		
1112.		
1113.		
1200. **GOVERNMENT RECORDING AND TRANSFER CHARGES**		
1201. Recording fees: Deed $; Mortgage $; Releases $		
1202. City/county tax/stamps: Deed $; Mortgage $		
1203. State tax/stamps: Deed $; Mortgage $		
1204.		
1205.		
1300. **ADDITIONAL SETTLEMENT CHARGES**		
1301. Survey to		
1302. Pest inspection to		
1303.		
1304.		
1305.		
1400. **TOTAL SETTLEMENT CHARGES** (enter on lines 103, Section J and 502, Section K)		

Glossary

Abstract of title: A condensed version of the history of property title to a piece of land that lists all ownership transfers as well as any liabilities attached to it, such as liens or mortgages.

Acceleration clause: A provision in a mortgage that—in the event of default on the part of the borrower—makes the entire principal and interest amount due and payable immediately.

Acceptance: A buyer's or seller's agreement to enter into a contract and be bound by the offer's terms.

Additional principal payment: A payment by a borrower of an amount that exceeds the actual payment due in order to reduce the loan's remaining balance.

Adjustable-rate mortgage (ARM): A mortgage loan with a fluctuating interest rate.

Agency: Legal relationship between a principal (such as the home seller) and an agent (a real estate agent, for example). In such a relationship the seller delegates to the agent the right to act on her behalf in business transactions and to exercise discretion while doing so.

Amortization: The act of paying off indebtedness, such as a mortgage, in an installment fashion, typically fifteen or thirty years.

Appraisal: Determination of the value of a home or other piece of property.

Appreciation: Increase in value or worth of a piece of property.

Balloon mortgage: A loan in which the final payment is much larger than any preceding payments. The mortgage's final payment is known as a balloon payment.

Breach of contract: Failure of one of the parties to a contract to act according to the contract.

Brokerage: A firm that engages in the act of bringing together parties who will buy, sell, exchange, or lease property for a commission or flat fee.

Buyer's broker: A real estate licensee who represents only the buyer in a transaction, regardless of which party is paying the commission.

Capital gains: Profit on the sale of property or other capital asset.

Ceiling: Maximum allowable interest rate over the life of an adjustable-rate mortgage.

Chattel: Any personal property related to the home.

Clear title: Land title that has no liens (mortgages included) against it.

Closing: Final step in the sales transaction where the seller transfers title to the buyer in exchange for consideration.

Closing costs: Costs that the buyer and seller must pay for at the time of closing, including points, down payment, credit report fee, and other charges.

Closing statement: Written summary of the financial settlement of a real estate transaction, showing all charges and credits made, and all cash received and paid out.

Commission: Compensation paid to a licensed real estate broker in exchange for services rendered. Commissions generally range from 5 to 7 percent, depending on location.

Condominium: Commonly known as a condo, a property in which individual owners possess separate portions of the building, plus shared ownership of common areas.

Contingency: Contract provision stating that some or all contract terms will be altered or voided should a specific event occur, such as the buyer's inability to obtain financing.

Contract: Legally enforceable agreement used in the purchase or sale of real estate.

Cooperative housing: Commonly known as a co-op, a dwelling in which residents own shares but do not directly own the space where they live.

Counteroffer: Rejection of an offer to buy or sell that simultaneously makes a different offer, thus changing the terms in some way.

Covenant: Restriction on the use of real estate that governs its use. Covenants are typically found in deeds or documents that bind all property owners in a specific development and are often referred to as deed restrictions.

Credit report: Account of an individual's credit history, prepared by a credit bureau and used to compile a credit score that lenders use to determine eligibility for a loan and its interest rate.

Deed: Written instrument by which title to land is conveyed.

Depreciation: Loss in value.

Disclosure: Making known a fact that had previously been hidden.

Discount points: Amount paid to either maintain or lower the interest rate charged. Each point is equal to 1 percent of the loan amount.

Down payment: An amount of money the buyer pays that represents the difference between the purchase price and the loan amount.

Earnest money: Deposit made by the buyer as evidence of good faith in offering to purchase real estate and to secure performance of the contract.

Easement: Right to use someone else's real estate for a specific purpose, such as a right-of-way.

Encroachment: Structure, such as a wall or fence, located on a portion of a property belonging to another.

Encumbrance: Anything that affects or limits the fee simple title to a property, such as mortgages, leases, easements, or restrictions.

Equity: Monetary difference between a home's value and the loan amount.

Escrow: Trust arrangement by which one or more parties deposit something of value with an authorized escrow agent in accordance with the terms of a real estate agreement.

Fixed-rate mortgage: Mortgage with an interest rate and monthly payment that do not vary for the life of the loan.

Fixture: Personal property that has been attached to real estate so as to become part of the real property. To be a fixture, the item must be attached in a permanent manner, specially adapted to the property, or intentionally made part of the real property.

Flood insurance: Special and separate type of homeowners insurance that provides coverage for damages resulting from flooding.

Foreclosure: Legal process by which a mortgagee or lien creditor sells a home when the debtor defaults on his or her obligations.

For sale by owner (FSBO): Piece of property sold by an individual home owner without a real estate broker.

Gross income: Income of the borrower before deducting taxes or expenses.

Hazard insurance: Contract between a purchaser and an insurer that compensates the former for loss of property due to hazards (fire, hail damage, etc.), for a premium.

Homeowners association: Organization that collects dues from home owners and is made up of neighbors concerned with managing the common areas of a subdivision or condominium complex.

Homeowners insurance: Insurance policy designed to protect home owners from financial losses related to the ownership of real property. Most policies also provide theft and liability coverage.

Home warranty: Service contract that covers a major housing system, such as plumbing or electrical wiring, for a set amount of time after closing—typically one year. The warranty is often renewable and guarantees repairs to the covered system(s).

Improvements: Valuable additions to the land, such as buildings, fences, and roads, that increase the value of the property.

Inspection clause: Stipulation in an offer to purchase that makes the sale contingent on the findings of a home inspector.

Latent defect: Hidden structural defects and flaws in a property.

Lease purchase: Contract in which an owner leases his home to a tenant for an increased monthly rent and that gives the tenant the right to purchase the home at the end of the lease period for a predetermined price.

Legal description: Description of a specific parcel of real estate that is acceptable to the courts in that state and that allows an independent surveyor to locate and identify it.

Lien: Monetary claim against a property that must be settled before the sale is finalized.

Loan-to-value ratio (LTV): Comparison of the amount being loaned and the appraised value of the property, usually expressed as a percentage.

Lock-in: Commitment from a lender assuring a particular interest rate or feature or a definite time period.

Market approach to value: Estimate of property value based on the actual sales prices of comparable properties.

Misrepresentation: False statement, or concealment, of material fact with the intention of inducing action of another.

Mortgage: Contract providing security for the repayment of a loan, registered against property, with stated rights and remedies in the event of default.

Mortgage banker: Company that originates mortgage loans, loans the lender's funds, and closes the loan in the lender's name.

Mortgage broker: Individual or company that works with financial institutions or individuals who invest in mortgages.

Multiple listing service (MLS): System by which real estate firms share information about homes that are for sale.

Offer: Proposal to enter into an agreement with another person. The offer must express the intent of the person making the offer to form a contract, contain some essential terms (including the price and subject matter of the contract), and be communicated by the person making the offer.

Open house: Opportunity for prospective buyers to view a home without having to deal with high-pressure sales tactics.

Points: Fees paid to induce lenders to make mortgage loans at a particular interest rate. Each point is equal to 1 percent of the loan principal.

Power of attorney: Written authorization by one person to another person to act on his or her behalf.

Prepayment: Paying off all or part of the mortgage before the scheduled date.

Prepayment clause in a mortgage: Statement of the terms upon which the borrower may pay the entire or stated amount on the mortgage principal at some time prior to the due date.

Prepayment penalty: Fee paid to the lending institution for paying a loan prior to the scheduled maturity date.

Principal: Amount of money owed to the lender, not including interest.

Property taxes: Taxes paid yearly on real estate property, based on the assessed value (ad valorem) of the real property.

Prorate: Divide or distribute proportionally. At closing, various expenses such as taxes, insurance, interest, and rents are prorated between the seller and buyer.

Qualify: Meet a mortgage lender's approval requirements.

Recording: Act of entering in the public records the written record of title to real property, thereby giving constructive notice to the public.

Sales contract: Written agreement stating the terms of the sale agreed to by both buyer and seller.

Setback: Distance a building must be set back from the property lines in accordance with local zoning ordinances or deed restrictions.

Steering: Illegal practice of directing members of minority groups to—or away from—certain areas or neighborhoods.

Term: Actual life of a mortgage, at the end of which the mortgage becomes due and payable unless the lender renews the mortgage.

Time is of the essence: Clause that makes failure to perform by a specified date a material breach or violation of the contract.

Title company: Provides title insurance policies and, in some states, holds real estate closings.

Title insurance: Protection for lenders or home owners against financial loss resulting from legal defects in the title.

Title search: Check of all records relating to the property to determine whether the seller can sell the property in a lien-free manner.

Town house: Unit comprising two, three, or four floors with structural walls shared with another unit.

Underwriting: Process of verifying data and approving a loan.

Variable rate: Interest rate that changes periodically in relation to an index. Payments may increase or decrease accordingly.

Variance: Exception to a zoning ordinance, usually granted by a local government.

Walk-through: Buyer's on-site inspection of the property being purchased, just prior to closing.

Zoning: A legal mechanism for local governments to prevent conflicts in land use and promote orderly development by regulating the use of privately owned land through enforcement.

Resources

Credit

For information, contact your local chapter of the Consumer Credit Counseling Service, whose umbrella organization is the National Foundation for Credit Counseling. Use the member agency locater at www.debtadvice.org to find your nearest counseling resource. For more information, contact the organization at 801 Roeder Road, Suite 900, Silver Spring, MD 20910, (301) 589-5600.

First-Time Homebuyer Assistance

Nearly all states and/or municipalities offer a range of programs designed to help first-time buyers purchase homes. Try keying the words "first-time homebuyer assistance" and your county's name into a search engine like www.google.com, or contact your city or county's government offices for further information.

Home Inspectors

The American Society of Home Inspectors (ASHI) calls itself the "largest and most respected professional association" for home inspectors in North America. From the group's Web site at www.ashi.com, you can learn more about the organization and even search for qualified home inspectors in your area.

Legal Assistance

In addition to checking your local yellow pages for a real estate attorney, you can use an online resource like www.realestatelawyers.com, which will give you a list of potential candidates in your region. Check them out thoroughly, ask for references, and be sure they're keyed into the local real estate industry and related laws before starting a relationship.

Lenders

Most lenders have their own Web sites, which can be accessed by searching for the name (Countryside Home Loans, Wells Fargo, etc.) using your favorite search engine. You can also use a service like LendingTree.com, where you can submit information and let the most appropriate lenders contact you directly. Your local bank or credit union is another good source of mortgage funds.

Online Home Search Tools

There are literally dozens of different Web sites where you can go to search for homes by price, size, and locale while also viewing complete virtual tours of the homes you're interested in. Among the most popular are the following sites:

Assist2Sell
www.assist2sell.com

BuyOwner.com
www.buyowner.com

Foxtons
www.foxtons.com

Harmon Homes
www.harmonhomes.com

HomeFinder
www.homefinder.com

HomePreviewOnline
www.homepreviewonline.com

HouseHunt
www.househunt.com

Houses4Sale-Online
www.houses4sale-online.com

HouseSeeker4U
www.houseseeker4u.com

MSN House and Home
http://houseandhome.msn.com

NewHomeOnline
www.newhomeonline.com

Realtor.com
www.realtor.com

Yahoo! Real Estate
www.realestate.yahoo.com

ZipRealty
www.ziprealty.com

Individual real estate agents (and even for sale by owners) often have their own Web sites where they post listings. If you see a yard sign with a company and agent name on it, you might also want to do a separate search online for that agent to see if she offers more details, price, and a virtual tour online.

Real Estate Agents/Brokers
Nearly all licensed real estate agents and brokers are members of the National Association of REALTORS®, and as such use the "REALTOR" designation after their names. To search for agents in your area, visit NAR's Web site at www.realtor.org for more information, or go directly to the site's search function at www.realtor.org/rodesign.nsf/pages/FS_FREALTOR? OpenDocument, to search for a real estate professional in your area who subscribes to the organization's strict code of ethics.

Taxes
The Internal Revenue Service's Publication 530 is specifically for first-time home buyers who need help deciphering and taking advantage of the various tax breaks they're entitled to. You can obtain the publication either through the IRS's Web site at www.irs.gov by entering "Publication 530" in the publication-search function, or by contacting the IRS's forms and publications department by phone at (800) 829-3676.

Index